Gods, Judges, and Presidents

Gods, Judges, and Presidents

Trifunctional Archetypes in American Law and Government

Charles Lincoln

BLOOMSBURY ACADEMIC
NEW YORK • LONDON • OXFORD • NEW DELHI • SYDNEY

BLOOMSBURY ACADEMIC
Bloomsbury Publishing Inc, 1359 Broadway, New York, NY 10018, USA
Bloomsbury Publishing Plc, 50 Bedford Square, London, WC1B 3DP, UK
Bloomsbury Publishing Ireland, 29 Earlsfort Terrace, Dublin 2, D02 AY28, Ireland

BLOOMSBURY, BLOOMSBURY ACADEMIC and the Diana logo are trademarks of Bloomsbury Publishing Plc

First published in the United States of America 2026

A catalog record for this book is available from the Library of Congress.

ISBN: HB: 978-1-6669-5776-1
ePDF: 979-8-216-26555-9
eBook: 978-1-9787-6231-2

Typeset by Integra Software Services Pvt. Ltd.

For my grandmothers,
Alice and Nina,
who showed me Athens before I knew I was looking for it.

Contents

Tables

A Note on the Text

With the goal of interpreting the understanding and meaning of the *ur-text* as an author—whether the text is written by Plato, Montesquieu, or James Madison—presented it to us, I have attempted to modernize, the spelling, punctuation, and grammatical structures of the primary sources I cite. However, I often let the ur-text speak for itself without any edits—especially in the form of James Madison's notes around the time of the American Constitutional Convention of 1787. Nevertheless, every quotation in this book has a footnote citing the original source. My goal has not been to alter any meaning of a text. However, the eminent literary academic Harold Bloom argued for the necessity of misreading a text. I apologize for any *misreadings* that do not produce helpful understandings. I hope the reader will forgive them as inadvertent or fruitful in Bloom's sense of misreading.

Preface

Most of the chapters here initially appeared as law review articles. Now they are collected into one volume with the view that they all deal with one problem: the problem of understanding the US Constitution in relation to trifunctionalism in the law. I have tried to state this problem from the perspective of law, philosophy, anthropology, and history.

For the chapter on Plato, I have made free use of my article *A Structural Etiology of the U.S. Constitution*, 43 J. Legis. 122 (2016). The chapter on Dumézilian trifunctionalism was first published in *Elon Law Review* in 2023.

I wish to thank the editors and proprietors of the above-mentioned works and for their kind permission to use them.

On the origin of this book:

This book represents a culmination of research for the past decade on the structures of the government. In 2012 and 2013, as an undergraduate student at Harvard University under the direction of Akiba Covitz of Harvard Law School, I delved into Hegelian thought. My senior thesis under Professor Covitz's guidance formed the basis of my first book, *The Dialectical Path of Law*. During that time with Professor Covitz's supervision in the fall of 2012, I sought to use the philosophy of the German philosopher Georg Wilhelm Friedrich Hegel's *The Phenomenology of Spirit* (German: *Phänomenologie des Geistes*) to analyze the changes of US voting rights from exclusive to inclusive over time.

In the course of this tutoring and mentoring, Professor Covitz and I discussed notions of the three-part structure of the federal government as representing the three parts of the US federal government. His PhD dissertation greatly influenced my thought. I saw his work as unification of the thought of Athens and Jerusalem. While a JD student at Texas A&M University School of Law, I pursued as an independent student during the spring semester of 2015 under the direction of Professor Franklin G. Snyder, focusing on Hegelian thought and using German idealism as a prism through which one could interpret the development of American law. Later during my JD studies, I took a seminar on Jurisprudence focusing on the philosophy and ethics of law with Professor Deni Garcia. In preparation of Professor Garcia's seminar, I discussed plans for writing a swerve of my thought that used Professor Covitz's theory of Plato's tripartite soul in analyzing the US Constitution and changing the constituent elements. I spent that entire semester under Professor Garcia's direction working on that swerve of thought.

My swerve from Professor Covitz's thought can likely be accurately interpreted as a similar swerve Harold Bloom articulates in his *Anxiety of Influence* (1973). In *Anxiety of Influence*, Bloom describes how poets interact with works of previous poets. As such Bloom's theory of influence, later developed in his *A Map of Misreading* (1975), outlines six revisionary steps—or using Bloom's term "revisionary ratios"—where a poet works to separate himself from a poet that the poet once admired. Bloom's first step of the six revisionary ratios is a *clinamen*. Bloom takes the term "clinamen" from the Roman poet and philosopher Lucretius's philosophical poem *De rerum natura* (English: *On the Nature of Things*) (written in the first century BCE). In *De rerum natura*, Lucretius suggests that atoms merely have a clinamen—Latin for "swerve." Bloom takes this swerve to articulate how a successor poet takes a first step away from a former poet.

Ultimately, the drive of curiosity that has influenced all my mentors and advisors in my life also drove me. It does not appear immediately obvious why one finds certain topics more curious than others or why one aims in one direction over others. Perhaps William Shakespeare in his *Romeo & Juliet* put it in words the best through Juliet regarding her love for Romeo:

> My bounty is as boundless as the sea,
> My love as deep; the more I give to thee,
> The more I have, for both are infinite.[1]

In this astonishing way, Shakespeare outdoes himself. Likewise, if allowed to grow, curiosity, too, is as boundless as the sea. The more you give to curiosity, the more you have, for both are infinite.

[1] William Shakespeare, *Romeo & Juliet*, Act 2, Scene 2, lines 133–6.

Acknowledgments

I'd like to give a special thanks to my PhD advisors at the University of Groningen, Irene Burgers, Raymond Adema, and Justin Lindeboom. Their urging me to pursue my intellectual curiosity has proven invaluable. Indeed, they all shared ways I could expand my research. In the words of Alfred Lord Tennyson's poem *Ulysses*, they help me realize " 'Tis not too late to seek a newer world." They are right. It is not too late to seek out new avenues of research and new ways of examining the law.

I'd like to thank Professor Calvin Johnson of the University of Texas for being a mentor on and off, since I was a seventeen-year-old high school student in 2010. Going back to when I was in twelfth grade when Professor Johnson interviewed me for Columbia University undergraduate students, Professor Johnson started the interview with "What books have you read recently?" Professor Johnson has urged me in the direction of the Great Books of the Western World series published by the Encyclopædia Britannica and the Classics. Moreover, especially for the contents of this book dealing with *Federalist Papers*, the Framers of the Constitution, and especially notions of *Federalist Paper No. 10*, Professor Johnson shared deep insights during the Spring semester and early summer of 2023. After purchasing Professor Johnson's book *Righteous Anger at the Wicked States: The Meaning of the Founders' Constitution* (2005), I immersed myself and wrote notes and questions on every single page. I thank Professor Johnson for his patience in answering my questions in person and over email.

For the chapter on Homeric poetry, I'd like to thank Professor Graeme D. Bird for his insights on Milman Perry, Albert Lord, and Gregory Nagy on the Greek hero. Just as when I was an undergraduate student taking Professor Bird's class, and many years after, Professor Bird would entertain my questions. I especially thank him for his time, hours after class would end into the night when he would entertain questions. Professor Bird gave me everlasting insight into classical Greek literature and comparative literature. Professor Bird fulfills the ideal in Plato's *Phaedo*, where Socrates says, "[a]nd I fancy that those men who established the mysteries were not unenlightened, but in reality had a hidden meaning when they said long ago that whoever goes uninitiated and unsanctified to the other world will lie in the mire, but he who arrives there initiated and purified will dwell with the gods. For as they say in the mysteries, 'the thyrsus-bearers are many, but the mystics few'; and these mystics are, I believe, those who have been true philosophers." Professor Bird not only bears the thyrsus but has the very visage of the philosopher himself.

In undergraduate studies, I took a course in the fall term of 2011 titled Current Constitutional Issues with Professor David Manwaring. I visited almost all his office hours and received excellent feedback on my understanding of American Constitutional law. Though Professor Manwaring is no longer with us, his influence remains in my thoughts of American political and Constitutional law.

Again, in the course of my undergraduate studies, Professor Akiba Covitz taught a course titled Constitutional Law in the spring term of 2012. From the first course with Professor Covitz, I was enchanted with his understanding of American Constitutional law. In his course, we read Harvard Law School Professor Richard Fallon's book titled *The Dynamic Constitution*. We also read Harvard Law School Professor Charles Fried's book *Saying What the Law Is*. Both Professors Fallon and Fried gave guest lectures. Those books and guest lecturers proved uniquely infinitely influential on my ways of thinking about American Constitutional law.

I would be remiss not to mention the Harvard Summer School course titled International Law I took during the summer of 2012 with Professor Beth Simmons—who at the time was director of the Weatherhead Center for International Affairs at Harvard University. Professor Simmons helped me understand the nature of human rights from a comparative constitutional perspective. Moreover, simultaneously that same summer at Harvard Summer School, I took a helpful course titled Crime and the Constitution with former law clerk to Associate Justice of the Supreme Court of the United States Antonin Scalia and current professor at Harvard Law School.

In the spring term of 2013, I took Global History of Modern Times (H-1920) at Harvard College. That course turned out to be one of the best courses in my life. Professor Charles Maier, the Leverett Saltonstall Research Professor of History at Harvard University, taught the course. He encouraged us to read and explore history in a way I never had previously. The works we read still impact my thinking to this day.

Later in law school, in the fall semester of 2014, I took an inspiring course titled Constitutional Law with Professor H. Brian Holland of Texas A&M University School of Law. He reignited another love for American Constitutional law interwoven with a historical interpretation. Moreover, his classes on the

Dormant Commerce Clause could not have been more prescient of my future research. Indeed, the Dormant Commerce Clause still remains a key factor generating my interest in tax law and my PhD research at the University of Groningen.

In the spring semester of 2015, Professor Franklin Snyder of Texas A&M University School of Law took me under his wing in the second year of law school for an independent study. We discussed Hegelian dialectics, the path of law, the future of law, and the history of law during our weekly and often biweekly talks. His guidance helped me from the beginning. I still thank him for the books he offered to me before anyone else when he was cleaning out his office. They turned out to guide the future of my thinking.

Professor Deni Garcia of Texas A&M's Law School gave us an intensive course on Jurisprudence, meeting most Saturdays during the fall semester of 2015. In her course, we explored Lon L. Fuller's *The Case of the Speluncean Explorers* (1949), Plato's *Apology*, the social contract, and Hans Kelsen, among other great legal minds. I wish more courses were like this. Professor Garcia's seminars explored so much-needed territory for which I still benefit from regularly.

I'd like to thank my high school history teacher, David Foster. His lectures and inspiration lived with me from ninth grade to the current day.

Professor Thomas Pangle—the Joe R. Long Chair in Democratic Studies in the Department of Government and Co-Director of the Thomas Jefferson Center for Core Texts and Ideas at the University of Texas at Austin—graciously communicated with me about this project over email. Furthermore, Professor Pangle extended an invitation to meet with me at his office at the University of Texas to provide generous feedback on this project to specifically discuss Plato's *Republic*. I am deeply appreciative for his time and generosity.

I would like to thank Professor Bruce Lincoln for communicating with me over email and providing valuable feedback on my ideas on Dumézilian trifunctionalism in relation to Plato and the US Constitution. Professor Jaan Puhvel also provided valuable criticism of Dumézilian trifunctionalism.

Professor Jack Rakove of Stanford University thoughtfully responded to several of my emails and questions in relation to my research into American Constitutional law based on my reading of his book titled *Original Meanings: Politics and Ideas in the Making of the Constitution* (1996)—that won the 1997 Pulitzer Prize for History.

I cannot overlook Professor Richard Vlekley of Tulane University for his email correspondence since early 2015. I am also thankful for my correspondence and insights from Professor Miguel Vatter at Deakin University, Professor Roger Woodward at the University of Buffalo, and Professor Emily Lyle at the University of Edinburgh.

Finally, no acknowledgments would be total without thanking my professor and longtime mentor, William Byrnes. Without his help, teaching, and guidance, much of what occurred in my life would have occurred differently. He is the reason I found out about and went to the University of Amsterdam's Advanced LLM program. A life-changing experience that pays dividends every day. Much of what I experienced academically and personally came through the direction he shared with me, as well as the career and academic direction he still shares with me.

Thank you, Professor Byrnes, for showing me the wonderful frontier of the tax law world. Much of philosophy and jurisprudence has a lot of work to do in tax law. Your work in the field of law has been invaluable to practitioners, academics, and students like me. Your passion resides in us. Thank you.

Finally, I thank Wesley De Sena, who read various drafts of this book even while he pursued his Master of Theological Studies at Harvard Divinity School. His insights provided me with new ways to think about my subject matter and unique insight into comparative mythology.

A Special Thank You to Libraries and Bookstores

The summer of 2012 proved to be one of the most productive summers for me. As a nineteen-year-old, I read every day at Harvard's Widener Library, Lamont Library, or Langdell Library. And often at all three in a day. Through the Harvard Library system and the library's HOLLIS catalog, I grew unlike ever before. In that summer in Cambridge, I developed the ideas and firsthand written notes for my first book *The Dialectical Path of Law*, which ultimately led me to the ideas in this book. In this sense, I would like to thank the Harvard Library as well as all those who work there for all that the system has done for my education and the development of my thought. A sincere and dear thank you to the Harvard Library.

But across Massachusetts Avenue, I found myself on pleasant, rainy, dry, or warm summer nights at the Harvard Book Store. As a student with a tight budget, my purchases found an inherent limit. But of the books I perused and those that I bought and the books I still have—including the books with the receipts, of the exact moment I bought the book, tucked away in the cover or to be used as a bookmark—showed me a new world of thought. I would like to thank the Harvard Book Store for its book signings, the smells of the used books downstairs, and the fabulous smells of the new books upstairs. Thank you to the Harvard Book Store.

Much of my research for this book occurred through the Texas A&M University Library System. The Aggie Library System has been one of the key fixtures of my life since I started law school in 2013. Again, I must thank Professor William Byrnes for keeping me as his research assistant and guaranteeing me access to the Aggie system online and in person. But the University of Groningen Library online now assists my use of the Aggie Library System.

Many public libraries—such as the District of Columbia Public Library, New Orleans Public Library, Central Texas Digital Consortium, Round Rock Public Library, Harris County Public Library, Houston Area Digital Media Catalogue, Houston Public Library, Corpus Christi Public Library Broward County Library, Austin Public Library, Las Vegas—Clark County Library District, Alexandria Library (Northern Virginia outside of Washington, DC), New York Public Library, San Jose Public Library, and Sunnyvale Public Library—provided digital books and support for my research even if I did not physically visit during the COVID-19 pandemic lockdown.

Given that I have been living in the Austin, Texas area for most of the writing of this book since I published my last book, *The Dialectical Path of Law* (2021), the Austin Public Library's various branches have served as a place of meditation, contemplation, and inspiration. Moreover, the Austin Public Library Recycled Reads Bookstore allowed me to pick up and discover books that I would not have likely seen before. In that same vein, I thank the Half-Price Books locations in Austin for inspiring me since I was a child.

Ever since I was a child, my parents took me to the Barnes & Noble at the Arboretum in Austin. As a teenager, I kept going there for dates and finding new books. Since then, I still go every chance I get, making new memories and discovering new books. The Barnes & Noble in Cedar Park near Lakeline Mall still is a home away from home—but really just five minutes from home.

Regarding the love of Austin bookstores, I cannot neglect to mention Book People in downtown Austin, where as a child I used to hide in the small caves and cubby holes for kids, losing myself in books. These days, I find myself on the other end of the bookstore in philosophy, history, politics, and fiction, losing myself in other concepts. Book People's discount section often proves and shows itself to be a treasure trove.

But outside of the United States, I found other homes from home. Amsterdam is filled with bookstores and booksellers around the University. I am infinitely thankful for having lived in such a bookish city. Many of the ideas in this book originated in the Amsterdam University Library in Single. A special thanks to The American Book Center and the Athenaeum Boekhandel Spui en Nieuwscentrum that Brodie McGhie-Fraser introduced me. Another thanks to Waterstones on Kalverstraat in Amsterdam as well.

And in recent years, I have had the opportunity to become inspired in the bookstores of Groningen and the University of Groningen's library system. Again, another lovely bookish city has drawn me nearby to its commodious stacks of books and the aroma of books. The stacks and smell of books lead to endless discovery and exploration.

But every trip to Groningen brings me back to Amsterdam. There, I'm reminded of how I used to walk to class every day in Oudemanhuispoort in Amsterdam, the book market—*boekenmarkt*—in the hallways of that old courtyard filled me with inspiration daily. Now, each new visit creates memories and ideas.

Principal Characters

- John Adams (1735–1826), second president of the United States and prolific author during the American Revolutions of 1776 and 1787
- Alexander Hamilton (1755–1804), prolific author and author of fifty-one *Federalist Papers*
- James Madison (1751–1836), fourth president of the United States, author of twenty-nine *Federalist Papers*, one of the chief architects of the American Constitution drafted in 1787, and a key figure in the creation of the Bill of Rights of 1781
- John Marshall (1755–1835), Justice of the Supreme Court from 1801 to 1835, firmly established the notion of judicial review
- Thomas Jefferson (1743–1826), third president of the United States, author of the Declaration of Independence
- Georges Edmond Raoul Dumézil (1898–1986), French structuralist anthropologist, formulated a trifunctional hypothesis to describe Proto-Indo-European mythology and society
- Sigmund Freud (1856–1939), founder of modern psychology and framed the tripartite distinction of the psyche through the *id*, *super-ego*, and *ego*
- George Washington (1732–99), First president of the United States, committed to ancient Roman and Greek republican notions of virtue
- Charles Louis de Secondat, Baron de La Brède et de Montesquieu (1689–1755), French political philosopher who influenced the Framers of the US Constitution on the three parts of government—a judiciary, executive, and legislative
- Plato (427/428 BC–348/347 BC), ancient Greek philosopher, author of *The Republic* and *Phaedrus* that outlined the three parts of the Platonic soul—*Thumos*, *eros*, and *logos*
- Polybius (200/197 BC–118/116 BC), ancient Greek historian who argued the reasons the Romans achieved so much success in his *Histories*. He attributed that success to the tripartite constitution of the Roman Republic comprising of the Assemblies, the Senate, and the magistrates

- Socrates (469/470 BC–399 BC), ancient Greek philosopher who has no recorded writings but was Plato's teacher and is the main character in most of the Platonic dialogues
- Homer (*c.* eighth century BC), The specific birth and death years of the ancient Greek poet are unknown. A blind poet who is attributed as the author of the prominent works *Iliad* and the *Odyssey* within the Greek oral tradition

Introduction

This book presents one general theory. That theory is that the US Constitution has three-part function that represents a pattern in political and philosophical thought, namely, that of trifunctionalism. This book explains why such an approach suits the structure of government well. But this book does not explain why such a three-part function of society exists.

The three parts of the US Constitution are the legislative, the executive, and the judicial. The cliché of such a structure of government that frequently elementary or middle school students learn in the United States is that the legislative branch creates the laws; the executive branch carries out the laws; and the judicial branch interprets the laws. Such an articulation reflects reality, but does not holistically explain the functioning of the US Constitution and its effect on the laws of the country. Such an accounting represents the total accumulation of laws, regulations, proposed laws, legislative history, regulatory history, case law, executive orders, treaties, and so on—perhaps *ad infinitum*. But it also has bearing on the private arrangements individuals enter into, such as contracts, deeds, titles, wills, codicils, trusts all from the prosaic to the hyper-complicated substance of law. As such, these represent the written words and text of the organization of our society.

Whether our social norms influence the creation of laws or the laws influence the creation of norms of such laws is not always clear. Indeed, there likely exists some back and forth: social norms influence laws and laws can influence social norms. They cyclically influence each other.

But what does a trifunctional analysis have to do with analyzing social norms? The answer is that the US Constitution is the basis of all law and private legal contracts in the country. If one can understand the nature of the Constitution, then the laws of the country may also be illuminated. Thus, this book seeks to shed light on the origin of the US Constitution and its true functioning.

This is not merely a legal book, but a book that relies on philosophical, political, literary, anthropological, and social thought to interpret a legal document—the US Constitution. Both in the inverse can shed light on the former. The Constitution can help understand social thought and social thought can help understand the Constitution.

An Encomium on Deep Reading

> I turn my body from the sun. What ho, Tashtego! let me hear thy hammer. Oh! ye three unsurrendered spires of mine; thou uncracked keel; and only god-bullied hull; thou firm deck, and haughty helm, and Pole-pointed prow—death—glorious ship! must ye then perish, and without me? Am I cut off from the last fond pride of meanest shipwrecked captains? Oh, lonely death on lonely life! Oh, now I feel my topmost greatness lies in my topmost grief. Ho, ho! from all your furthest bounds, pour ye now in, ye bold billows of my whole foregone life, and top this one piled comber of my death! Towards thee I roll, thou all-destroying but unconquering whale; to the last I grapple with thee; from hell's heart I stab at thee; for hate's sake I spit my last breath at thee. Sink all coffins and all hearses to one common pool! and since neither can be mine, let me then tow to pieces, while still chasing thee, though tied to thee, thou damned whale! Thus, I give up the spear!
>
> —Herman Melville, *Moby Dick*, Chapter 135

James Madison's *Federalist Paper No. 10* can be interpreted in two ways. Both ways have validity and worth in their interpretation. However, the second way has an esoteric reading that Madison encapsulated in the text.

Esotericism is meant here in the context of holding heterodoxic views and hiding alternative readings within a text. German-Jewish twentieth-century philosopher Leo Strauss laid out the meaning of esotericism in his *Persecution and the Art of Writing* (1952). Strauss's simple argument that encapsulates esotericism is that some beliefs are not politically viable and thus must be represented in language that is not immediately apparent in a first or subsequent reading. A reader must endeavor to delve deeply into a text to understand it. A simple text example comes from the Sephardic Jewish philosopher Maimonides, who lived in the Islamic Caliphate of Spain during the twelfth century in Medieval Europe. Strauss claimed that Maimonides wrote in an esoteric way because Maimonides did not actually believe in religion, Maimonides had to obfuscate his true meanings for political reasons.

Strauss notes that moral, religious, and political philosophers in prior centuries had to hide their actual views from the public for fear of persecution of heterodox beliefs. However, Strauss writes in *Persecution and the Art of Writing* (1952) that in esoteric writing because "[p]ersecution cannot prevent even public expression of the heterodox truth, for a man of independent thought can utter his views in public and remain unharmed, provided he moves with circumspection. He can even utter them in print without danger, provided he can write between the lines." Thus, in Strauss's view, the most excellent and in-depth texts require multiple readings with deep analysis. Strauss's view may be read as a variation and recognition of the existence of Plato's *noble lie*—where a political system must maintain a lie to maintain authority over the populace. Strauss suggested in his book *The City and Man* (1964) that a *noble lie* was necessary for political systems to exist.

Thus, in summary, there are at least two ways to read a text. One is a simple and direct reading. It is not meant to be an incorrect reading. It is an exoteric reading. However, such a reading is an incomplete reading. The second can only be discovered through intensive reading through a trained eye. It is a difficult task to accomplish, and Strauss reserves such reading for a select few members of society.

The first interpretation of Madison's *Federalist Paper No. 10* is not an esoteric reading. It is that minority rights must be preserved over majority rights. It occurs through factionalism, where minorities in some states will support minorities in other states, or majorities in some states will support minorities in other states. Madison defines factionalism as "a number of citizens, whether amounting to a minority or majority of the whole, who are united and actuated by some common impulse of passion, or of interest, adverse to the rights of other citizens, or to the permanent and aggregate interests of the community." Madison further states that "the most common and durable source of factions has been the various and unequal distribution of property." Madison here means that factions come to exist through unequal distributions of property. This seems like an egalitarian statement. Factions occur because people have equal property. Thus, a surface-level reading of *Federalist Paper No. 10* suggests that Madison wants to reduce economic inequality.

The second way is an esoteric reading. Starting from the exoteric meaning, Madison shows that the primary concern of government is economic. But the government's economic concern is to stop the factionalism that would affect unequal distribution of property. It seems reasonable to interpret Madison as writing that capitalists and businesses can exploit and create factions of whomever they want as well as those with less and unequal property. The business owners and monied interest will have this ability because they would prevent laws which would restrain factions taking away property from the wealthier factions. Any attempts at achieving goals to help poorer people will be constantly under attack and almost always prevented from ever becoming law. Thus, Madison wants to limit the means to which economic inequality may be ameliorated by taking away property from the monied interests in the country. *Federalist Paper No. 10* can be read to say that government ensures factions can't aggregate power to use the government to take from the property class.

This esoteric reading becomes clearer in the following section:

> As long as the reason of man continues fallible, and he is at liberty to exercise it, different opinions will be formed. As long as the connection subsists between his reason and his self-love, his opinions and his passions will have a reciprocal influence on each other; and the former will be objects to which the latter will attach themselves. The diversity in the faculties of men, from which the rights of property originate, is not less an insuperable obstacle to a uniformity of interests. The protection of these faculties is the first object of government. From the protection of different and unequal faculties of acquiring property, the possession of different degrees and kinds of property immediately results; and from the influence of these on the sentiments and views of the respective proprietors, ensues a division of the society into different interests and parties.

Here, Madison states that different opinions and faculties of people lead to different levels of property accumulations. In other words, the different skills and passions people have, the differing levels of property they will acquire. This makes sense. But these differing interests often lead to differing interests, which can lead to factions and different parties. Madison acknowledges the government must protect these faculties because each of them can be productive. But he acknowledges that these differing parties of interest lead to a division in society. Madison wants to maintain this difference of skills. And thus, he wants to maintain the unequal distribution of property. This is the esoteric reading. He does not explicitly say it, but equal distribution of property will not be allowed under the Constitution. Logically in this section, Madison admits he is against the idea of equality in property ownership.

Madison couches his language appropriately, but he explicitly states government intends to prevent equal distribution of property. He writes this in the second to last paragraph:

> The influence of factious leaders may kindle a flame within their particular States, but will be unable to spread a general conflagration through the other States: … for an abolition of debts, for an equal division of property, or for any other improper or wicked project, will be less apt to pervade the whole body of the Union, than a particular member of it.

In other words, the factious leaders may attempt to create laws for equal division of property—which Madison labels as a wicked project—but the structure of the Union under the US Constitution would now allow that.

1

The US Constitution's Three Parts

A Legal Analysis

The accumulation of all powers, legislative, executive, and judiciary, in the same hands, whether of one, a few, or many, and whether hereditary, selfappointed, or elective, may justly be pronounced the very definition of tyranny.

—James Madison, *Federalist Paper No. 47* (1788)

In republican government, the legislative authority necessarily predominates.

—James Madison, *Federalist Paper No. 51* (1788)

All the powers of government, legislative, executive, and judiciary, result to the legislative body [in the Virginia Constitution of 1776]. The concentration these in the same hands is precisely the definition of despotic government.

—Thomas Jefferson, *Notes on the State of Virginia* (1785)

The Goal of This Chapter

The goal of this chapter is to lay out the three-part structure of the US Constitution: the legislative, executive, and judicial. This tripartite structure will remain one of the key premises of this entire book. Subsequent chapters will analyze the three functions and classes represented in the three parts of the US Constitution. However, this chapter will not analyze the functions. This chapter aims to lay out the framework and functions. In a Straussian sense, this chapter seeks to lay out the "exoteric" meaning of the Constitution.

To lay out the Constitution, this chapter uses case law and history. Case law remains a key domain of the judiciary. However, given that the judiciary can analyze the other three parts in such detail without losing the other functions' ethos remains a good source.

Ideally, the best description would be other branches describing a third branch or completely different sources—such as secondary sources—describing a branch of government.

With these limitations in mind, this chapter hopes to provide a compelling conception of the three parts of the US Constitution. Such a chapter could be used for future research for purposes of understanding what the US Constitution does.

The Judiciary

The role of the judiciary depends on the interpreter's perspective. The formation of the judiciary underwent several debates during the Constitutional Convention of 1787. Indeed, James Madison's notes provided the delegates to the Constitutional Convention debated competing theories for how the judiciary should have functioned during the Convention.[1]

From a formalistic perspective, the role of the judiciary frequently follows a logical and syllogistic application of law found in the notion of *stare decisis et non quieta movere.*[2]

Such a system provides legitimacy and predictability.[3] Affirming this idea, the Ninth Circuit Court of Appeals wrote, "Stare decisis is the policy of the court to stand by precedent; the term is but an abbreviation of stare decisis et non quieta movere—'to stand by and adhere to decisions and not disturb what is settled.'"[4]

But, the pure use of syllogisms as it appears in the use of stare decisis does not always occur. Justice Rehnquist admits in the majority opinion of *Payne v. Tennessee* that "*Stare decisis* is the preferred course because it promotes the evenhanded, predictable, and consistent development of legal principles, fosters reliance on judicial decisions, and contributes to the actual and perceived integrity of the judicial process"[5] (emphasis in original). Furthermore, on a policy note Rehnquist writes, "Adhering to precedent 'is usually the wise policy, because in most matters it is more important that the applicable rule of law be settled than it be settled right.'"[6] However, he goes on to write that "when governing decisions are unworkable or are badly reasoned, 'this Court has never felt constrained to follow precedent,'" meaning in other words, "*Stare decisis* is not an inexorable command; rather, it 'is a principle of policy and not a mechanical formula of adherence to the latest decision.'"[7] Rehnquist further states that not using stare decisis is "true in constitutional cases, because in such cases 'correction through legislative action is practically impossible.'"[8]

Subsequent Supreme Court opinions have reaffirmed and restated Rehnquist's opinion on *stare decisis*. Justice Scalia more recently in *Johnson v. United States*, writing for the majority opinion, provided that "[t]he doctrine of stare decisis allows us to revisit an earlier decision where experience with its application reveals that it is unworkable." Here Scalia showed how experience can inform the application of *stare decisis*.[9]

Indeed, such an experience informed use of judicial reasoning does not conform to the Roman idea of pure logic envisioned in the term *elegantia juris*.[10] Instead such an idea is a balanced view more akin to Oliver Wendell Holmes's pronouncement of legal realism that he outlines in his book *The Common Law*, "[t]he life of the law has not been logic: it has been experience."[11] Holmes adopted a critical view on the scientific and logical methods that Harvard University School of Law Professor Christopher Columbus Langdell proposed and used.[12] Holmes wrote that Langdell "could be suspected of ever having troubled himself about Hegel, we might call him a Hegelian in disguise, so entirely is he interested in the formal connection of things, or logic, as distinguished from the feelings which make the content of logic, and which have actually shaped the substance of the law."[13]

Holmes's mode of legal realism could appear in judicial reasoning and decisions as a type of "sociological jurisprudence." The former Dean of Harvard Law School Roscoe Pound proposed the notion of sociological jurisprudence. In sociological jurisprudence courts are allowed or even encouraged to consider social factors in decision-making.[14] Moreover, Holmes argued that decisions that appear to be based on strict logical formalism are actually masquerading policy decisions. Holmes argues this by stating "[p]erhaps one of the reasons why judges do not like to discuss questions of policy, or to put a decision in terms upon their views as law-makers, is that the moment you leave the path of merely logical deduction you lose the illusion of certainty which makes legal reasoning seem like mathematics."[15] However, Holmes admitted that the premises for an argument still itself was a choice of policy in line with Pound's sociological jurisprudence—whereby afterwards judges could use logical deductions—"certainty is only an illusion, nevertheless."[16]

Executive

An illustrative example defining the Constitutional limits of the Executive branch's power is seen in *Youngstown Sheet & Tube Co. v. Sawyer.*[17] The facts of the case originated as a result of the steel labor strikes during the Truman administration during the Korean War. President Truman sought to take executive control over the steel producers under the inherent powers doctrine. *Youngstown Sheet & Tube Co. v. Sawyer.*[18]

Justice Black writing the Supreme Court's majority opinion provided that the Presidential and Executive power "must stem either from an act of Congress or from the Constitution itself." *Youngstown Sheet & Tube Co. v. Sawyer.*[19]

Justice Black wrote that the could not "with faithfulness to our constitutional system hold that the Commander in Chief of the Armed Forces has the ultimate power as such to take possession of private property in order to keep labor disputes from stopping production. This is a job for the Nation's lawmakers, not for its military authorities." *Youngstown Sheet & Tube Co. v. Sawyer*, 343 US 579, 587.

Moreover, Justice Black writing for the Court indicated that "[i]n the framework of our Constitution, the President's power to see that the laws are faithfully executed refutes the idea that he is to be a lawmaker."[20] This means that the Constitution limits the Executive's rulemaking force. Instead, the Court continues interpreting the Constitution so as to give power to the legislature to make rules, "[a]ll legislative Powers herein granted shall be vested in a Congress of the United States." After granting many powers to the Congress, Article I goes on to provide that Congress may "make all Laws which shall be necessary and proper for carrying into Execution the foregoing Powers, and all other Powers vested by this Constitution in the Government of the United States, or in any Department or Officer thereof."[21]

Specifically in terms of taking of private property for public use the Court stated only Congress is authorized for "the taking of private property for public use."[22]

Perhaps using the logic of originalism, the Court declared: "The Founders of this Nation entrusted the lawmaking power to the Congress alone in both good and bad times. It would do no good to recall the historical events, the fears of power and the hopes for freedom that lay behind their choice. Such a review would but confirm our holding that this seizure order cannot stand."[23]

As a result of the case, in the concurring opinion Justice Frankfurter wrote, "Loose and irresponsible use of adjectives colors all nonlegal and much legal discussion of presidential powers. 'Inherent' powers, 'implied' powers, 'incidental' powers, 'plenary' powers, 'war' powers and 'emergency' powers are used, often interchangeably and without fixed or ascertainable meanings."[24]

Justice Frankfurter writing in a concurring opinion on the Separation of Power provided that "[t]he doctrine of the separation of powers was adopted by the Convention of 1787, not to promote efficiency but to preclude the exercise of arbitrary power. The purpose was, not to avoid friction, but by means of the inevitable friction incident to the distribution of the governmental powers among three departments, to save the people from autocracy."[25]

In relation to the *super ego*, *Youngstown Sheet & Tube Co.* represents how the Executive branch is limited in its functions of making laws but it carries out these laws. The Executive may resolve conflicts through agencies.

The concept of the super ego most clearly appears in the notion of *Chevron* deference doctrine. In the *Chevron* deference doctrine, the Supreme Court decided that "considerable weight should be accorded to an executive department's construction of a statutory scheme it is entrusted to administer, and the principle of deference to administrative interpretations."[26]

Justice Stevens wrote the case involved that "[i]n the Clean Air Act Amendments of 1977, Pub. L. 95–95, 91 Stat. 685, Congress enacted certain requirements applicable to States that had not achieved the national air quality standards established by the Environmental Protection Agency (EPA) pursuant to earlier legislation."[27] He continued stating that "[t]he amended Clean Air Act required these 'nonattainment' States to establish a permit program regulating 'new or modified major stationary sources' of air pollution."[28] Moreover, the EPA required that plants comply with a certain level of conditions.[29] The issue of the case was "whether EPA's decision to allow States to treat all of the pollution-emitting devices within the same industrial grouping as though they were encased within a single 'bubble' is based on a reasonable construction of the statutory term 'stationary source.'"[30]

The Court concluded that when any court in the judiciary function reviews an agency's action, the court must take two questions into consideration.[31] The first question the court must ask is "whether Congress has directly spoken to the precise question at issue. If the intent of Congress is clear, that is the end of the matter; for the court, as well as the agency, must give effect to the unambiguously expressed intent of Congress."[32] The second question the court must ask is if "Congress has not directly addressed the precise question at issue … the question for the court is whether the agency's answer is based on a permissible construction of the statute," meaning the court defers to an agency's interpretation.[33] Likewise, if the agency does not have an interpretation, the court would interpret the statute.[34]

In *Chevron*, the Court reasoned and "justified this new general rule of deference by positing that Congress has implicitly delegated interpretive authority to all agencies charged with enforcing federal law."[35] Indeed, the Court provided that "the decision [made] administrative actors the primary interpreters of federal statutes and relegate courts to the largely inert role of enforcing unambiguous statutory terms."[36]

The Legislative

In 1917, Congress proposed the Eighteenth Amendment. That law represented a *will* of portions of the country to ban alcohol. But in 1933, the Twenty-first Amendment repealed that 1917 ban. The 1933 repeal also represented a will at the time. Alternatively, the 1933 Amendment could have also represented that the 1917 Congress did not accurately represent what people desired in 1917—but it took over a decade to change the law. In a sense, the Eighteenth Amendment represented the soul of the polity going out of control. That action in 1917 was initially an unjust result although deemed necessary just at the time. Then Congress repealed it deciding that the Twenty-first Amendment was just—meaning the Eighteenth was deemed unjust. Examples of such laws presented and passed by Congress are clearer. Often Congress passes unclear laws that are difficult to understand.

The need for rules of statutory interpretation indicates that there is a need to interpret laws that are often difficult to understand.[37] This could be the result of many factors, such as rushed drafting,[38] political maneuvering to gain enough votes, or the lack of any of these.[39] Professor Abbe Gluck of Yale Law School has pointed out that a major reason for the public outcry against the courts and the legislature is because we do not have a clear understanding of their respective roles:

> These moves have been grounded in a spectacular lack of theory about the role that courts should play in the legislative process itself—which is, after all, the fundamental constitutional question of the Court-Congress relationship in statutory cases. Should courts try to understand how Congress works, or is Congress too complex to understand? Should courts be "tough" on Congress, perhaps to incentivize Congress to draft better the next time, or should courts cut Congress some slack, and even correct enacted imperfections? Perhaps courts are best conceived as guardians of the US Code, obligated to shape increasingly imperfect statutes into a more coherent product for the public, no matter how disconnected that result may be from Congress's own intentions. The Court has long resisted definitively answering these basic questions, even as the most difficult statutory cases turn on them.[40]

The problem of the legislature not conforming to its theoretical role within the three branches of government has occurred in other branches as well, including the judiciary with the Supreme Court. Even "[t]he Warren Court understood the problems and the promises of politics from its own experience. The Court numbered among its members former senators, representatives, and state legislators, a former governor and a former mayor, and former cabinet members."[41]

Furthermore, there does not seem to be a uniform system of interpreting statutes, despite its importance for courts upholding the rules.[42] Some argue for the adoption of a uniform system of statutory interpretation.[43] Indeed, there could be problems with using different methods of statutory analysis within courts, because one method may work in one case, but not in another; yet, the subsequent courts would be urged to use precedent from the former case.[44] Alternatively, others argue against a uniform system of statutory interpretation, because such a system could lead to a rigid application of *stare decisis* for interpreting statutes.[45] However, despite several states having adopted "methodological" and "formalistic" *stare decisis*,[46] it is unclear whether the method produces equitable results.[47]

Although the legislatures have utmost formality, exemplified by guides such as Robert's *Rules of Order*[48] or Thomas Jefferson's *Manual of Parliamentary Practice*,[49] statutes that come from Congress are often vague and unclear.[50] The respective roles of the three branches of government are summarized in Table 1.1.

Summary of Chapter

Table 1.1 The Three Branches of the US Government and Their Constitutional Functions

Branch of Government	Highest Body	Function
Judiciary	Supreme Court	Judicial Review John Marshall wrote: "It is emphatically the province and duty of the judicial department to say what the law is. Those who apply the rule to particular cases, must of necessity expound and interpret that rule. If two laws conflict with each other, the courts must decide on the operation of each." —*Marbury v. Madison*, 5 US 137 (1803) Alexander Hamilton in *Federalist Paper No. 78* wrote: "If it is said that the legislative body is themselves the constitutional judges of their own powers and that the construction they put upon them is conclusive upon the other departments, it may be answered, that this cannot be the natural presumption, where it is not to be collected from any particular provisions in the Constitution. It is not otherwise to be supposed, that the Constitution could intend to enable the representatives of the people to substitute their will to that of their constituents. It is far more rational to suppose, that the courts were designed to be an intermediate body between the people and the legislature, in order, among other things, to keep the latter within the limits assigned to their authority."
Executive	Presidency	Alexander Hamilton in *Federalist Paper No. 78* wrote: "The Executive not only dispenses the honors but holds the sword of the community."
Legislative	Congress—Bicameral Chambers with a House of Representatives apportioned for representation by state and a Senate having two senators per state	Alexander Hamilton in *Federalist Paper No. 78* wrote: "The legislature not only commands the purse but prescribes the rules by which the duties and rights of every citizen are to be regulated."

Notes

1 James Madison, *Notes of Debates in the Federal Convention of 1787* (Ohio University Press, Athens, 2022).

2 Petersen v. Magna Corp., 773 N.W.2d 564, 571 (Mich. 2009). "*Stare decisis* is short for *stare decisis et non quieta movere*, which means 'stand by the thing decided and do not disturb the calm.' *Stare decisis* attempts to balance two competing considerations: the need of the community for stability in legal rules and decisions and the need of courts to correct past errors. This doctrine has been part of the American legal landscape since the country's formation." See Thomas Healy, *Stare Decisis as a Constitutional Requirement*, 104 W. VA. L. REV. 43, 56–62 (2001).

However, the article itself notes that very few cases were recorded during the Anglo-Saxon period. However, there were many records of Anglo-Saxon and Norman history such as the "Anglo-Saxon Chronicle," 1067 AD, version D, (B. L. Cott, Tiber B. iv), English Historical Documents, 2nd Ed., Vol. 2, Ed. David C. Douglass and G. W. Greenaway (London: Oxford University Press, 1981) 150. Indeed, there are even artistic representations, such as the Bayeux Tapestry. See *The Bayeux Tapestry, A Comprehensive Survey* (Sir Frank Stenton ed., Phaidon, New York, 1957).

But earlier Roman law was itself a compilation of cases in digests, which Roman lawyers would reference. See Shael Herman, *Legacy and Legend: The Continuity of Roman and English Regulation of the Jews*, 66 TUL. L. REV. 1781, 1797 (1992). Even as early as the first century BC "Cicero praised his friend, the jurist Servius Sulpicius Rufus for using dialectic and treating law as [a science]," indicating that—much like the modern method of using case law—Romans treated like cases alike. James Gordley, *The Method of Roman Jurists*, 87 TUL. L. REV. 933, 947 n.73 (2013). See generally Peter Stein, Regulae Iuris: From Juristic Rules to Legal Maxims (1966).

By 1256, Henry de Bracton wrote of the importance of using past precedent he experienced previously to decide current cases before him, "if any new and unusual matters arise, which have not before been seen in the realm, if like matters arise let them be decided by like since the decision is a good one for proceeding a similibus ad similia." Thomas Healy, *Stare Decisis as a Constitutional Requirement*, 104 W. VA. L. REV. 43, 56–7 (2001).

3 Henry Paul Monaghan, *Stare Decisis and Constitutional Adjudication*, 88 COLUM. L. REV. 723, 749–52 (1988).

4 *In re* Osborne, 76 F.3d 306, 309 (9th Cir. 1996)

Moreover, the Court unpacked the etymology of *stare decisis* writing, "Consider the word 'decisis.' The word means, literally and legally, the decision. Nor is the doctrine stare dictis; it is not 'to stand by or keep to what was said.' Nor is the doctrine stare rationibus decidendi—'to keep to the rationes decidendi of past cases.' Rather, under the doctrine of stare decisis a case is important only for what it decides—for the 'what,' not for the 'why,' and not for the 'how.' Insofar as precedent is concerned, stare decisis is important only for the decision, for the detailed legal consequence following a detailed set of facts." *id.*

5 *Payne v. Tennessee*, 501 U.S. 808, 827 (1991).

6 *Id.* at 827.

7 *Id.*

8 *Id.* at 828–9.

9 *Johnson v. United States*, 576 U.S. 591, 605 (2015).

10 Thomas C. Grey, *Holmes and Legal Pragmatism*, 41 STAN. L. REV. 787, 861 (1989).

11 Oliver Wendell Holmes, Jr., The Common Law 1 (Mark DeWolfe Howe ed., Harvard University Press 1963) (1881).

12 Andrew P. Morriss, *Codification and the Right Answers*, 74 CHI.-KENT L. REV. 355 (1999)

Compare with *Id.* n. 161 "The Civil Code of the State of New York (pt. 1), 2 ALB. L.J. 385, 385 (November 19, 1870). This was the idea behind the case method introduced by Christopher Columbus Langdell at Harvard Law School in 1870, where Carter had trained. See Wiecek, *supra* note 10, at 92–3."

Indeed, many legal scholars have long viewed Christopher Columbus Langdell, the dean of Harvard Law School from 1870 to 1895, as the prototypical American jurist of the late nineteenth century. He portrayed the common law as a conceptually ordered scientific system in which rigorous logical reasoning trumped concerns about the just resolution of particular cases. In Langdell's Orthodoxy, probably the most influential modern article on Langdell, Thomas Grey dubbed this system of legal thought "classical orthodoxy." Others have labeled it "mechanical jurisprudence," "classical legal thought," "liberal legal science," or "Langdellian formalism." Whatever term they have preferred, scholars have long agreed that Gilded Age legal thinkers viewed the common law as a rigidly logical, amoral system.

Lewis A. Grossman, *Langdell Upside-Down: James Coolidge Carter and the Anticlassical Jurisprudence of Anticodification*, 19 YALE J.L. & HUMAN. 149, 150 (2007).

13 Holmes, *supra* note 36, at 1. Holmes continued a sentence later, "[t]he form of continuity has been kept up by reasonings [*sic*] purporting to reduce every thing to a logical sequence; but that form is nothing but the evening dress which the newcomer puts on to make itself presentable according to conventional requirements. The important phenomenon is the man underneath it, not the coat; the justice and reasonableness of a decision, not its consistency with previously

held views. … As a branch of anthropology, law is an object of science; the theory of legislation is a scientific study; but the effort to reduce the concrete details of an existing system to the merely logical consequences of simple postulates is always in danger of becoming unscientific, and of leading to a misapprehension of the nature of the problem and the data."

14 *Roscoe Pound, Mechanical Jurisprudence*, 606 COLUMBIA L. REV. 8th ed. (1908).

15 Holmes, *Privilege, Malice, and Intent*, 8 HARV. L. REV. 1, 7 (1894).

16 *Id.* at 7.

17 *Youngstown Sheet & Tube Co. v. Sawyer*, 343 U.S. 579 (1952).

18 *Id.* at 582–5.

19 *Id.* at 585.

20 *Id.* at 587.

21 *Id.* at 588.

22 *Id.*

23 *Id.* at 589.

24 *Id.* at 646–7.

25 *Id.* at 629.

26 *Chevron, U.S.A., Inc. v. NRDC, Inc.*, 467 U.S. 837, 844 (1984).

27 *Id.* at 839–40.

28 *Id.* at 840.

29 *Id.*

30 *Id.*

31 *Id.* at 843.

32 *Id.* at 843–4.

33 *Id.* at 844.

34 *Id.*

35 Thomas W. Merrill, *Judicial Deference to Executive Precedent.*, 101 YALE L.J. 969 (1992).

36 *Id.* at 969–70.

37 Abbe R. Gluck, *The Supreme Court 2014 Term—Comment: Imperfect Statutes, Imperfect Courts: Understanding Congress's Plan in the Era of Unorthodox Law Making*, 129 HARV. L. REV. 62, 63 (2015).

38 Whether a law was passed too quickly is a matter of public opinion as well. Some commentators argued that Congress "rushed so fast through a short-circuited lawmaking process" to create the Act to provide for reconciliation pursuant to titles II and V of the concurrent resolution on the budget for fiscal year 2018, Pub. L. 115–97 also known as the Tax Cuts and Jobs Act of 2017 law. Albert R. Hunt, Republican Haste Warps Tax Bills, Bloomberg View (November 29, 2017).

39 See Cristina Marcos & Sarah Ferris, *House Votes to Repeal ObamaCare,* The Hill (February 3, 2015, 5:07 PM), http://thehill.com/policy/healthcare/231638-house-votes-to-repeal-obamacare [http://perma.cc/C7FH-LV65].

40 Gluck, *supra* note 62, at 63.

41 Pamela S. Karlan, *The Supreme Court 2011 Term: Foreword: Democracy and Disdain*, 126 HARV. L. REV. 1, 5 (2012).

42 Carlos E. González, *Reinterpreting Statutory Interpretation*, 74 N.C. L. REV. 585, 587 (1996).

43 "Methodological stare decisis—the practice of giving precedential effect to judicial statements about methodology—is generally absent from federal statutory interpretation, but appears to be a common feature of some states' statutory case law." Abbe R. Gluck, *The States as Laboratories of Statutory Interpretation: Methodological Consensus and the New Modified Textualism*, 119 YALE L.J. 1750, 1754 (2010).

44 See Brian G. Slocum, *Overlooked Temporal Issues in Statutory Interpretation*, 81 TEMP. L. REV. 635, (2008) (illustrating some of the problems with courts using different types of statutory analysis).

45 *See* Glen Staszewski, *The Dumbing Down of Statutory Interpretation*, 95 B.U. L. REV. 209, (2015) (arguing against a uniform system of statutory interpretation).

46 Professor Gluck expands on the terms methodological and formalistic: "By 'formalistic,' I mean clearly defined, ex ante interpretive rules arranged to be applied in a consistent order. But the characteristics of the particular rules chosen (for instance, whether and when legislative history may be consulted) need not themselves be rigid. *Cf.* Cass R. Sunstein, *Must Formalism Be Defended Empirically?*, 66 U. CHI. L. REV. 636, 638 (1999) ('Formalist strategies … entail three commitments: to promoting compliance with all applicable legal formalities (whether or not they make sense in the individual case), to ensuring rule-bound law … and to constraining the discretion of judges …')." Gluck, *supra* note 67, at 1754 n.8.

47 *Cf.* Alternatively, this article argues that courts should use *stare decises* to interpret statutes. Moreover, the article argues that courts should always use *stare decisis.* Sydney Foster, *Should Courts Give Stare Decisis Effect to Statutory Interpretation Methodology?*, 96 GEO. L.J. 1863 (2008).

48 Henry M. Robert, Robert's Rules of Order Newly Revised (12th ed. 2020); *See generally* Saul Levmore, *Parliamentary Law, Majority Decision Making, and the Voting Paradox,* 75 VA. L. REV. 971 (1989).

49 Thomas Jefferson, a Manual of Parliamentary Practice (1801).

50 Einer Elhauge, *Statutory Default Rules: How to Interpret Unclear Legislation* (Harvard University Press, Cambridge, MA, 2008).

2

A Homeric Analysis of the US Constitution

A Poetic Paradigm to Interpret the US Constitution

> μῆνιν ἄειδε θεὰ Πηληϊάδεω Ἀχιλῆος
> οὐλομένην, ἣ μυρί᾽ Ἀχαιοῖς ἄλγε᾽ ἔθηκε,
> πολλὰς δ᾽ ἰφθίμους ψυχὰς Ἄϊδι προΐαψεν
> ἡρώων, αὐτοὺς δὲ ἑλώρια τεῦχε κύνεσσιν
> οἰωνοῖσί τε πᾶσι, Διὸς δ᾽ ἐτελείετο βουλή,
> ἐξ οὗ δὴ τὰ πρῶτα διαστήτην ἐρίσαντε
> Ἀτρεΐδης τε ἄναξ ἀνδρῶν καὶ δῖος Ἀχιλλεύς.

> Sing, O goddess, the anger [mênis] of Achilles son of Peleus, that brought countless ills upon the Achaeans. Many a brave soul [psukhê] did it send hurrying down to Hades, and many a hero did it yield a prey to dogs and vultures, for so was the will of Zeus fulfilled from the day on which the son of Atreus, king of men, and great Achilles, first fell out with one another.
>
> —Homer, *The Iliad* (Samuel Butler translation)

Summary of Chapter

This chapter offers an interpretation of the US' structure of government outlined in the Constitution from the perspective of ancient Greek poetry—specifically the Homeric tradition based on *The Iliad* and *The Odyssey*. Simultaneously, it seeks to analyze and explain the continued three-part structure of the US federal government as outlined in the Constitution. Subsequently, this chapter defines the three parts of the federal government—judiciary, executive, and legislative—as explained through the lens of the Homeric ancient Greek account of the Judgment of Paris, where Paris of Troy is given a "choice" to pick among three goddesses regarding the fate of Troy: Hera, Athena, and Aphrodite.

Paradigmatically, the goddesses as such are Hera, Aphrodite, and Athena, whereby *Aphrodite* represents the legislative function, *Hera* represents the executive function, and *Athena* represents the judicial functions of the US system of government. This chapter picks up a previous law review article by this author titled *A Structural Etiology of the US Constitution*.[1] That predecessor article also provided a tripartite analysis of the US Constitution. However, the analysis occurred through the lens of Plato's tripartite conception of the soul where (*logos* = word = law), (*thumos* = external driving spirit = executive), and (*eros* = general welfare = legislative) extrapolated from Plato's dialogues.

First, this chapter establishes a working understanding of the Homeric account and references to the Judgment of Paris. The Homeric account of the Judgment of Paris and the representation of the three goddesses is the central premise—as in a syllogism. Second, the chapter lays out the generally accepted division of the US Constitution of 1789 as laying out three parts to the federal government—the legislative as described in Article I, the executive as described in Article II, and the judicial as described in Article III. This second part represents the minor premise. Third, the syllogism is completed by weaving the central premise of the three goddesses in the Judgment of Paris into the three parts of the US federal government. This third step of application suggests possible future evolution of the structure.

This chapter fits into the broader issue of the US federal government's functionally efficient and naturally adaptive structure. Providing a historical and poetic context to this structural analysis will serve as a framework for future research on the federal government's operation. When the branches of the federal government step out of their roles, the balance of the federal government structure becomes disrupted in liminal periods of paradigmatic change.

Introduction to Homeric Poetry

This chapter argues that the tripartite system of government in the United States can be viewed through the ancient Greek poetic account of the Judgment of Paris.[2] The central premise of this chapter is the definition and narrative summary of the Homeric and ancient Greek poetic account of the Judgment of Paris. The minor premise is that the US federal government has three major parts: the judiciary, the executive, and the legislative. The syllogism and argument of this chapter is that the three federal parts of government represent the Homeric mythological choice: the judiciary being the Greek goddess *Athena*, the executive being the Greek goddess *Hera*, and the legislative being the *Aphrodite*. This chapter will explore these concepts in greater depth. As a corollary, when the anthropological etiology of the polity—arguably archetypal structure—becomes unbalanced, people become dissatisfied with the government because the government does not fulfill its function administratively—acting in opposition to the laws—and promoting justice.

Premises and Structures of Analysis

The chapter takes the story of the Judgment of Paris and the causes of the Trojan War as representative of the Greek story. The primary interest this chapter shares is in the accessible and readable style Homer and other writers from antiquity present the story—particularly the three-part choice that Paris must face in the wedding. This chapter will rely mainly on primary source written material by Homer, namely, *The Iliad* and *The Odyssey*. However, the chapter will examine various translations to understand the meaning rather than focusing on one translation. This chapter will also look at secondary sources from antiquity and modernity.

Fundamentally, the validity of Homer's historical assertions appeals less to a reader than the results that can come about from utilizing his paradigm of the psyche. Considering the Homeric account holds literary value over historical accuracy, this chapter focuses more on an interpretation of the literary devices in Homer and ancient Greek poetry. The paradigm Homer applies to the structure of the US Constitution—much like literary analysis interprets legal principles. Thus, Homeric and ancient Greek poetry provided by the stories surrounding the Trojan War provides a way to read the US Constitution. Likewise, it is just as important to focus on the primary sources of Homer and ancient Greek authors' writings to apply Homeric and ancient Greek thought as literary devices. Thus, there is an even more critical need to focus on the primary texts. Indeed, given that literature and stories can represent mythological constructs, such an analysis can ultimately inversely affect the psyche—not through the validity of ancient Greek poetry's claims but through its literary value.[3]

Furthermore, this chapter presumes that the world has an order founded on reason that mirrors nature.[4] In Plato's *Timaeus*, the interlocutor—Timaeus himself—proposes that nature possesses discernible and organized structures.[5] Relevant to Plato's substantive inquiry in the *Timaeus* of order in nature, Plato inquires whether randomness or patterns are provable or real.[6] How do we decide what is random if not through statistical or other mathematical analysis?[7] Philosophically speaking, there could be a discrepancy between a series following a mathematical rule or being genuinely random. In his *Philosophical Investigations,* Ludwig Wittgenstein explained how randomness can be explained in terms of the increasing complexity of following a rule. However, paradoxically, if everything can be shown to be following a rule, it can also, at the same time, be shown not to follow a rule.[8]

The alternative to this presumption holds that there exists no order in the universe or world, and humans attempt to impose order.[9] Lucretius introduced such a view in his *On the Nature of the Universe.*[10] Consequently, nature can represent itself in the structure of law, specifically the law of the United States.[11]

Why a Structured Approach at All? A Philosophical-Psychoanalytic Explanation

To understand why analyzing and comparing the US government with the account of the Judgment of Paris as the central focal point in the origin of the Trojan War, the key event in Homeric poetry, is essential, it is helpful to first consider the broader philosophical and anthropological context. The following paragraph briefly overviews relevant historical analysis to provide context related to structural and "trifunctionalist" analysis.

Indeed, many anthropological-philosophical theories exist for understanding the fundamental structures of societies and governments. The twentieth-century French anthropologist and ethnologist Claude Lévi-Strauss promoted structuralism theories in his writings.[12] In the late twentieth century, French philosopher and historian Michel Foucault wrote that individual desire to gain power is the impetus behind government function.[13] Also, in the late twentieth century, the American anthropologist Marvin Harris contended that the practice of gift-giving within a society's structure enhances incentives to maintain the existing social dynamics and fortify the existing cultural foundations of that culture.[14] Likewise, the idea of a "tripartite" structure of society being inherent to human cultures is not new but has been written about extensively by George S. Dumézil.[15] The idea has even been discussed in Plato's dialogues regarding the three functions of the soul.[16] Indicative of the universal nature of the "trifunctionalist," Dumézilian approach has even been applied to Pre-Columbian Yucatán Mayan societies.[17]

Poetically, in the Homeric Greek account of the Judgment of Paris—prior to the beginning of the Trojan War in Homer's *Iliad*—Paris of Troy is given a Dumézilian "choice," a beauty contest among three goddesses Hera, Athena, and Aphrodite.[18] Applying the ancient Greek concept of the Platonic soul to governmental structure seems fitting because the "trifunctionalist" approach originates in ancient Greece but can also be seen in non-Western civilizations.

As the French political philosopher Montesquieu argued, a balanced view of government may exist in the separation of powers, "that of enacting laws, that of executing the public resolutions, and of trying the causes of individuals."[19] Exploring this thought "[i]n The Federalist No. 47, Madison explained that while Montesquieu was correct in saying that the separation of the legislative, executive, and judicial powers was essential to liberty, that conclusion did not purport to tell us how strict the resultant separation had to be."[20] This author suggested in a previous article that based on their education, the Framers of the Constitution may have even had Plato's Soul in mind when they framed the Constitution.[21] Granted, the Framers of the Constitution perhaps did not consciously and explicitly reference the Judgment of Paris in their deliberations, but there is evidence of knowledge of a tripartite paradigm reflected in government. Whether such a paradigm was discussed at the Constitutional Convention is unknown; it at least subconsciously existed in part of their educations.[22] Even if the Framers did not have Plato in the back of their minds, the idea of Plato's Soul is arguably inherent in humans regardless of how it is defined.[23] Moreover, a structured approach to the philosophical underpinnings of a government can be assumed to have been in the framer's mind—consciously or subconsciously. Likewise, poetry thought has similar undertones.

Why Ancient Greek Poetry and Homer?

If one embraces structured and poetical approaches as a reasonable mode of analysis, then why should one use ancient Greek poetry, and Homer specifically?

The idea of comparing a tripartite conception of the human mind—or mode of existence—is not original. Indeed, the idea of comparing the Platonic soul to the US federal system of government has been written previously by Akiba Covitz in *The Soul of the Polity* as explored in more depth in this book.[24] Covitz argued the syllogism as the judiciary is the *thumos*, the executive is the *logos*, and the legislative is the *eros*. This author and article greatly appreciate Covitz's theory and writing. The predecessor to this chapter by this author on the Platonic interpretation of the US Constitution switched correspondences from *thumos* to *logos* for judiciary, *logos* to *thumos* for executive, and maintains Covitz's conception of legislative as eros.[25] Indeed, Covitz used a different terminology of (1) artifice, (2) nature, and (3) history/divinity/myth instead of *logos*, *eros*, and *thumos*, respectively.[26] Covitz argues that the constitution had a psychoanalytic dimension, and these Platonic elements essentially represented this psychoanalysis.[27]

Professor Covitz sincerely wanted to explore what a constitution is. He asked, "ti esti or 'what is?'" translated from Greek. This classic question drove the ancient Greeks to a purely innocent love for searching for knowledge. This chapter has sourced inspiration from such an inquiry.

The inquiry here is what psychoanalytic characteristics can we extrapolate from the US Constitution using the Homeric paradigm of the human condition of choices that individuals must face as represented in the Judgment of Paris. Ultimately, this experimental test could lead to insights into the etiology or cause of the US Constitution from a teleological perspective—but not direct practical inquiries. Like classical Graeco-Roman studies, myths are frequently used to interpret why a specific custom existed in ancient Greece or Roman antiquity.

In his *Myth and History in Ancient Greece: The Symbolic Creation of a Colony* (2003), Claude Calame drew on work by George Dumézil, arguing that the ancient Greeks would not have viewed what we consider to be their mythology as fiction but rather the historical archaeological basis of their society.[28] It is fair to say that ancient Athenian citizens believed in the mythological stories allegedly authored by the blind poet Homer.

Likewise, the enshrining of the US Constitution carries some mythological status through its interpretation in popular culture—despite a more abundant aggregation of resources than in ancient Greece. However, regardless of whether such an event is fictional, its representation as an etiology for the subsequent events in US history is reasonable. Thus, analyzing the Constitution much like a literary document makes sense following the classical Graeco-Roman tradition of archaeological analysis.

Likewise, in returning to Covitz's initial inquiries of "what a constitution is," Covitz suggests an easy answer to these questions would be to "provide satisfying answers to my questions would be to choose the Constitution of the United States and a more contemporary and more straightforward text (at least in terms of form) such as [John] Locke's *Second Treatise on Government*, or Montesquieu's *Spirit of the Laws*." But Professor Covitz sought a "more than a deeper understanding of the American Constitution; [he sought the Constitution's original] beginnings." Thus, seeking to the origins of the Constitution may shed light on what the Constitution is.

Covitz followed in the path of answering these questions through Platonic dialogues because, if one is to understand the beginning of the US Constitution, one must be familiar with not only the circumstances that gave its birth, but also the great books that the authors of the Constitution read. Covitz supports this standpoint by writing, "[i]f one is to search out the theoretical beginnings of American constitutional thought, one must come to grips with the textual beginnings of the Western constitutional thought in which the American experience is itself framed," this can be interpreted as the books and laws the Framers were most familiar, "regardless of our views of Plato's tyrannical or democratic qualities. Important, underlying aspects of this broader realm of Western constitutional thought began in the dialogic pages and the constitutional theory of Plato's *Republic*."

This author gained much inspiration from such inquiries. It seems reasonable and in the spirit of Covitz's analysis to pursue the Homeric paradigm. This analysis will extend beyond the works available to the Framers of the Constitution from 1789, specifically into the Homeric and ancient Greek poetic traditions. The symbolic roles of the three Greek goddesses are summarized in Table 2.1.

The Judgment of Paris in Ancient Greek Poetry

Summary of Three Greek Goddesses

Table 2.1 Symbolic Interpretations of the Three Greek Goddesses in Political Allegory

Greek Goddess	Interpretation of the Goddesses' symbolic representation
Athena	Athena (Attic Greek: Αθηνά) the goddess of wisdom and logical thinking represents how the judiciary must act logically. Both Homer and Hesiod use the epithet "gray-eyed Athena."[29] In Attic Greek, translators usually convey γλαυκῶπις as "bright-eyed" or "grey-eyed."
Hera	Hera (Attic Greek: Ἥρα) the goddess married to the leader of the Olympian Greek gods, Zeus. Homer describes Hera frequently with the epithet βοῶπις ("cow-eyed").[30]
Aphrodite	Aphrodite (Attic Greek: Ἀφροδίτη) the goddess of love and fertility, lust, pleasure, and procreation. Homer frequently refers to Aphrodite with the epithet "φιλομμειδής" meaning "smile-loving."[31]

Welcome to Cause of the Trojan War

Before understanding how the Homeric Judgment of Paris functions within the US federal government, a brief outline of Homeric and ancient Greek conception of the events is required.

The primary sources from Homer do not explicitly reference the Judgment of Paris. Instead, the Homeric account in *The Iliad* alludes to the Judgment of Paris.[32] Such an allusion indicates that ancient Greek audiences knew of the Judgment of Paris. Later poets, including the Roman poets from the reign of Augustus Ovid[33] and Lucian,[34] the Greek writer Pseudo-Apollodorus,[35] and the Latin poet Gaius Julius Hyginus—a freedman from Augustus.[36] The Greek traveler and geographer Pausanias provides a more vivid account in his Descriptions of Greece.[37] Pausanias writes:

> Hermes bringing to Alexander [*i.e.*, who is also known as Paris] the son of Priam the goddesses of whose beauty he is to judge, the inscription on them being: "Here is Hermes, who is showing to Alexander, that he may arbitrate concerning their beauty, Hera, Athena and Aphrodite."

Here, Priam is the king of Troy. Alexander is also known as Paris. Hermes, one of the Greek gods, tells Paris that Paris may decide who is the most beautiful goddess among the three.

The myth occurs when Zeus organizes a banquet for the Olympian gods to celebrate the marriage of Peleus and Thetis.[38] Thetis and Peleus are the parents of Achilles—the hero whose wrath caused countless ills on the Achaeans in *The Iliad*.[39] Among those not invited included Eris. Eris was the goddess of chaos. Eris becomes angered at not being invited. Eris arrives uninvited to the wedding feast.

Nevertheless, Eris brings a golden apple from the Garden of the Hesperides.[40] The purpose of throwing this golden apple was to cause "strife," according to the Frazer translation of Pseudo-Apollodorus's *Bibliotheca*.[41] Indeed, Eris's name as a goddess means "strife." Some accounts provide that the golden apple had the word "καλλίστῃ."[42] The word is the dative form of καλός, meaning "good" or "beautiful," whereby καλλίστῃ means "to/for the fairest one."[43] This apple is generally known as the Golden Apple of Discord.[44]

In due course, three of the goddesses claim the apple thrown in by Eris. Those goddesses are Hera, Athena, and Aphrodite. The goddesses speak with Zeus to ask him to decide. However, Zeus does not want to decide. Instead, Zeus chooses a mortal from Troy—Paris. This part of the scene of the Judgment of Paris is the only scene alluded to in Homer's *Iliad*:

> All were of this mind save only Hera, Poseidon, and Zeus' gray-eyed daughter, who persisted in the hate which they had ever borne towards Ilion with Priam and his people; for they forgave not the wrong [atê] done them by Alexander in disdaining the goddesses who came to him when he was in his sheepyards, and preferring her who had offered him a wanton to his ruin. (Samuel Butler 1898 translation)[45]

The proceeding section indicates how Zeus was reluctant to make any judgment, and Paris was the one who had to judge.[46] The god Hermes shows Paris each of the goddesses. Each goddess makes an offer. Hera offers Paris to be king of Europe and Asia. Athena makes a promise of wisdom and skill in war. Aphrodite provides the promise of the most beautiful woman in the world. Paris decides to pick Aphrodite's offer. In turn, Helen of Sparta—collectively known as Helen of Troy—is identified by Aphrodite. Paris ends up with Helen. The problem is that Helen was married to the Spartan king, Menelaus. This is the immediate and proximate cause of the Trojan War. Menelaus raises a Greek army to bring war on the Trojans to bring Helen back to Greece. Homer's *Iliad* picks up in the middle of the Trojan War.

But this chapter is not concerned with the more significant portions of the Homeric poetic tradition. This chapter only focuses on the Judgment of Paris. To summarize the three-part choice, Paris had to choose among three goddesses. Each goddess represented a type of mythological wish that someone could attain. Athena represents the choice of wisdom and knowledge. Hera represents the choice of power and rulership. Aphrodite represents the more erotic of the choices leading to emotion.

Comparing the Structure of the Federal Government to the Three-Part Choice in the Ancient Greek Account of the Judgment of Paris

Judiciary as Athena

The judiciary[47] in this chapter's paradigm represents the ancient Greek goddess, Athena. The judicial function in the US Constitution is outlined in Article III of the US Constitution. Article III judges—as intended by the Framers of the Constitution—were not and are not politicians seeking re-election. Nevertheless, instead, they are aloof from the political system, seeking to interpret and apply the law. This logical analysis—which can be informed by the other elements of the soul—is the guiding principle of the judiciary. The judiciary represents *Athena.*

Why the Judiciary Represents the Ancient Greek Goddess Athena

In the Judgment of Paris, Athena promises Paris wisdom and knowledge—the most intangible of all the promises from the goddesses. Homer described Athena as the goddess most in charge of wisdom and knowledge in making wise choices.[48] Likewise, Chief Justice Marshall said, "It is emphatically the province and duty of the judicial department to say what the law is."[49] The Supreme Court uses judicial review and interprets the Constitution and legislatively passed statutes to keep them in check, much like the analogy of the rider being the ego.

Although ideally, the Court would follow *logic* of Athena, the catch is that the members of the Court are not purely guided by the *logos* of Athena—as to be expected—because all humans have the three-part paradigm of the psyche operating within them. The idea of a three-part psyche may be intended to understand the essential functions of an aspect of government; each member has an entire psyche governing their mind. This leads to more nuanced decisions in the judiciary and all three branches of the government.

In terms of the judiciary, stepping out of the bounds of the separate powers or the role in the soul of the policy can have bad and good outcomes.

Justice from the judiciary could come in various forms. In this case, the ego likely guides to just results by keeping emotions, represented through the id, and repressive forces, represented through the *superego*, in check.

Executive as the Ancient Greek Goddess Hera

In this chapter, the executive[50] represents *Hera. Hera* is the goddess who promised Paris to be king and ruler of Europe and Asia. This promise is more in line with administration and ruling a nation.

This indicates that one who would pick Hera will likely turn to politics. At the same time, in the tension of the other two goddesses (Athena and Aphrodite), and other words, has become the Hera—a force attempting to mediate the two. This is more akin to the president—rather than a member of the judiciary—who, in all likelihood, is searching for honors and recognition much like other politicians.

Such recognition of a politician's ability is not necessarily a negative aspect of the executive. Because if the country's executive did not seek honor or maintain some "haughtiness," other politicians and world leaders would take advantage of us. As president, she must be decisive, not merely passively following rules. However, the other goddesses' aspects may and must exist within her, but she must, as president, have a prevailing element similar to the goddess Hera.

At first, this moves away from purely logical toward using "experience," which may seem like a contradiction of the purely non-emotional and non-pleasure-seeking aspect of the *promise of Hera as represented in the Judgment of Paris.*

Why the Executive Represents Hera

Here, the *goddess Hera* manifests itself when a part of the Executive branch of government—such as the Department of the Treasury or the Food and the Federal Reserve System—interprets a statute from the legislature and implements it. This occurs through the rules laid out by the Supreme Court and the judiciary, as seen in the *Chevron* case.

Frequently, the president of the government issues executive orders. Moreover, frequently, Courts of Appeals declare executive orders unconstitutional. Whether the executive orders are eventually upheld as constitutional or not, they represent the Executive branch of government conducting actions with the administration's justification that they are the most in line with societal values to various problems. In this sense, such executive orders act in line with the promise of Hera at the Judgment of Paris. Suppose the orders are upheld to be constitutional after all. In such a case, the judiciary or the legislature will consider the executive orders to have been the more effective way to prevent a great disaster later. Conversely, if the orders are not upheld to be constitutional, then the judiciary or the legislature will have deemed them not the most effective approach.

Because the executive—and the legislature—is also charged with carrying out the daily activities of the nation, international relations appear to be of paramount importance with spirited leadership that represses immediate instincts of pleasure—as represented by the goddess Aphrodite.

Thus, the leadership and executive actions may not or may be based on *the notions represented in the goddesses Athena and Aphrodite,* but through the regulating force represented in the promise of Hera, which this chapter argues fits into the paradigm of the executive branch of government in the US Constitution.

The Legislature as the Ancient Greek Goddess Aphrodite

In this chapter, the legislature[51] represents *the promises of the ancient Greek goddess Aphrodite*. Aphrodite represents the basic instincts and desires of the subconscious of the preconscious. The Congress, in theory, acts the will of the people and is the closest interaction most of the population can have with the three main branches of government—arguably other than through taxation in the executive branch. Thus, many proposals in Congress can represent more emotional responses to issues—indeed, some are passed, and the other branches of government thwart some.

As such, the desires and pleasures of the Congress may seem contradictory—indeed, they often are—but over time, they become more precise and less clear. Indeed, one of the most challenging things to divine is the legislative intent of a Congressional act. Much like the notions that the goddess Aphrodite represents, an act of Congress can exhibit contradictory aims at the same time. The analogy between the Greek goddesses and the branches of the US Constitution is summarized in Table 2.2.

Summary of Analogy and Argument in This Chapter

Table 2.2 Summary of the Analogy between Greek Goddesses and the Branches of the US Constitution

Greek Goddess	US Constitution Branch	Interpretation in the Context of the Analogy of the Greek Goddess to the US Constitution
Athena	Judiciary	Athena represents wisdom and logic or *logos* in Attic Greek. Likewise, the judiciary needs to carry out its decisions with impartiality and with the guidance of the wisdom of previous decisions and the *logos* aforethought in analyzing current cases.
Hera	Executive	Hera fits into the role of the executive. Hera offers Paris all of Europe. Likewise, out of all the functions, only the executive can carry out such military expeditions similar to that of all of Europe.
Aphrodite	Legislative	Aphrodite representing the productive and erotic functions easily represents how the legislative functions of government representing the immediate wants of the people can function.

Conclusion

To reiterate, this chapter has demonstrated that to interpret the problems and the eventual purpose of the US government while simultaneously explaining its continued existence by analyzing the three-part structure of the US federal government as outlined in the Constitution—and subsequently interpreted by all three parts of the government—through the lens of the Judgment of Paris as represented in the ancient Greek goddesses, Hera, Athena, and Aphrodite as explained in Homer's as a primary source but also other secondary sources from antiquity. The chapter's central premise is the Homeric tripartite choice that Paris faces and the indications that Greek poetry has for individual choices humans face. The minor premise is the three-part structure of the US government. The syllogism is the analysis in the chapter that attempts to show how each part of the promises of the ancient Greek goddesses represents itself in the three parts of judiciary for *Athena*, executive for *Hera*, and legislature for *Aphrodite*.

Overall, this Homeric and poetic analysis of the Constitution's structure and function could add to the dialogue of Constitutional analysis. Indeed, there are arguments for living constitution, purposivism, and political process theory, but there also seems to be a basis for a poetic interpretation of the Constitution.

In line with a balanced soul of the polity and a balanced government, it would seem that each part of government would not reach into another's duties in line with the outline of *Federalist Paper No. 47*.[52]

As Homer and the other authors of antiquity wrote, each person—in the paradigm of Paris's decision—encounters the three goddesses in some form. Although an individual may act in one part of the federal government, each person has all three parts of the Homeric structure operating within their psyche. Thus, it is expected that different parts of the poetic notions of the goddesses would manifest in a different part of the federal government from various individuals.

Regardless of the correct formulation of the Homeric paradigm, in short, it seemed that there was an archetype of government that seemed suited for long-term existence that Plato had touched upon and perhaps Freud had illuminated in the individual sense through his theory of psychoanalysis.[53] From a Homeric perspective, is it fair to say that the best government, at least in part, represents the individual's most balanced choices or the individual's psyche? Likewise, it seems fair to say that a mythopoetic archetype of government could exist. The topic of a mythopoetic archetype of government would fall into the scope of a different article and further research.

Notes

1 The analysis of this chapter represents a similar structure as the article this author wrote: Charles Lincoln, A Structural Etiology of the U.S. Constitution, 43 J. Legis. 122 (2016). But instead of using Plato's theory of the soul, the article uses the theory of the Judgment of Paris in Homer's epic poem.

2 Pausanias, Pausanias Description of Greece with an English Translation by W.H.S. Jones, Litt.D., and H.A. Ormerod, M.A., in 4 Volumes. Cambridge, MA, Harvard University Press; London, William Heinemann Ltd. 1918. Online version at the Perseus Digital Library. 5.19.5.

3 See for further analysis of legal principles of law through literary traditions, such as J.R.R. Tolkien's writings. Lincoln, Charles Edward Andrew IV (2020) "A Literary Lens Into Constitutional Interpretation and a Possible Synthesis of Natural and Positive Law: The Silmarillion," *Mitchell Hamline Law Journal of Public Policy and Practice*: Vol. 41: Iss. 1, Article 4.

4 Cicero, *De Republica* (Loeb Classical Library, Cambridge, MA, 1928), 3.22.33.

5 Plato, *Timaeus* (Oxford University Press, Oxford, trans., Robin Waterfield, 2008) at 30a–31b. The page numbers used throughout this chapter to refer to Platonic texts are in accord with the Stephanus pagination.

6 See regarding the questions dealing with the notion of whether the demiurge (ancient Greek: δημιουργός (*dēmiourgós*) to be interpreted as the handicraftsman creator of the universe) made the universe in order or in chaos. Plato, *Timaeus* at 28a6.

7 Plato, *Timaeus* at 28a6.

8 This was our paradox: no course of action could be determined by a rule because every course of action can be made out to accord with the rule. The answer was: if everything can be made out to accord with the rule, then it can also be made out to conflict with it. And so there would be neither accord nor conflict here. It can be seen that there is a misunderstanding here from the mere fact that in the course of our argument we give one interpretation after another; as if each one contented us at least for a moment, until we thought of yet another standing behind it. What this shows is that there is a way of grasping a rule which is not an interpretation, but which is exhibited in what we call "obeying the rule" and "going against it" in actual cases. Hence there is an inclination to say: every action according to the rule is an interpretation. But we ought to restrict the term "interpretation" to the substitution of one expression of the rule for another. Ludwig Wittgenstein, *Philosophical Investigations § 201* (G.E.M. Anscombe & R. Rhees eds., G.E.M. Anscombe trans., 1972).

This makes one question whether randomness really exists or does everything follow a set rule? See, e.g., Ahilan T. Arulanantham, *Breaking the Rules?: Wittgenstein and Legal Realism*, 107 YALE L.J. 1853, 1869–71 (1998). Dennis Patterson, *Wittgenstein and Constitutional Theory*, 72 TEX. L. REV. 1837, 1851

(1994). Scott Hershovitz, *Wittgenstein on Rules: The Phantom Menace*, 22 OXFORD J. OF LEG. STUD. 619, 639–40 (2002).

9 Such an example can be seen in literature,

Borges's *The Library of Babel* implicitly undercuts all the written structures—religion, science, art—through which human beings strive to impose order on an unruly world. It consists of a fantastic monologue in which a Librarian, who lives in a Library which is also the universe, tries unsuccessfully to describe the chaotic infinity (or near infinity) that surrounds him. According to the Librarian, the Library may or may not be endless; but it is certainly meaningless, being made up of numberless books in a Babel of tongues. Because it contains all the possible combinations of letters in all languages, many of the books contain only an intelligible word or two, or are only partially true copies of books contained in their proper form elsewhere in the Library. The librarians spend their time, among other ways, searching for the true catalogue that would bring order and meaning to their incomprehensible collection.

Susan Mann, *The Universe and the Library: A Critique of James Boyd White as Writer and Reader*, 41 STAN. L. REV. 959, 965 (1989).

10 *Lucretius: On the Nature of Things* (H. A. J. Munro trans.), reprinted in 12 *Great Books of the Western World* 1, 12 (Robert Maynard Hutchins ed., 1952).

Concurrently, directly contrasting the Platonic theory of order the universe,

The contrary materialist view characterizes archetypes as speculative constructs. Aristotle and Plato had their ancient Greek materialist counterparts in Epicurus, Democritus, and Lucretius, who in his *On the Nature of the Universe* wrote that all things began from "the purposeless congregation and coalescence of atoms." There are uniform and entirely natural causes in a closed system not ordered or otherwise affected by the presence of a higher mind capable of recognizing and ordering information. Thus Epicurus could hold that morality was merely a sensual matter of seeking pleasure and avoiding pain, not a sensitivity issue to any particular purpose or design. Aristotle's teleological universe was rejected for an atomistic universe without purpose or form in which biological forms and the ordered universe in which they exist were not the fixed product of information, intelligence, or design but of random accretion. Nobel Prize-winning biologist George Wald, physicist Freeman Dyson, and astronomer George Greenstein explain the improbability of the universe's remarkable order by suggesting either that the universe did not exist until humans observed it and (in Wald's words) that "[t]he universe wants to be known."

Marion Hilligan, Nelson P. Miller, Don Petersen & Chris Hastings, *Symposium Issue: World Views Collide: A Dialogue on State-Authored Embryonic Stem-Cell Research, Human Enhancements, Physician-Assisted Suicide and the Value of Life: Superhuman-Biotechnology's Emerging Impact on the Law*, 24 T.M. COOLEY L. REV. 1, 25–6 (2007).

11 Such as the interlocutor suggests nature represented itself in Athens. *Timaeus* 90b–c. See recent work suggesting there is an order to the world's structure. "About fifty years ago a physicist called Paul Dirac asked himself why the number ten to the fortieth power keeps occurring. The square of this number, ten to the eightieth power, is the mass of the visible universe, measured in terms of the mass of the proton. The number itself, ten to the fortieth, is the present age of the universe, expressed in units of time it takes light to travel across a proton. And, get this, the constant that measures the strength of gravity in terms of the electrical force between two protons is ten to the fortieth times weaker! Also, ten to the fortieth to the one-fourth, or ten to the tenth, just about equals the number of stars in a galaxy, the number of galaxies in the universe, and the inverse of the weakfine structure constant! John Updike, Roger's Version 23–4 (1986); George Johnson, A *Fire in the Mind: Science, Faith, and the Search for Order* 308–16 (1996)." Robert Birmingham, *Proving Miracles and the First Amendment*, 5 Geo. Mason L. Rev. 45, 60 (1996).

12 "To illustrate the nature of structuralist theory, this discussion will concentrate on the work of Claude Levi-Strauss. Levi-Strauss has made the search for the fundamental properties of human thought the focus of his work. His basic objective is uncovering the universal, basic structure of human thought, which is deep below the surface but is manfested [*sic*] in myth, language, cooking, table manners, and the general structures of social life. This basic structure, which is termed 'deep structure,' will identify cross-cultural similarities." Donald H. J. Hermann, *Phenomenology, Structuralism, Hermeneutics, and Legal Study: Applications of Contemporary Continental Thought to Legal Phenomena*, 36 U. Miami L. Rev. 379, 390–1 (1982).

13 "Michel Foucault's compelling and poetic methodological manifesto describes the nature of "critique" and, thereby, the proper role of the critic. For Foucault, "critique" was more than a means to an end; criticism was itself an act of resistance and refusal. Toward this end, Foucault sought to decouple criticism from positive programs for social and political change. "Criticism is, according to this view, a negative operation—'essays in refusal'—resisting and rejecting 'what is' without regard for 'what needs to be done'. For this reason, Foucault's views have occasionally been labeled 'rejectionist.' Such 'rejectionist' claims, in turn, exemplify the most feared aspects of a new challenge to traditional legal thought: postmodernism." Derek P. Jinks, *Essays in Refusal: Pre-Theoretical Commitments in Postmodern Anthropology and Critical Race Theory*, 107 Yale L.J. 499, 499–500. (1997). *See also*. For a discussion on Foucault's ideas on law and sovereignty: Tom Frost, "Agamben's Sovereign Legalization of Foucault." *Oxford J Legal Studies* 30, 3 (2010): 545.

14 Marvin Harris, The Rise of Anthropological Theory (1968). See Perry Dane, *Jurisdictionality, Time, and the Legal Imagination*, 23 Hofstra L. Rev. 1, 94.

(1994). See "The reciprocity concept justifies the assumption that one who gives will receive in return, though there are no hard promises as to timing, quality, or quantity." John W. Ragsdale, Jr., *The Rise and Fall of the Chacoan State*, 64 UMKC L. Rev. 485, 528. See Perry Dane, *Jurisdictionality, Time, and the Legal Imagination*, 23 Hofstra L. Rev. 1, 94. (1994). See Bronislaw Malinowski, Argonauts of the Western Pacific 72–76 (Routledge 1961) (1922) (discussing gift giving cultures).

15 According to Dumézil, the division of society—government—into three parts was inherent in all Indo-European societies. The trifunctional pattern (and implicit political separation of powers) is manifest among the Hindus in the original Castes: Brahmana (teachers, priests, keepers of the law), Ksatriya (Warrior Kings), and Vaisya (Farmers, Producers, Merchants and Doctors). "For classic development of this so-called 'tripartite hypothesis' concerning the division of social roles in Proto-Indo-European societies, see generally Georges Dumézil, *Flamen-Brahman* (1935); Georges Dumézil, *Mitra-Varuna: An Essay on Two Indo-European Representations of Sovereignty* (Derek Coltman trans., 2d ed. 1988)." Robin Bradley Kar, *Western Legal Prehistory: Reconstructing the Hidden Origins of Western Law and Civilization*, 2012 U. Ill. L. Rev. 1499, 1525 n. 71. (2012). See Georges Dumézil, *Archaic Roman Religion* 585 (1966). See also for critiques of the Trifunctional Hypothesis: Wouter W. Belier, *Decayed Gods: Origin and Development of Georges Dumézil's "Ideologie Tripartie"* 17–20 (1991).

16 David S. Caudill, *Freud and Critical Legal Studies: Contours of a Radical Socio-Legal Psychoanalysis*, 66 Ind. L.J. 651, 658–9. (1991). See S. Freud, *The Ego and the Id*, in 19 The Standard Edition of the Complete Psychological Works of the Complete Psychological Works of Sigmund Freud 3 (J. Strachey ed. 1951).

17 Lincoln, Charles E., *Ethnicity and Social Organization at Chichen Itza, Yucatan, Mexico* (PhD. dissertation, Department of Anthropology, Harvard University) Advisors Mathews, Peter, and Gordon R. Willey (1990). See Charles E. Lincoln, *The Chronology of Chichen Itza: A Review of the Literature. In Late Lowland Maya Civilization: Classic to Postclassic* (Jeremy A. Sabloff and E. Wyllys Andrews V ed., University of New Mexico Press, Albuquerque, 1986), 141–56.

18 *The Iliad of Homer* 14:28–30 (Richmond Lattimore trans., 25th reprint ed. 1976) (1951). See "[T]he well known Judgment of Paris, which Homer apparently knew. Although it is not directly recounted in the Iliad, there is a clear reference to it in Book 14, where Hera's displeasure with the other gods (i.e., gods who were urging Achilles to treat Hector's corpse with respect) was attributed to the Judgment of Paris: 'because of the delusion of Paris / who insulted the goddesses when they came to him in his courtyard / and favoured her who supplied the lust that led to disaster.' The myth of the Judgment of Paris began when Peleus and Thetis did not invite Eris, the goddess of discord, to their wedding. Eris, feeling snubbed, concocted one of literary history's most evil schemes. She procured a golden apple

and inscribed it 'For the fairest.' She then crashed the wedding feast and tossed the apple onto the table. Three goddesses, Hera, Athena, and Aphrodite, each argued that it should be her's. They asked Zeus to decide. He refused because he feared his wife's anger in the event that he did not choose her. He passed the buck and suggested that the Trojan prince Paris, the son of Priam, act as arbiter." Russ VerSteeg, *A Contract Analysis of the Trojan War*, 40 Ariz. L. Rev. 173, 192. (1998).

19 Montesquieu, *The Spirit of the Laws* bk. XI, ch. 6, at 152 (Thomas Nugent trans., Hafner Pub. 1949) (1748).

20 John F. Manning, "Separation of Powers as Ordinary Interpretation." 124 Harv. L. Rev. 1939, 2004 (2010).

21 Charles Edward Andrew Lincoln IV, *A Structural Etiology of the U.S. Constitution*, 43 J. Legis. 122 (2016). James J. Walsh, *Education of the Founding Fathers of the Republic: Scholasticism in the Colonial Colleges* 104–5 (1970).

22 This author has communicated with and spoken with Professor Thomas L. Pangle—who holds Joe R. Long Chair in Democratic Studies in the Department of Government and is Co-Director of the Thomas Jefferson Center for Core Texts and Ideas at the University of Texas at Austin—asking about trifucntionalism and the Constitution. Professor Pangle said there is no direct evidence. Moreover, this author has not found any. Professor Pangle met with the author and graciously offered feedback on this project.

23 Jean-Francois Pradeau, *Plato and the City* (University of Exeter Press, Exeter, 2002) at 129.

24 As far as the author knows, Akiba Covitz is the only person to have written on this subject.

25 Charles Lincoln, *A Structural Etiology of the U.S. Constitution*, 43 J. Legis. 122 (2016).

26 Covitz, xxii–xxv.

27 *Id.* xviii–xx.

28 Claude Calame, Mythe et Histoire Dans L'antiquité Grecque (2003).

29 Hesiod recounts Athena's bird from Zeus's headache in the following way:

> Zeus himself produced, from his own head,
> Grey-eyed Athena, fearsome queen who brings
> The noise of war and, tireless, leads the host,
> She who loves shouts and battling and fights.
> *Theogony* 53 (Dorothea Wender trans. Penguin Classics ed. 1973).

Likewise, in the "First Homeric Hymn to Athena," Homer recounts the gods being awestruck by Athena's appearance—even Helios stops his chariot in the sky. Jeffrey M Hurwit, *Helios Rising: The Sun, the Moon, and the Sea in the Sculptures of the Parthenon*, 121 Am. J. Archaeol. 527 (2017).

30 Rightfully called one of the Charles Darwin of Homeric epics, the scholar Milman Parry who died an all too young death at age thirty-three noted that, Homeric epithets, such as Achilles "swift-footed," Hector "shining-helmet," Hera "cow-eyed," "divine Odysseus," Athena "gray-eyed," the "rosy fingered dawn," or the sea "as dark as wine," changed according to the needs of meter, not according to the needs of the narrative context. Parry concluded that the repetition of ready-made expression would have found no meaningful explanation, unless that text predated its origin in an oral tradition. Giancarlo F. Frosio, *Rediscovering Cumulative Creativity from the Oral Formulaic Tradition to Digital Remix: Can I Get a Witness?*, 13 J. MARSHALL REV. INTELL. PROP. L. 341, 346 (2014). Parry further argued that the poet's and recitation "formulae were only functional devices to be used and re-used to help the aoidous to remember and perform in the given length of the verse." *Id.*

31 Monica S Cyrino, Aphrodite (2012).

32 *Iliad* (24.25–30).

33 Ovid writes in Heroides 16.71ff, 149–52, and 5.35f of the Judgment of Paris.

34 Lucian writes of the Judgment of Paris in his Dialogues of the Gods 20.

35 Pseudo-Apollodorous wrote of the account in his Bibliotheca, E.3.2.

36 Hyginus wrote of the event in his Fabulae 92.

37 Pausanias, Description of Greece, 5.19.5 https://www.perseus.tufts.edu/hopper/text?doc=Paus.+5.19.5

38 Randall L. Schweller (April 3, 2014). *Maxwell's Demon and the Golden Apple: Global Discord in the New Millennium.* JHU Press. pp. 10–12.

39 "Sing, O goddess, the anger [mênis] of Achilles son of Peleus, that brought countless ills upon the Achaeans." Samuel Butler translation. http://www.perseus.tufts.edu/hopper/text?doc=Perseus:text:1999.01.0217:book=1

40 According to the Sir James George Frazer translation of Apollodorus, EpitomeSir James George Frazer, Ed E.3.2. http://www.perseus.tufts.edu/hopper/text?doc=urn:cts:greekLit:tlg0548.tlg002.perseus-eng1:e.3.2

41 Sir James George Frazer, Ed E.3.2. http://www.perseus.tufts.edu/hopper/text?doc=urn:cts:greekLit:tlg0548.tlg002.perseus-eng1:e.3.2

42 Peter Yioutsos Nektarios, "Order in Ancient Greek Dance Rituals: The Dance of Pan and the Nymphs." *Dramaturgias* 5 (2017): 211–34.

43 Perseus Digital Library, "Greek Word Study Tool." Accessed October 14, 2023. http://www.perseus.tufts.edu/hopper/morph?l=kalli%2Fsth%7C&la=greek&can=kalli%2Fsth%7C0&prior=th=|&d=Perseus:text:1999.01.0173:text=Phaedrus:section=244c&i=1.

44 Randall L. Schweller, *Maxwell's Demon and the Golden Apple: Global Discord in the New Millennium* (Johns Hopkins University Press, 2014).

45 Samuel Butler, *The Iliad*, http://www.perseus.tufts.edu/hopper/text?doc=Hom.+Il.+24&fromdoc=Perseus%3Atext%3A1999.01.0217 (last visited October 14, 2023).

46 Nektarios, 211–34.

47 "The judicial Power of the United States, shall be vested in one supreme Court, and in such inferior Courts as the Congress may from time to time ordain and establish." U.S. Const. art. III, 1

Further, Chief Justice Marshall in *Marbury v. Madison* stated, "The particular phraseology of the constitution of the United States confirms and strengthens the principle, supposed to be essential to all written constitutions, that a law repugnant to the constitution is void; and that courts, as well as other departments, are bound by that instrument." 5 U.S. (1 Cranch) at 180.

48 Carol A. Sommer, Panagiotis Markopoulos, and Shana L. Goggins. "Mentoring master's level students: Drawing upon the wisdom of Athena as Mentor in Homer's *Odyssey*." *Journal of Poetry Therapy* 26, 1 (2013): 1–12.

49 *Marbury v. Madison*, 5 U.S. (1 Cranch) 137, 177 (1803); accord *United States v. Nixon*, 418 U.S. 683, 703–5 (1974).

50 With its source of power from U.S. Const. art. II, § 1, cl. 1.

51 With its power generally emanating from U.S. Const. art. 1.

52 The Federalist No. 47, at 301 (James Madison) (Clinton Rossiter ed., 1961).

53 Charles Lincoln, *The Dialectical Path of Law* viii (2021).

3

The Soul of the Republic

Plato's Tripartite Psychology and the Structure of the US Constitution

SOCRATES: You, Gorgias, like myself, have had great experience of disputations, and you must have observed, I think, that they do not always terminate in mutual edification, or in the definition by either party of the subjects which they are discussing; but disagreements are apt to arise—somebody says that another has not spoken truly or clearly; and then they get into a passion and begin to quarrel, both parties conceiving that their opponents are arguing from personal feeling only and jealousy of themselves, not from any interest in the question at issue. And sometimes they will go on abusing one another until the company at last are quite vexed at themselves for ever listening to such fellows. Why do I say this? Why, because I cannot help feeling that you are now saying what is not quite consistent or accordant with what you were saying at first about rhetoric. And I am afraid to point this out to you, lest you should think that I have some animosity against you, and that I speak, not for the sake of discovering the truth, but from jealousy of you. Now if you are one of my sort, I should like to cross-examine you, but if not I will let you alone. And what is my sort? you will ask. I am one of those who are very willing to be refuted if I say anything which is not true, and very willing to refute any one else who says what is not true, and quite as ready to be refuted as to refute; for I hold that this is the greater gain of the two, just as the gain is greater of being cured of a very great evil than of curing another. For I imagine that there is no evil which a man can endure so great as an erroneous opinion about the matters of which we are speaking; and if you claim to be one of my sort, let us have the discussion out, but if you would rather have done, no matter—let us make an end of it.

GORGIAS: I should say, Socrates, that I am quite the man whom you indicate; but, perhaps, we ought to consider the audience, for, before you came, I had already given a long exhibition, and if we proceed the argument may run on to a great length. And therefore I think that we should consider whether we may not be detaining some part of the company when they are wanting to do something else.

—Plato's *Gorgias* (written around 380 BCE), translated by Benjamin Jowett—on the importance of dialogue and conversation.

Introduction to Plato's Thought

This chapter argues that the tripartite system of the federal government in the United States can be viewed through the Platonic concept of the soul (ψυχή).[1] The major premise is that the US federal government has three major parts: the judiciary, the executive, and the legislative. The minor premise of this chapter is that the Platonic soul is divided into three parts, the *logos* (λογιστικόν),[2] the *thumos* (θυμοειδές),[3] and the *eros* (ἐπιθυμητικόν).[4] The syllogism and argument of this chapter are that the three federal parts of government represent the Platonic soul: the judiciary being the *logos*, the executive being the *thumos*, and the legislative being the *eros*. This chapter will explore these concepts in greater depth. As a corollary, when the soul of the polity[5] becomes unbalanced, then people become dissatisfied with the government because the government does not fulfill its function administratively—as in acting in opposition to the laws—and in promoting justice. However, sometimes overstepping a role in the Platonic soul of the polity is a necessary change.[6]

Premises and Structures of Analysis of This Chapter

Presumed throughout this chapter—as is presumed throughout this book—is that the world has order based on reason that reflects nature.[7] In Plato's *Timaeus*, the interlocutor suggests that nature is organized and is thus intelligible.[8] The alternative to this presumption is that there is no order to the universe or world and humans try to impose order to it.[9] Lucretius in his *On the Nature of the Universe* introduced such a view.[10] Consequently, nature can represent itself in the structure of law, specifically the law of the United States.[11]

Why a Structured Approach at All? An Anthropological-Philosophical Explanation

To understand why it is appropriate to analyze and compare the structure of the US federal government—as outlined by the US Constitution of 1789—with the Platonic concept of the soul, it is helpful to have some understanding of the context of philosophical-anthropological thought related to it. The following paragraph is a brief overview of relevant historical analysis to provide context related to structural and "trifunctionalist" analysis. Indeed, many anthropological-philosophical theories exist for understanding the basic structures of societies and governments, from Claude Lévi-Strauss's structuralism theories,[12] to Michel Foucault on the impetus behind government function,[13] and Marvin Harris on the gift-giving incentives in a society's structure.[14] Concurrently, the idea of a "tripartite" structure of society being inherent to human cultures is not new, but has been written about extensively by George S. Dumézil,[15] and has been written by Sigmund Freud's division of psychoanalysis.[16] Indicative of the universal nature of the "trifunctionalist" Dumézilian approach has even been applied to Pre-Columbian Yucatán Mayan societies.[17] Poetically, in the Homeric Greek account of the Judgment of Paris—before the beginning of the Trojan War in Homer's *Iliad*—Paris of Troy is given a Dumézilian "choice," a beauty contest among three goddesses Hera, Athena, and Aphrodite.[18] It seems fitting to apply the ancient Greek concept of the Platonic soul to governmental structure because the "trifunctionalist" approach has origins in ancient Greece but can be seen in non-Western civilizations as well.

A balanced view of government may exist in the separation of powers as Montesquieu laid out "that of enacting laws, that of executing the public resolutions, and of trying the causes of individuals."[19] Exploring this thought "[i]n The Federalist No. 47, Madison explained that while Montesquieu was correct in saying that the separation of the legislative, executive, and judicial powers was essential to liberty, that conclusion did not purport to tell us how strict the resultant separation had to be."[20] Based on their education, the Framers of the Constitution may have even had Plato's Soul in mind when they framed the Constitution.[21]

Granted, trifunctionalism existed in Montesquieu's writings and Montesquieu explicitly referenced Polybius who wrote on the trifunctional nature of the Roman Republic's Constitution. Polybius attributed Rome's success in maintaining its large empire and conquering the known world due to the Roman Republic's

Constitution allowing for three parts. However, the *Federalist Papers* as a whole only refer to Polybius. The author of *Federalist Paper No. 63*—either Hamilton or Madison—explicitly refers to Polybius writing, "To these examples might be added that of Carthage, whose senate, according to the testimony of Polybius, instead of drawing all power into its vortex, had, at the commencement of the second Punic War, lost almost the whole of its original portion."[22]

However, even if the Framers did not have Plato in the back of their minds, the idea of Plato's Soul is arguably inherent in humans regardless of how it is defined.[23] Moreover, a structured approach to the philosophical underpinnings to a government can be assumed to have been in the framer's mind—whether consciously or subconsciously.

Why Plato? Truth and Justice in Plato

If one accepts the premises that structured and philosophical approaches are a reasonable mode of analysis, then why should one use Plato's approach specifically?

This idea of comparing the Platonic soul to the US federal system of government has been written previously been written about by Akiba Covitz in *The Soul of the Polity*.[24] Covitz argued the syllogism as the judiciary is the thumos, the executive is the logos, and the legislative is the eros. This chapter greatly appreciates and gains much inspiration from Covitz's theory, but switches correspondences from thumos to logos for the judiciary, logos to thumos for executive and maintains Covitz's conception of legislative as eros.[25] However, Covitz uses a different terminology of (1) artifice; (2) nature; and (3) history/divinity/myth in lieu of logos, eros, and thumos, respectively.[26] Covitz argues that the constitution had a psychoanalytic dimension and these Platonic elements in large part represented this psychoanalysis.[27]

As discussed previously in this book, Professor Covitz sincerely wanted to explore what a constitution is. He asked "*ti esti* or 'what is?'" translated from Greek.[28] This is a classic question that drove the Greeks as a purely innocent love for searching for knowledge. This chapter has a sourced inspiration from such an inquiry. Covitz asks, "Why, then, have I chosen Plato's *Republic* along with the Constitution of the United States as the two main texts that I will analyze?"[29] He answers, "My broadest goal is to seek the beginnings of American constitutional thought, and my related, narrower goal is to respond to the question of why the American Constitution is seen to be such a success." Indeed, this represents a variation of the two-pronged endeavor, which this chapter searches to solve: What does it mean for the three parts of the government to interact with one another? The second is: Why has the American Constitution lasted so long? Indeed, with relatively few amendments.

Covitz suggests an easy answer to these questions would be to "provide satisfying answers to my questions would be to choose the Constitution of the United States and a more contemporary and more straightforward text (at least in terms of form) such as Locke's Second Treatise on Government, or Montesquieu's Spirit of the Laws." But Professor Covitz sought a "more than a deeper understanding of the American Constitution; [he sought] its beginnings."

Professor Covitz quotes an introduction to an edition of Plato's works by Erich Segal where Segal quotes "Spanish neo-Kantian social theorist, José Ortega y Gassett," that succinctly indicates Professor Covitz's and this chapter's focus on the *Republic*. Covitz writes, "Ortega y Gassett describes Plato's influence on Western thought in the following manner: 'It is impossible to tell [to] what deep levels of the Western mind Platonic notions have penetrated. The simplest sort of person regularly employs expressions and portrays views which are derived from Plato (Plato 1986, vii).'"

Covitz lays out the great appeal to using Plato's work, "Put more simply, Plato has provided for the West a fertile image, founded on a complex theory of psychology and politics, of how the soul is seen as working and how it is intimately connected with politics and constitutions." However, Covitz admits there is a darker—more tyrannical and dictatorial—side to Plato's works. Specifically, "according to [Karl] Popper, Plato's Republic is the handbook of tyranny and the guide to constructing a society closed to all change and freedom. Plato's use of lies, myths, and the powers of divinity as aspects of constitutional life, are indicative for Popper of Plato's falsity and duplicity (see Popper 1945)." This is a relevant argument because, despite the appeal of Plato's work for positive ideas, there has also been an evil side to the works going to support fascism and Nazism.[30]

However, if one is to understand the beginning of the US Constitution, one must be familiar with—not only the circumstances that gave its birth—but also the great books that the authors of the Constitution read. Covitz supports this standpoint by writing "if one is to search out the theoretical beginnings of American constitutional thought, one must come to grips with the textual beginnings of the Western constitutional thought in which the American experience is itself framed," this can be interpreted as the books and laws the

Framers were most familiar, "regardless of our views of Plato's tyrannical or democratic qualities. Important, underlying aspects of this broader realm of Western constitutional thought began in the dialogic pages and the constitutional theory of Plato's Republic."

Truth and Plato's Forms

Indeed, it must be mentioned that Plato's soul has a special connection to truth and Plato's "Forms" in his philosophy, as explained by American legal scholar Kenji Yoshino of Yale University.[31] Unlike, "the poet [who] always misrepresents the truth," Yoshino claims, "[i]n the Republic, Plato describes the existence of immutable, abstract, and invisible Forms."[32] Yoshino states that "[t]hese Forms are the ideals to which Plato seeks to anchor the state and the human soul, which is the microcosm of the state. The highest Platonic aspiration for human beings is to bring us closer to these Forms. The difficulty is that our ordinary modes of perception—such as our senses—cannot seize these ideas." However, Yoshino interestingly writes, "Only right reason, as exercised through dialectic, can do so in any systematic way."[33]

Plato's—and Professor Yoshino's—intersection of truth, as represented by the forms and justice compels one to look further into why the two are related.

Professor Yoshino's formulation of "right reason,"[34] sounds akin to the concept of natural law. Natural law exists in religion and higher ethics, which may or may not exhibit themselves in statutes and case law. Natural can be defined as that which is not positive law, but it can also be defined as follows, "Natural law refers to the ethic of justice, fairness, or right. Although denominated 'law,' it is not positive law at all, but rather is a sense derived from God-given or rational sources."[35] Such a definition emphasizes the importance of religion as a base for natural law. But it can also be based on rational reason or right reason as Professor Yoshino or St. Thomas Aquinas would argue.[36] This means natural law can come from secular sources and an atheist could believe in natural law through right reason or rational sources.

Although an all-encompassing definition of natural law would not only contrast itself with positive law, but would rather show how it, "relates to positive law by serving as a standard against which positive law can be judged. Natural law is frequently cited as the 'ought' and positive law as the 'is,' meaning that natural law is what should be done and positive law is what exists as the rule established by the sovereign."[37]

Alternatively, positive law is commonly referred to as law passed by legislatures or case law. For a succinct definition, "positive law, or every law simply and strictly so called, is set by a sovereign person, or a sovereign body of persons, to a member or members of the independent political society wherein that person or body is sovereign or supreme."[38] Moreover, "Every positive law, or every law simply and strictly so called, is set by a sovereign person, or a sovereign body of persons, to a member or members of the independent political society wherein that person or body is sovereign or supreme."[39]

Justice and Plato

In regard to the Platonic soul, a person acts justly if the soul acts in concordance with each constituent part without overstepping its reach, and unjustly if the soul acted in an unbalanced manner.[40] Likewise, an unbalanced soul may follow any means necessary in Machiavellian fashion to reach a desirable goal.[41] Choosing between what is viewed as natural law and positive law can depend on the balance of the soul.[42] Indeed, in Sophocles's play *Antigone*, the eponymous character suffered such a choice between following positive law or natural law when deciding to follow the edicts of King Creon not to bury her brother or her religious beliefs to bury her brother.[43] Perhaps this choice between natural law[44] and positive law[45]—also phrased as choosing between what is "right" and following the law—is one of the fundamental cruxes of jurisprudence.[46] An informed viewpoint on the Platonic conception of the soul can help analyze choices between positive and natural law, understand the structure of the Constitution, and explain why former choices had been made, as well as why some decisions in the Supreme Court and Congress are made the way they are.

Truth, Justice, and Plato

Thus, Plato intimately intertwines truth and justice. The Platonic Forms—eternal ideals—represent truth.[47] It is worth briefly exploring Plato's idea of what truth is.[48] In Plato's *Republic* Book VII, Socrates starts off describing an analogy of people living in a cave with their heads fixed and chained to the wall.[49] These cave dwellers can only see shadows and hear voices performed by puppeteers in the background, but those who are chained do not know where the voices come from.[50] These cave dwellers cannot see or turn their head around. Their heads are fixed. Later, if one of the members fixed in the cave is loosened, he can see the puppets and realize that the shadows were not the "truth." They were just shadows. Then the person can turn around and see what caused the shadows. This is the first step of the truth. But he can also exit the cave and see the sun and the truth. The sun is the metaphor of truth. Socrates, in Plato's *Republic*, uses this analogy of the cave and sun as a way to metaphorically represent truth.[51]

Socrates then in dialectical mode of discourse provokes the interlocutor think how hard it would be for this person who has seen truth to go back into the cave and explain what truth is to those who were in the cave with their heads fixed on the shadows.[52] The cave dwellers who remained in the cave might not believe the person who returned from the sun. The cave dwellers might even react violently to the person bringing the truth. It is worth quoting this difficulty in teaching in detail:[53]

> SOCRATES: And consider this also, said I. If such a one should go down again and take his old place would he not get his eyes full of darkness, thus suddenly coming out of the sunlight?
>
> GLAUCON: He would indeed.
>
> SOCRATES: Now if he should be required to contend with these perpetual prisoners in "evaluating" these shadows while his vision was still dim and before his eyes were accustomed to the dark—and this time required for habituation would not be very short—would he not provoke laughter, and would it not be said of him that he had returned from his journey aloft with his eyes ruined and that it was not worth while even to attempt the ascent? And if it were possible to lay hands on and to kill the man who tried to release them and lead them up, would they not kill him?
>
> GLAUCON: They certainly would, he said.
>
> SOCRATES: This image then, dear Glaucon, we must apply as a whole to all that has been said, likening the region revealed through sight to the habitation of the prison, and the light of the fire in it to the power of the sun. And if you assume that the ascent and the contemplation of the things above is the soul's ascension to the intelligible region, you will not miss my surmise, since that is what you desire to hear. But God knows whether it is true. But, at any rate, my dream as it appears to me is that in the region of the known, the last thing to be seen and hardly seen is the Idea of Good, and that when seen it must needs point us to the conclusion that this is indeed the cause for all things of all that is right and beautiful, giving birth in the visible world to light, and the author of light and itself in the intelligible world being the authentic source of truth and reason, and that anyone who is to act wisely in private or public must have caught sight of this.

GLAUCON: I concur so far as I am able.

. . .

SOCRATES: But a sensible man, I said, would remember that there are two distinct disturbances of the eyes arising from two causes, according as the shift is from light to darkness or from darkness to light, and, believing that the same thing happens to the soul too, whenever he saw a soul perturbed and unable to discern something, he would not laugh unthinkingly, but would observe whether coming from a brighter life its vision was obscured by the unfamiliar darkness, or whether the passage from the deeper dark of ignorance into a more luminous world and the greater brightness had dazzled its vision. And so, he would deem the one happy in its experience and way of life and pity the other, and if it pleased him to laugh at it, his laughter would be less laughable than that at the expense of the soul that had come down from the light above.

GLAUCON: That is a very fair statement, he said.

SOCRATES: Then, if this is true, our view of these matters must be this, that education is not in reality what some people proclaim it to be in their professions. What they aver is that they can put true knowledge into a soul that does not possess it, as if they were inserting vision into blind eyes.[54]

Such a pedagogical task to teach those in the cave what "truth" is outside of the cave or even that the shadows are created by puppets guided by puppeteers would seem incredibly difficult to overcome.[55] Indeed, those only knowing of the shadows would likely chastise and say the person who claims to know the truth is a lunatic. But Socrates suggested that those in the cave could be taught—even those without educations, such as the slave boy in Plato's *Meno*—through memory and recollection. Socrates's idea of memory, recollection, and teaching is perhaps best summed up in Plato's *Meno* where Socrates states:

The soul then, as being immortal, and having been born again many times, and having seen all things that exist, whether in this world or in the world below, has knowledge of them all; and it is no wonder that she (the soul) should be able to call to remembrance all that she ever knew about virtue and about everything; for as all nature is akin, and the soul has learned all things, there is no difficulty in her eliciting, or as men say "learning," out of a single recollection, all the rest, if a man is strenuous and does not faint; for all inquiry and all learning is but recollection.[56]

Returning to the cave analogy, the metaphor was explored in a novelistic format in the late-nineteenth-century book titled *Flatland*, where a world of two-dimensional beings only knows points and triangles, squares, and circles and where senses can only explore the first and second dimensions.[57] But then one day, the protagonist who is a triangle is taken into the third dimension. Imagine how hard it would be to describe the third dimension to two-dimensional beings! This is the task that Plato sets out for those who have seen the sun and left the cave when they return back to the cave.

Now, the cave is just a metaphor. But Plato urges us to conceive truth as that which his outside of the cave and is metaphorically represented as the sun. For Plato, truth is justice. Likewise, justice represents human activity carrying out and adhering to the truth of the eternal Forms. The Forms are the eternal concepts of things. For example, when we interact with a chair, we interact with the idea of a chair. But a chair can come in various shapes, sizes, or even a box can be a chair. The idea of a chair is the Form of the chair. Thus, all things have Forms. A tree, and indeed all trees, comes in infinitely different shapes, sizes, and configurement of branches, but they all partake in the idea of a tree.[58] That idea of the tree is the Form of the tree. Trees and chairs are simple ideas and Forms. And we do not always access these Forms. Sometimes we can access the Forms through mathematics. This might be one way to escape the cave in Plato's analogy of the cave dwellers. Another is through music. In Plato's *Symposium*, Socrates suggests that humans regularly interact directly with the Forms through music. Well played beautiful music puts us directly in contact with the Form of music. The music as played is given to us in a true sense and we partake in the Form of beauty and music.

But there are also Forms of truth and justice. The Platonic soul partakes in these Forms. How can human activity carry truth to achieve justice? How can humans apprehend the Form of justice? This requires the elements of the Platonic soul to exist in a balance. But what is the Platonic soul? What are its elements? How can they exist in harmony?

In answer, the parts of the Platonic soul can exist in harmony by living a polity that allows expression of each part of the soul in a balanced way. This would mean that the eros part of the soul can be expressed in one branch of government, the thumos expressing itself in another, and the logos expressing itself in another. Such a government would be the ideal government that Plato indirectly and esoterically refers to in his *Republic*.

Three Parts of the Federal Government

The Judiciary

At first, a move away from purely logical toward using "experience" may seem like a contradiction of the purely logical aspect of the *logos* in the Platonic soul. Indeed, this is not akin to the *elegantia juris* using pure logic in law as envisioned by the Romans.[59] Rather it is more similar to Oliver Wendell Holmes's legal realism where he writes in his book *The Common Law*, "The life of the law has not been logic: it has been experience."[60] Indeed, Holmes criticized the purely scientifically logical methods proposed by Professor Christopher Columbus Langdell[61] that he "could be suspected of ever having troubled himself about Hegel, we might call him a Hegelian in disguise, so entirely is he interested in the formal connection of things, or logic, as distinguished from the feelings which make the content of logic, and which have actually shaped the substance of the law."[62]

Indeed this mode of realism could come into action in judicial decisions specifically with "sociological jurisprudence"—proposed by Roscoe Pound—whereby courts could consider social factors in decision-making.[63] Furthermore, Holmes wrote that even decisions that appear to be based on firm logical deductions are decisions of policy by stating, "Perhaps one of the reasons why judges do not like to discuss questions of policy, or to put a decision in terms upon their views as law-makers, is that the moment you leave the path of merely logical deduction you lose the illusion of certainty which makes legal reasoning seem like mathematics."[64] But declared that choosing the premises—being the choice of policy—then using logical deductions from there for "certainty is only an illusion, nevertheless."[65]

Executive

As discussed earlier in this book, a prime example of the outline of the definition of the Executive branch's power is seen in *Youngstown Sheet & Tube Co. v. Sawyer*.[66] The case rose as a result of the steel strikes during the Truman administration during the Korean War, President Truman sought to take executive control over the steel producers under the inherent powers doctrine. *Youngstown Sheet & Tube Co. v. Sawyer*.[67]

Writing for the majority opinion Justice Black stated the Presidential and Executive power "must stem either from an act of Congress or from the Constitution itself." *Youngstown Sheet & Tube Co. v. Sawyer*.[68]

The Court's majority opinion stated that the Court could not "with faithfulness to our constitutional system hold that the Commander in Chief of the Armed Forces has the ultimate power as such to take possession of private property in order to keep labor disputes from stopping production. This is a job for the Nation's lawmakers, not for its military authorities." *Youngstown Sheet & Tube Co. v. Sawyer*, 343 US 579, 587.

Furthermore, the Court declared that "[i]n the framework of our Constitution, the President's power to see that the laws are faithfully executed refutes the idea that he is to be a lawmaker."[69] This means that the Constitution limits the Executive's rulemaking force. Instead, the Court continues interpreting the Constitution so as to give power to the legislature to make rules, "[a]ll legislative Powers herein granted shall be vested in a Congress of the United States." After granting many powers to the Congress, Article I goes on to provide that Congress may "make all Laws which shall be necessary and proper for carrying into Execution the foregoing Powers, and all other Powers vested by this Constitution in the Government of the United States, or in any Department or Officer thereof."[70]

Specifically in terms of taking of private property for public use the Court stated only Congress is authorized for "the taking of private property for public use."[71]

Finally—perhaps in an originalist interpretation fashion—the Court declared: "The Founders of this Nation entrusted the lawmaking power to the Congress alone in both good and bad times. It would do no good to recall the historical events, the fears of power and the hopes for freedom that lay behind their choice. Such a review would but confirm our holding that this seizure order cannot stand."[72]

As a result of the case, in the concurring opinion Justice Frankfurter wrote, "Loose and irresponsible use of adjectives colors all nonlegal and much legal discussion of presidential powers. 'Inherent' powers, 'implied' powers, 'incidental' powers, 'plenary' powers, 'war' powers and 'emergency' powers are used, often interchangeably and without fixed or ascertainable meanings."[73]

Discussing the Separation of Powers, a concurring opinion written by Justice Frankfurter stated, "The doctrine of the separation of powers was adopted by the Convention of 1787, not to promote efficiency but to preclude the exercise of arbitrary power. The purpose was, not to avoid friction, but by means of the inevitable friction incident to the distribution of the governmental powers among three departments, to save the people from autocracy."[74]

In relation to the thumos, *Youngstown Sheet & Tube Co.* represents how the Executive branch is limited in its functions of making laws but it carries out these laws. The Executive may resolve conflicts through executive agencies tasked with carrying out the duties the Executive has in carrying out the law.

Specifically, through the *Chevron* deference doctrine whereby the Supreme Court decided that "considerable weight should be accorded to an executive department's construction of a statutory scheme it is entrusted to administer, 14 and the principle of deference to administrative interpretations."[75]

Justice Stevens wrote the case involved that "[i]n the Clean Air Act Amendments of 1977, Pub. L. 95–95, 91 Stat. 685, Congress enacted certain requirements applicable [840] to States that had not achieved the national air quality standards established by the Environmental Protection Agency (EPA) pursuant to earlier legislation."[76] He continued stating that "[t]he amended Clean Air Act required these 'nonattainment' States to establish a permit program regulating 'new or modified major stationary sources' of air pollution."[77] Furthermore, the EPA required that plants comply with a certain level of conditions.[78] The issue of the case was "whether EPA's decision to allow States to treat all of the pollution-emitting devices within the same industrial grouping as though they were encased within a single 'bubble' is based on a reasonable construction of the statutory term 'stationary source.'"[79]

The Court reasoned when reviewing an agency's construction of a statute, it must ask two questions.[80] The first question is "whether Congress has directly spoken to the precise question at issue. If the intent of Congress is clear, that is the end of the matter; for the court, as well as the agency, must give effect to the unambiguously expressed intent of Congress."[81] The second question arises if "Congress has not directly addressed the precise question at issue ... the question for the court is whether the agency's answer is based on a permissible construction of the statute," meaning the court defers to an agency's interpretation.[82] Concurrently, if the agency does not have an interpretation, the court would interpret the statute.[83]

The Court reasoned and "justified this new general rule of deference by positing that Congress has implicitly delegated interpretive authority to all agencies charged with enforcing federal law."[84] Indeed, "the decision [made] administrative actors the primary interpreters of federal statutes and relegate courts to the largely inert role of enforcing unambiguous statutory terms."[85]

The Legislative

With the example of the Eighteenth Amendment, the Congress passed a law represented a *will* of portions of the country to not allow alcohol. But it took the Twenty-first Amendment to realize that the Eighteenth Amendment did not accurately represent what people desired. In a sense, the Eighteenth Amendment represented the soul of the polity going out of control. This was initially an unjust result (although deemed just at the time), and then Congress repealed it deciding that the Twenty-first Amendment was just (meaning the Eighteenth was deemed unjust).

The need to have rules of statutory interpretation indicates that there is a need to interpret often difficult to understand laws.[86] This could be the effect of many reasons, such a quick drafting or function of political maneuvering to gain enough votes or lack thereof.[87] Professor Gluck has pointed out that a large part of the problem about public outcry against the courts and the legislature is because we do not have a clear idea of what they should be doing:

> These moves have been grounded in a spectacular lack of theory about the role that courts should play in the legislative process itself—which is, after all, the fundamental constitutional question of the Court–Congress relationship in statutory cases. Should courts try to understand how Congress works, or is Congress too complex to understand? Should courts be "tough" on Congress, perhaps to incentivize Congress to draft better the next time, or should courts cut Congress some slack, and even correct enacted imperfections? Perhaps courts are best conceived as guardians of the US Code, obligated to shape increasingly imperfect statutes into a more coherent product for the public, no matter how disconnected that result may be from Congress's own intentions. The Court has long resisted definitively answering these basic questions, even as the most difficult statutory cases turn on them.[88]

Indeed, the problem of the legislature or courts not conforming to what it's theoretical role within the three branches of government has occurred in other branches as well, including the judiciary with the Supreme Court. Even, "[t]he Warren Court understood the problems and the promises of politics from its own experience. The Court numbered among its members former senators, representatives, and state legislators, a former governor and a former mayor, and former cabinet members."[89]

Moreover, there does not seem to be a uniform system of interpreting statutes even despite its large importance for courts upholding the rules.[90] Others argue for adopting a uniform system of statutory interpretation.[91] Indeed, there could be problems using different types of statutory analysis within courts, because one method may work in one case, but not in another case; yet, the subsequent courts would be urged to use precedent from the former case.[92] Alternatively others argue against a uniform system of statutory interpretation, because such a system could lead to a rigid system of *stare decisis* for interpreting statutes.[93] However, despite several states having adopted "methodological" and "formalistic" *stare decisis*,[94] it is unclear whether the method produces equitable results.[95]

Although the legislatures have utmost formality, such as with Robert's *Rules of Order*[96] or Thomas Jefferson's *Manual of Parliamentary Practice*,[97] statutes that come from Congress are often unclear.

Plato's Soul

Welcome to Plato's Soul[98]

Before an understanding of how the Platonic soul functions within the US federal government, a brief outline of Plato's conception of the soul is required. Plato wrote that the soul (ψυχή) consists of three parts; the λογιστικόν (logical), the θυμοειδές (thumotic/spirit) and the ἐπιθυμητικόν (appetitive/erotic).[99] Concurrently, a person has all three parts within herself or himself, and acts justly if all the parts of the soul act as it is supposed to act.[100] If each part of the soul and each part of the city conduct their activities according to their "nature" or part of the soul, then all three parts of both city and individual will produce justice.[101]

Logos

Logos (λογιστικόν)[102] in the Platonic sense represents the part of the soul that loves knowledge and the search for knowledge.[103] The word in itself has a unique concept behind it: "λογιστικόν is one of Plato's many synonyms for the intellectual principle. *Cf.* 441 C, 571 C, 587 D, 605 B. It emphasizes the moral calculation of consequences, as opposed to blind passion."[104] This idea can be compared to the section in the *Phaedrus* where "Socrates compares the soul to a charioteer who controls two horses—one white and docile, the other black and intemperate. These three figures echo the division of the soul into reason, emotion, and appetite in Book IV of the Republic."[105] The charioteer is logos keeping control of the two horses.

Eros

Eros (ἐπιθυμητικός)[106] in the Platonic sense represents what Socrates says is "that with which it loves, hungers, thirsts, and feels the flutter and titillation of other desires, the irrational and appetitive—companion of various repletions [*sic*] and pleasures."[107]

Thumos

Thumos (θυμοειδές)[108] in the Platonic sense represents the "spirit"[109] of unifying with the logos but resisting the erotic part of the soul.[110] James Adams commented on this aspect of Plato's conception of the soul in the following way:

> There is also a third element or part of soul, that which we call the element of Spirit. It is distinct from the Appetitive element, with which, indeed, it frequently contends. Its function is to support the Rational part of the soul. In a man of noble character the spirited element is quiescent or the reverse in accordance with the commands of Reason. It must not however be identified with Reason; for it is present in children and the lower animals, whereas Reason is not. Homer also recognises that the two elements are distinct.

The analogy between the righteous city and the righteous soul is continued throughout this section. It should be noted however that the parallel is no longer quite exact. The difference between θυμοειδές and λογιστικόν in the soul is greater than that between auxiliaries and rulers in the State: for the λογιστικόν is not a select part of the θυμοειδές—as the rulers are of the soldiers—but something generically distinct from it. Otherwise, the analogy holds (with the reservations mentioned on 435 A).[111]

Further, this key concept of thumos/spirit (θυμός) is/can be described as in the distinctively

> Platonic sense of θυμός as the power of noble wrath, which, unless perverted by a bad education, is naturally the ally of the reason, though as mere angry passion it might seem to belong to the irrational part of the soul, and so, as Glaucon suggests, be akin to appetite, with which it is associated in the mortal soul of the *Timaeus* 69 D.[112]

However, one can contradict this to the idea in "[i]n *Laws* 731 B.C. Plato tells us again that the soul cannot combat injustice without the capacity for righteous indignation."[113] Later on in time, "[t]he Stoics affected to deprecate anger always, and the difference remained a theme of controversy between them and the Platonists." Cf. Schmidt, *Ethik der Griechen*, ii. pp. 321 ff., Seneca, De ira, i. 9, and *passim*. Moralists are still divided on the point. Cf. Bagehot, *Lord Brougham*: "Another faculty of Brougham … is the faculty of easy anger. The supine placidity of civilization is not favorable to animosity [Bacon's word for θυμός]."[114] Furthermore, "Leslie Stephen, *Science of Ethics*, pp. 60 ff. and p. 62, seems to contradict Plato: 'The supposed conflict between reason and passion is, as I hold, meaningless if it is taken to imply that the reason is a faculty separate from the emotions,' etc. But this is only his metaphysics. On the practical ethical issue he is with Plato."[115]

The Platonic Soul Overall

Essentially, the Platonic soul (ψυχή) consists of three parts; the λογιστικόν (logical), the θυμοειδές (thumotic/spirit), and the ἐπιθυμητικόν (appetitive/erotic). Each part represents an integral part to how a human functions. But there must exist a balance between the parts for justice to exist.

Comparing the Structure of the Federal Government to the Platonic Soul

Judiciary as Logos

Explaining Why the Judiciary Is Not Thumos

The judiciary[116] in this chapter's paradigm represents logos. *Logos* is part of the Platonic part of the soul that represents logic.[117] This contrasts with Professor Covitz's formulation of the judiciary representing the *thumos*. His argument is compelling. However, in the *Republic*, Socrates states, that a person "watering and fostering the growth of the rational principle [logos] in his soul and the others the appetitive and the passionate [two representing eros]," and this specific person "is not by nature of a bad disposition but has fallen into evil communications," meaning this person has not become evil, but just in between the pull of logos and eros.[118] Socrates says this tension will resolve in "a compromise and turns over the government in his soul to the intermediate principle of ambition and high spirit and becomes a man haughty of soul and covetous of honor [meaning a turn to the thumotic part of the soul]."[119]

This indicates that one will likely turn to politics while in the tension of logos and eros, and in other words has become thumotic. This is more akin to the president, a politician, who in all likelihood is in search of honor, much like other politicians. Because if the executive of the country did not seek honor or maintain some "haughtiness" other politicians and world leaders would take advantage of us. She must be a decisive president, not merely logical. Yet, logic—as well as eros—may exist within her, but she must as president have a prevailing thumotic element.

This is in sharp contrast to the Article III judges especially. These judges—as intended by the Framers of the Constitution—were not and are not politicians seeking reelection.[120] But rather they are aloof from the political system seeking to interpret and apply the law.[121] This logical analysis—which can be informed with the other elements of the soul—is the guiding principle of the judiciary. The judiciary represents *logos*.

Cases and Examples Showing Why the Judiciary Represents Logos

In the *Phaedrus*, Socrates designates the charioteer as logos keeping control of the eros and thumos. Likewise, Chief Justice Marshall said, "[I]t is emphatically the province and duty of the judicial department to say what the law is."[122] The Supreme Court uses judicial review and interprets the Constitution and legislatively passed statutes to keep them in check much like the charioteer in Plato's *Phaedrus*.

When constituent parts of the soul become imbalanced, then unjust results arise, such as *Plessy v. Ferguson*.[123] However, imbalance and stepping out of a role in the separate powers may lead to more just and fair results, such as *Brown v. Board of Education*.[124]

In *Plessy v. Ferguson*,[125] the Supreme Court stepped out of its judicial authority and took on a legislative function, but with an unjust result. The Court declared that a "State, shall provide equal but separate accommodations" for members of different races.[126]

In *Brown v. Board of Education*,[127] the Supreme Court stepped out of its judicial authority and took on a legislative function, but with a just result. In *Brown v. Board of Education*,[128] the Court noted that "[t]he doctrine of 'separate but equal' did not make its appearance in this Court until 1896 in the case of

Plessy v. Ferguson … involving not education but transportation," showing that the Court in *Plessy* stepped out of its mode of *stare decisis* and made law based on no previous law. *Brown v. Bd. of Educ.*[129]

Most recently, in *Obergefell v. Hodges*,[130] many in the United States appreciate the decision, but others see it as a violation of natural law. Either way, the Supreme Court took on a legislative role in deciding the case; as Professor Kenji Yoshino writes:

> While Obergefell's most immediate effect was to legalize same-sex marriage across the land, its long-term impact could extend far beyond this context. To see this point, consider how much more narrowly the opinion could have been written. It could have invoked the equal protection and due process guarantees without specifying a formal level of review, and then observed that none of the state justifications survived even a deferential form of scrutiny. The Court had adopted this strategy in prior gay rights cases.[131]

American legal scholar Professor Laurence Tribe of Harvard University supports this position by stating:

> Professor Kenji Yoshino's splendid Comment makes clear just how misguided these glib detractions are, and eloquently elaborates the important doctrinal work done by Justice Kennedy's decision, which represents the culmination of a decades-long project that has revolutionized the Court's fundamental rights jurisprudence. As Yoshino demonstrates, *Obergefell* has definitively replaced *Washington v. Glucksberg's* wooden three-prong test focused on tradition, specificity, and negativity with the more holistic inquiry of Justice Harlan's justly famous 1961 dissent in *Poe v. Ullman*, a mode of inquiry that was embodied in key opinions from the mid-1960s to the early 1970s.[132]

Over time, society may come to a consensus on whether the Court decided the case correctly. Nevertheless, it currently serves as an example of a Court decision stepping out of the bounds of the judiciary's role and acting in a legislative capacity with an unclear or clear result of justice.

Although ideally the Court would follow *logos*, the catch is that the members of the Court are not purely guided by *logos*—as to be expected—because all humans, according to Plato, have three aspects of the soul within themselves. The idea of a three-part soul may be intended to understand the basic functions of an aspect of government, each member has an entire soul (ψυχή) governing their aspects of existence. This leads to more nuanced decisions, not only in the judiciary but also in all three branches of the government.

In terms of judiciary, stepping out the bounds of the separate powers or the role in the soul of the policy can have bad and good outcomes.

Justice from the charioteer comes from consistency, as many philosophers have defined justice. In this case, the *logos* as seen through the Supreme Court and judiciary, applying and saying what the law is.

Executive as Thumos

In this chapter the executive[133] represents *thumos*. *Thumos* represents the spirit of the soul as represented by the white horse in the *Phaedrus*.[134] The white horse is spirited, but controlled with a sense of potential shame.[135]

Explaining Why the Executive Is Not Logos

However, in Professor Covitz's formulation, the executive represents *logos*. As mentioned previously, Socrates states in the *Republic* that a person "watering and fostering the growth of the rational principle [logos] in his soul and the others the appetitive and the passionate [two representing eros]," and this person "is not by nature of a bad disposition but has fallen into evil communications," meaning this person has not become evil, but just in between the pull of *logos* and the pull of eros, but is otherwise unable to make a decision.[136] Socrates says this tension will resolve in "a compromise and turns over the government in his soul to the intermediate principle of ambition and high spirit and becomes a man haughty of soul and covetous of honor [meaning a turn to the thumotic part of the soul]."[137]

This indicates that one will likely turn to politics while in the tension of logos and eros, and in other words has become thumotic. This is more akin to the president—rather than a member of the judiciary—who in all likelihood is in search of honors much like other politicians. This is not a negative aspect of the executive necessarily. Because if the executive of the country did not seek honor or maintain some "haughtiness" other politicians and world leaders would take advantage of us. She must be a decisive president, not merely logical. Yet, logic—as well as *eros*—may and must exist within her, but she must as president have a prevailing thumotic element.

Cases and Examples Showing Why the Executive Represents Thumos

Here, the *thumos* manifests itself where a part of the Executive branch of government—such as the Federal Communications Commission or the Securities and Exchange Commission—would interpret a statute from the legislature and implement it. This occurs through the rules laid out by the Supreme Court and the judiciary as seen in the *Chevron* case.

Through 2013–15, the Obama administration issued executive orders relating to immigration.[138] By November 2015, the Fifth Circuit Court of Appeals declared the executive orders unconstitutional.[139] Regardless whether the executive orders are eventually upheld as constitutional or not, they represent the Executive branch of government conducting actions with the administration's justification that they are the most "thumotic" solution to the immigration problem. If the orders are upheld to be constitutional after all, then the judiciary or the legislature will deem them to have been the most effective approach at the time to avoid a greater disaster later. If the orders are not upheld to be constitutional, then the judiciary or the legislature will have deemed them not the most effective approach at the time. In an ironic sense, the immigration orders—if deemed constitutional—will be seen as a way to unify the country in a spirited "thumotic" way to avoid a greater catastrophe.[140]

Because the executive—and the legislature as well—are charged with the carrying out the daily activities of the nation, international relations appear to be of paramount importance with spirited leadership.

Thus, the leadership and executive actions that may not or may be based in *logos* and eros, but through a combination of the two as is the Platonic paradigm for *thumos*, which this chapter argues fits into the paradigm of the Executive branch of government in the US Constitution.

The Legislature as Eros

In this chapter the legislature[141] represents eros. Eros represents the basic instincts and desires of the soul as represented by the black horse in the *Phaedrus*. The black horse can wear down the white horse and charioteer.

The Patient Protection and Affordable Care Act Patient Protection and Affordable Care Act[142] (Obamacare) as passed by the Congress and signed into law in 2010.[143] According the Supreme Court, "[T]he Act aims to increase the number of Americans covered by health insurance and decrease the cost of health care. The Act's 10 titles stretch over 900 pages and contain hundreds of provisions."[144]

This example shows how the concept of justice is inconsistent. At the time it may be clear what the eros, the legislature, sees as justice. Overtime, this may become clear and unclear.

Conclusion

To reiterate, this chapter has demonstrated that to interpret the problems and the eventual purpose of the US government while simultaneously explaining its continued existence by analyzing the three-part structure of the US federal government as outlined in the Constitution—and subsequently interpreted by all three parts of the government—through the lens of the Platonic paradigm of logos, thumos, and eros as explained in Plato's dialogues. The major premise of the chapter is Plato's three-part soul. The minor premise is the three-part structure of the US government. The syllogism is the analysis in the chapter attempts to show how each part of the Platonic soul represents itself in the three parts of judiciary for logos, executive for thumos, and legislature for eros. Plato's tripartite soul and its correspondence to the structure of the US federal government are summarized in Table 3.1.

Overall, this Platonic analysis of the Constitution's structure and function could add to the dialogue of Constitutional analysis. Indeed, there are arguments for originalist, textualist, evolving constitutional doctrine, but there seems to be a basis for a Platonic interpretation of the Constitution.

In line with a balanced soul of the polity and a balanced government, it would seem that each part of government would not reach into another's duties.[145]

Table 3.1 Plato's Tripartite Soul and the Structure of the US Federal Government

Plato's Soul Component	Psychological Function	US Government Branch	Institutional Role
Logos (Reason)	Rational guidance, pursuit of truth, deliberative and judicial	Judiciary	Applies legal reasoning, interprets the law, seeks justice
Thumos (Spirit)	Courage, willpower, ambition, drive toward honor and action	Executive	Enforces laws, leads action, embodies the assertive and directive force
Eros (Appetite)	Desire, longing, generative drive, oriented toward productivity	Legislative	Represents the people's will, generates law, and reflects the common desires and needs

As fate would have it, each person—in the Platonic paradigm—has the three parts of the Platonic soul. Although an individual may act in one part of the federal government, each person has all three parts. Thus, it is to be expected that different parts of the soul would manifest in a different part of the federal government.

Notes

1 This can perhaps be better understood for purposes of this chapter as "aspects of existence." Also, consider the similarity to Sigmund Freud's psychoanalysis. Sigmund Freud, *The Ego and the Id* (1923), in The Standard Edition of the Complete Psychological Works of Sigmund Freud (James Strachey ed. & trans., 1961) 3, 25.

The Liddell & Scott's *A Greek-English Lexicon* defines the word as, "ψυχή ψύχω I.breath, Lat. anima, esp. as the sign of life, the life, spirit." "Henry George Liddell, Robert Scott, *An Intermediate Greek-English Lexicon*, Ψυχή." Accessed May 19, 2021. http://www.perseus.tufts.edu/hopper/text?doc=Perseus%3Atext%3A1999.04.0058%3Aentry%3Dyuxh%2F.

2 Plato, *The Republic of Plato* (trans. Allan Bloom, 2d ed., Basic Books, New York, 1991) 435e–432a [hereinafter Plato, Republic].

3 *Id.* at 439a, 439e3–4.

4 *Id.* at 439d5–6a1-3.

5 "A particular form of government or political organization."

6 In the dialogue, Socrates suggested the three parts of the soul should not prevent the other parts from functioning appropriately. Id. at 433a.

7 Cicero, *De Republica* (Loeb Classical Library, Cambridge, MA, 1928), 3.22.33.

8 Plato, *Timaeus* (Oxford University Press, Oxford, trans., Robin Waterfield, 2008) at 30a–31b. The page numbers used throughout this chapter (and book) to refer to Platonic texts are in accord with the Stephanus pagination.

Substantively, are randomness or patterns provable or real? How do we even decide what is random if not through statistical or other mathematical analysis? Philosophically speaking there could be a discrepancy between a series following a mathematical rule or being truly random. Ludwig Wittgenstein in his *Philosophical Investigations* explained how randomness *can* really be explained in terms of increasing complexity of following a rule, but paradoxically if everything can be shown to be following a rule it can also at the same time be shown to not follow a rule.

201. This was our paradox: no course of action could be determined by a rule, because every course of action can be made out to accord with the rule. The answer was: if everything can be made out to accord with the rule, then it can also be made out to conflict with it. And so there would be neither accord nor conflict here. It can be seen that there is a misunderstanding here from the mere fact that in the course of our argument we give one interpretation after another; as if each one contented us at least for a moment, until we thought of yet another standing behind it. What this shews is that there is a way of grasping a rule which is not an interpretation, but which is exhibited in what we call "obeying the rule" and "going against it" in actual cases. Hence there is an inclination to say: every action according to the rule is an interpretation. But we ought to restrict the term "interpretation" to the substitution of one expression of the rule for another. Ludwig Wittgenstein, Philosophical Investigations (G.E.M. Anscombe & R. Rhees eds., G.E.M. Anscombe trans., 1972) § 201.

This makes one question whether randomness really exists or does everything follow a set rule? See, e.g., Ahilan T. Arulanantham, Breaking the Rules?: Wittgenstein and Legal Realism, *Yale L.J.* 107 (1998) 1853, 1869–71. Dennis Patterson, Wittgenstein and Constitutional Theory, *Tex. L. Rev.* 72 (1994) 1837, 1851. Scott Hershovitz, "Wittgenstein on Rules: The Phantom Menace." *Oxford J. of Leg. Stud.* 22 (2002): 619, 639–40.

9 Such an example can be seen in literature,

Borges's *The Library of Babel* implicitly undercuts all the written structures—religion, science, art—through which human beings strive to impose order on an unruly world. It consists of a fantastic monologue in which a Librarian, who lives in a Library which is also the universe, tries unsuccessfully to describe the chaotic infinity (or near infinity) that surrounds him. According to the Librarian, the Library may or may not be endless; but it is certainly meaningless, being made up of numberless books in a Babel of tongues. Because it contains all the possible combinations of letters in all languages, many of the books contain only an intelligible word or two, or are only partially true copies of books contained in their proper form elsewhere in the Library. The Librarians spend their time, among other ways, searching for the true catalogue that would bring order and meaning to their incomprehensible collection.

Susan Mann, "The Universe and the Library: A Critique of James Boyd White as Writer and Reader." *Stan. L. Rev.* 41 (1989) 959, 965.

10 *Lucretius: On the Nature of Things* (H. A. J. Munro trans.), reprinted in 12 *Great Books of the Western World* (Robert Maynard Hutchins ed., 1952) 1, 12.

Concurrently, directly contrasting the Platonic theory of order the universe,

The contrary materialist view characterizes archetypes as speculative constructs. Aristotle and Plato had their ancient Greek materialist counterparts in Epicurus, Democritus, and Lucretius, who in his *On the Nature of the Universe* wrote that all things began from "the purposeless congregation and coalescence of atoms." There are uniform and entirely natural causes in a closed system not ordered or otherwise affected by the presence of a higher mind capable of recognizing and ordering information. Thus Epicurus could hold that morality was merely a sensual matter of seeking pleasure and avoiding pain, not a sensitivity issue to any particular purpose or design. Aristotle's teleological universe was rejected for an atomistic universe without purpose or form in which biological forms and the ordered universe in which they exist were not the fixed product of information, intelligence, or design but of random accretion. Nobel Prize winning biologist George Wald, physicist Freeman Dyson, and astronomer George Greenstein explain the improbability of the universe's remarkable order by suggesting either that the universe did not exist until humans observed it and (in Wald's words) that "[t]he universe wants to be known."

Marion Hilligan, Nelson P. Miller, Don Petersen & Chris Hastings, SYMPOSIUM ISSUE: WORLD VIEWS COLLIDE: A Dialogue on State-Authored Embryonic Stem-Cell Research, Human Enhancements, Physician-Assisted Suicide and the Value of Life: Superhuman-Biotechnology's Emerging Impact on the Law, *T.M. Cooley L. Rev.* 24 (2007) 1, 25–6.

11 Such as the interlocutor suggests nature represented itself in Athens. *Timaeus* 90b–c. See recent work suggesting there is an order to the world's structure. "About fifty years ago a physicist called Paul Dirac asked himself why the number ten to the fortieth power keeps occurring. The square of this number, ten to the eightieth power, is the mass of the visible universe, measured in terms of the mass of the proton. The number itself, ten to the fortieth, is the present age of the universe, expressed in units of time it takes light to travel across a proton. And, get this, the constant that measures the strength of gravity in terms of the electrical force between two protons is ten to the fortieth times weaker! Also, ten to the fortieth to the one-fourth, or ten to the tenth, just about equals the number of stars in a galaxy, the number of galaxies in the universe, and the inverse of the weakfine structure constant! John Updike, Roger's Version 23–4 (1986); George Johnson, *A Fire in the Mind: Science, Faith, and the Search for Order* 308–16 (1996)." Robert Birmingham, "Proving Miracles and the First Amendment." *Geo. Mason L. Rev.* 5 (1996): 45, 60.

12 "To illustrate the nature of structuralist theory, this discussion will concentrate on the work of Claude Levi-Strauss. Levi-Strauss has made the search for the fundamental properties of human thought the focus of his work. His basic objective is uncovering the universal, basic structure of human thought, which is deep below the surface but is manfested [*sic*] in myth, language, cooking, table manners, and the general structures of social life. This basic structure, which is termed 'deep structure,' will identify cross-cultural similarities." Donald H. J. Hermann, "Phenomenology, Structuralism, Hermeneutics, and Legal Study: Applications of Contemporary Continental Thought to Legal Phenomena." *U. Miami L. Rev.* 36 (1982): 379, 390–1.

13 "Michel Foucault's compelling and poetic methodological manifesto describes the nature of 'critique' and, thereby, the proper role of the critic. For Foucault, 'critique' was more than a means to an end; criticism was itself an act of resistance and refusal. Toward this end, Foucault sought to decouple criticism from positive programs for social and political change. Criticism is, according to this view, a negative operation—'essays in refusal'—resisting and rejecting 'what is' without regard for 'what needs to be done.' For this reason, Foucault's views have occasionally been labeled 'rejectionist.' Such 'rejectionist' claims, in turn, exemplify the most feared aspects of a new challenge to traditional legal thought: postmodernism." Derek P. Jinks, "Essays in Refusal: Pre-Theoretical Commitments in Postmodern Anthropology and Critical Race Theory." *Yale L. J.* 107 (1997): 499, 499–500. See also for a discussion on Foucault's ideas on law and sovereignty: Tom Frost, "Agamben's Sovereign Legalization of Foucault." *Oxford J Legal Studies* 30, 3 (2010): 545.

14 Marvin Harris, *The Rise of Anthropological Theory* (1968). See Perry Dane, "Jurisdictionality, Time, and the Legal Imagination." *Hofstra L. Rev.* 23 (1994): 1, 94. See "The reciprocity concept justifies the assumption that one who gives will receive in return, though there are no hard promises as to timing, quality, or quantity." John W. Ragsdale Jr., "The Rise and Fall of the Chacoan State." *UMKC L. Rev.* 64 (1995): 485, 528. *See* Bronislaw Malinowski, Argonauts of the Western Pacific 72–76 (Routledge 1961) (1922) (discussing gift giving cultures). Perry Dane, "Jurisdictionality, Time, and the Legal Imagination." *Hofstra L. Rev.* 23 (1994): 1, 94. *See* In regard to gift giving cultures. Bronislaw Malinowski, Argonauts of the Western Pacific (Routledge 1961) (1922) 72–6.

15 According to Dumézil, the division of society—government—into three parts was inherent in all Indo-European societies. The trifunctional pattern (and implicit political separation of powers) is manifest among the Hindus in the original Castes: Brahmana (teachers, priests, keepers of the law), Ksatriya (Warrior Kings), and Vaisya (Farmers, Producers, Merchants and Doctors). "For classic development of this so-called 'tripartite hypothesis' concerning the division of social roles in Proto-Indo-European societies, see generally Georges Dumézil, *Flamen-Brahman* (1935); Georges Dumézil, *Mitra-Varuna: An Essay on Two Indo-European Representations*

of Sovereignty (Derek Coltman trans., 2d ed. 1988)." Robin Bradley Kar. "Western Legal Prehistory: Reconstructing the Hidden Origins of Western Law and Civilization." *U. Ill. L. Rev.* (2012): 1499, 1525 n. 71. *See also* Georges Dumézil, Archaic Roman Religion (1966) 585. See also for critiques of the Trifunctional Hypothesis: Wouter W. Belier, Decayed Gods: Origin and Development of Georges Dumézil's "Ideologie Tripartie" (1991) 17–20.

16 David S. Caudill, "Freud and Critical Legal Studies: Contours of a Radical Socio-Legal Psychoanalysis." *Ind. L. J.* 66 (1991): 651, 658–9. *See* S. Freud, *The Ego and the Id*, in 19 The Standard Edition of the Complete Psychological Works of the Complete Psychological Works of Sigmund Freud (J. Strachey ed. 1951) 3.

17 Lincoln, Charles E., *Ethnicity and Social Organization at Chichen Itza, Yucatan, Mexico* (PhD. dissertation, Department of Anthropology, Harvard University) Advisors Mathews, Peter, and Gordon R. Willey. (1990). *See* Lincoln, Charles E., *The Chronology of Chichen Itza: A Review of the Literature. In Late Lowland Maya Civilization: Classic to Postclassic* (Jeremy A. Sabloff and E. Wyllys Andrews V ed., University of New Mexico Press, Albuquerque, 1986), 141–56.

18 *The Iliad of Homer* 14:28–30 (Richmond Lattimore trans., 25th reprint ed. 1976) (1951). *See* "[T]he well known Judgment of Paris, which Homer apparently knew. Although it is not directly recounted in the Iliad, there is a clear reference to it in Book 14, where Hera's displeasure with the other gods (i.e., gods who were urging Achilles to treat Hector's corpse with respect) was attributed to the Judgment of Paris: 'because of the delusion of Paris / who insulted the goddesses when they came to him in his courtyard / and favoured her who supplied the lust that led to disaster.' The myth of the Judgment of Paris began when Peleus and Thetis did not invite Eris, the goddess of discord, to their wedding. Eris, feeling snubbed, concocted one of literary history's most evil schemes. She procured a golden apple and inscribed it 'For the fairest.' She then crashed the wedding feast and tossed the apple onto the table. Three goddesses, Hera, Athena, and Aphrodite, each argued that it should be her's. They asked Zeus to decide. He refused because he feared his wife's anger in the event that he did not choose her. He passed the buck and suggested that the Trojan prince Paris, the son of Priam, act as arbiter." Russ VerSteeg, *A Contract Analysis of the Trojan War*, Ariz. L. Rev. 40(1998) 173, 192.

19 Montesquieu, *The Spirit of the Laws* (Thomas Nugent trans., Hafner Pub. 1949) (1748) bk. XI, ch. 6, at 152.

20 John F. Manning, "Separation of Powers as Ordinary Interpretation." 124 Harv. L. Rev. 1939, 2004 (2010).

21 James J. Walsh, *Education of the Founding Fathers of the Republic: Scholasticism in the Colonial Colleges* (1970) 104–5.

22 *Federalist Paper No. 63* (James Madison).

23 Jean-Francois Pradeau, *Plato and the City* (University of Exeter Press, Exeter, 2002) 129.

24 As far as the author knows, Akiba Covitz is the only person to have written on this subject.

25 As well as long-term personal correspondence with Professor Akiba J. Covitz discussing the dissertation's ideas. Professor Covitz was the author's mentor during the author's undergraduate studies.

26 Covitz, xxii–xxv.

27 *Id.* xviii–xx.

28 *Id.* iv.

29 This chapter will also focus on the Constitution and Plato's *Republic*, but also other works that have interpreted the two of them—including some of mine.

30 "In his book, The Cave and the Light, Arthur Herman traces the gradual emergence of the view that rulers do not properly derive power from force of arms, but from the people, who both may chose and remove rulers. The idea began with William Ockham, was part of the philosophical underpinning of the 'Catholic Schism' (the only instance before recent times when a Pope voluntarily relinquished office), was famously developed by John Locke, and was memorialized by Thomas Jefferson in the Declaration of Independence." Kenneth S. Klein, *Weighing Democracy and Judicial Legitimacy in Judicial Selection*, 23 Tex. Rev. L. & Pol. 269, 278 (2018). Moreover, "The debate between theoretical and practical teaching contains elements of the multimillennial debate over the approaches of Plato and Aristotle. See generally Arthur Herman, The Cave and the Light: Plato Versus Aristotle, and the Struggle for the Soul of Western Civilization (2013)." S. Scott Gaille, *The ABA Task Force Report on the Future of Legal Education: The Role of Adjunct Professors and Practical Teaching in the Energy Sector*, 35 Energy L.J. 199, 213 n. 69 (2014).

31 Kenji Yoshino, *The City and the Poet*, Yale L.J. 114 (2005) 1835, 1842.

32 *Id.*

33 *Id.* 1842–3.

Conversely, Plato's idea of the soul is similar but different from Aristotle's view.

Aristotle's use of the vocabulary of dunamis is unusually complex and requires clarification. A typical example of the first meaning ("innate") is found at Aristotle, Ethica Nicomachea, *supra* note 13, at 1105b20–28, which contrasts dunamis with a developed capacity. But in other passages, dunamis is clearly used in the sense of a developed capacity. *Id.* at 1094b2, 1101b13, 1143a28. Finally, the term is sometimes used when the capacity is already active, and thus the conditions for its activation must be present. See Aristotle, De Anima 412a1–13a10 (W.D. Ross ed., 1956) (defining psuche as the active organization of a body that has life, potentially, or dunamei). Of course, as Aristotle immediately points out, one is alive only when the body is actually alive, thus meeting all the "external" conditions for the presence of psuche. See *id.*; see also Martha C. Nussbaum, *Commentary on Aristotle, De Motu Animalium* 271, 363–4 (Martha Craven Nussbaum trans., 1978) (discussing Aristotle, De Motu Animalium 702a30–1, 703b29–32).

Martha Nussabaum, "The Supreme Court: 2006 Term: Foreword: Constitutions and Capabilities: 'Perception' against Lofty Formalism." *Harv. L. Rev.* 121 (2007) 4, 34.

34 *Id.*

35 Bruce D. Fisher, "The Ethical Consumer: A Rejecter of Positive Law Arbitrage." *Seton Hall L. Rev.* 25 (1994): 230, 245.

36 Natural law can find its roots as far as the ancient Greeks and Aquinas. Martin Rhonheimer, "Natural Law as a Work of Reason: Understanding the Metaphysics of Participated Theonomy." *Am. J. Juris.* 55 (2010): 41, 47, 50. See generally, Philip A. Hamburger, "Natural Rights, Natural Law, and American Constitutions." *Yale Law Journal* (1993): 907–60.

37 *Id.*

38 Linda Meyer, "'Nothing We Say Matters': Teague and New Rules." *The University of Chicago Law Review* 61, 2 (1994): 423–92, 460.

39 *Id.*

The author goes on to explain how: "[Positive law] … is set by a monarch, or sovereign number, to a person or persons in a state of subjection to its author." John Austin, The Province of Jurisprudence Determined (1832), reprinted in John Austin, The Province of Jurisprudence Determined and The Uses of the Study of Jurisprudence 132 (Noonday, 1954). See also Frederick Schauer, "Constitutional Positivism," 25 *Conn L Rev* 797, 799 (1993) (Legal positivism takes the position that the law "is not derived necessarily from fundamental moral principles, but rather is simply 'posited' by human beings and human institutions"), and the bibliography of major theorists cited therein. *Id.* at 799 n 3.

However, Professor Nonet, discusses the essence of positive law in relation to Nietzsche's philosophy, "What is positive law? We may begin with the familiar account that the word 'positive' suggests immediately: positive law (Nietzsche calls it Gesetz) is law that exists by virtue of being posited (gesetzt), laid down and set firmly, by a will empowered so to will. Such law 'exists' in the sense that it has validity (Geltung). It has validity if the will (Wille) from which it issues has the power (Macht) to impose it, to demand and secure obedience to its command." Nonet, Philippe. "What Is Positive Law?." *The Yale Law Journal* 100, no. 3 (1990): 667–99, 667–8.

40 Plato, Republic at 608c–621d.

41 Niccolo Machiavelli, The Prince (Luigi Ricci and E.R.P. Vincent trans.), reprinted in Social and Political Philosophy: Readings from Plato to Gandhi (John Somerville & Ronald E. Santoni eds., 1963) 123.

42 *Cf.* Christopher Bobonich, "Persuasion, Compulsion, and Freedom in Plato's 'Laws.'" in *Plato*, ed. Gail Fine (Oxford: Oxford University Press, 2000), 884.

43 Albert Grande, "Education as a Natural Right." *John's J. Legal Comment* 21 (2006): 53, 53–6. "Antigone, with clear conscience, deliberately violates King Creon's law that denies her brother a decent burial. Her brother had been a rebel and was thereby denied the honor of a proper burial. Antigone appeals to the higher unwritten laws of God, the eternal natural laws. While it is unknown when those laws originated, Antigone's act of defiance violates written laws in favor of natural law, which respects a sister's right to bury her brother, despite the king's prohibition." *Id.*

44 Bruce D. Fisher, *The Ethical Consumer: A Rejecter of Positive Law Arbitrage*, 25 Seton Hall L. Rev. 230, 245 (1994).

45 *Id.*

46 Cicero, De legibus, 1.18, at 316–17 (Clinton Walker Keyes trans., 1928) ("Law is the highest reason, implanted in Nature, which commands what ought to be done and forbids the opposite"). It's interesting to consider how positive law is rooted in nature.

47 Veronica Gentilli, "A Double Challenge for Critical Race Scholars: The Moral Context." 65 *S. Cal. L. Rev.* 2361, 2368 (1992).

On the Platonic view, concepts are immutable and eternal; they exist independently of the world around us. Plato calls these concepts of independent and necessary truths "Forms." For Plato, the Forms, or concepts, are reality; things in the world have only diminished reality since they are imperfect replicas of the Forms. Thus, a chair in the world is but an imperfect reflection of the concept, the abstract idea, of "Chairhood." The material world is true and real only to the degree that it accurately reflects the Forms. We call a particular object a chair because we recognize it as an instantiation of the Form of Chairhood.

48 "Plato is discussing the deepest of epistemic questions, but the imagery that he crafts in the dialogue helps us to address the central problems that Sherwin raises regarding contemporary legal practice. To doubt that the sight lovers can sustain law is to assume with Plato that it is possible to break away from the multitude, escape from the cave, and gain access to the forms of legal certainty." Francis J. Mootz III, *Law among the Sight Lovers*, 57 N.Y.L. Sch. L. Rev. 61, 62 (2013).

49 "The first reading assignment in my undergraduate courses in constitutional law is Plato's analogy of the cave. I then ask students to imagine the Supreme Court justices standing at the rear of the cave, casting shadows (decisions) upon the front wall. Seated in successive rows are constitutional scholars, members of the intelligentsia (lawyers, political scientists, and educators), and behind them elected officials and media representatives. Common citizens fill the remainder of

the cave. As in Plato's analogy all those seated are prisoners with chains about their necks, their heads fixed to view the shadows on the front wall." William Gangi, *A Scholar's Journey on the Dark Side*, 11 CHAP. L. REV. 1, 8 (2007).

50 Plato, Republic (*c.* 360 BC), reprinted in *The Collected Dialogues of Plato* 575, bk. VI, 510d–e, at 746 (Edith Hamilton & Huntington Cairns eds., Paul Shorey trans., Princeton University Press 1961). (The original dialogue provides that "[t]he very things which they mould and draw, which have shadows and images of themselves in water, these things they treat in their turn as only images, but what they really seek is to get sight of those realities which can be seen only by the mind.")

51 "Applying this dialectic model, Plato develops the famous 'cave' analogy, wherein the philosopher purges himself from the vision of mere images by escaping into the sunlight of the day, whereupon he grasps the true form of the 'Good.'" Edward C. Lyons, *Reason's Freedom and the Dialectic of Ordered Liberty*, 55 Clev. St. L. Rev. 157, 184 (2007).

52 This was explored in a novelistic format in the late nineteenth century in a book titled *Flatland* where a world of two-dimensional beings only know points and triangles, and so on. But then one day a triangle is taken into the third dimension. Imagine how hard it would be to describe the third dimension to two-dimensional beings.

53 I use the Paul Shorey translation for this section. I have a deep affinity for this translation as I first read it when I was eighteen and still refer to this translation frequently.

54 Plato, Republic (Paul Shorey trans.), reprinted in *The Collected Dialogues of Plato* 575, 749–50 (516e–518c) (Edith Hamilton & Huntington Cairns eds., 1961).

55 "Socrates' theory of education presents a disarmingly simple, albeit puzzling, answer to the first question "what should we teach to our students?" His answer is nothing. According to Socratic educational theory, students already know what we as teachers are attempting to teach to them; they just do not know that they know it. This is Socrates' theory that "all inquiry and learning is but recollection." James R. Beattie, Jr., *Socratic Ignorance: Once More into the Cave*, 105 W. Va. L. Rev. 471, 475 (2003).

56 Plato, Meno (W.K.C. Guthrie trans.), reprinted in *The Collected Dialogues of Plato*, 353, 364 (81c–d). I follow closely the analysis outlined by Professor James Beattie who writes, "For Socrates, we cannot teach students something they do not already know for that is to aver 'that (we) can put true knowledge into a soul that does not possess it, as if (we) were inserting vision into blind eyes.' What teachers can do for their students is to get them to recognize explicitly what they already know implicitly. Rather than transferring information to our students, we should elicit information from them; information, which in some significant sense, they already possess." James R. Beattie, Jr., *Socratic Ignorance: Once More into the Cave*, 105 W. VA. L. REV. 471, 475–6 (2003).

57 "Edwin A. Abbott, *Flatland: A Romance of Many Dimensions* (Harper & Row 1963) (1880) (philosophical parable of a two-dimensional planar world and the epochal discovery by one inhabitant of the revolutionary notion of height)." Mark A. Levin, *Essential Commodities and Racial Justice: Using Constitutional Protection of Japan's Indigenous Ainu People to Inform Understandings of the United States and Japan*, 33 N.Y.U. J. Int'l L. & Pol. 419, 526 n. 265 (2001).

58 Theophrastus the successor to Aristotle in the School of Athens wrote extensively on the parts and Forms of plants and trees. *Theophrastus: Enquiry into Plants and Minor Works on Odours and Weather Signs*, vol. 2, trans. Sir Arthur Hort (London: William Heinemann, 1916).

59 Thomas C. Grey, *Holmes and Legal Pragmatism*, 41 Stan. L. Rev. 787, 861 (1989).

60 Oliver Wendell Holmes, Jr., *The Common Law* (Mark DeWolfe Howe ed., Harvard University Press, 1963) (1881), p. 1.

61 Andrew P. Morriss, Codification and the Right Answers, *Chi.-Kent L. Rev.* 74 (1999) 355.

Compare with *Id.* n. 161 "The Civil Code of the State of New York (pt. 1), 2 Alb. L.J. 385, 385 (November 19, 1870). This was the idea behind the case method introduced by Christopher Columbus Langdell at Harvard Law School in 1870, where Carter had trained. See Wiecek, *supra* note 10, at 92–3."

Indeed, many legal scholars have long viewed Christopher Columbus Langdell, the dean of Harvard Law School from 1870 to 1895, as the prototypical American jurist of the late nineteenth century. He portrayed the common law as a conceptually ordered scientific system in which rigorous logical reasoning trumped concerns about the just resolution of particular cases. In Langdell's Orthodoxy, probably the most influential modern article on Langdell, Thomas Grey dubbed this system of legal thought "classical orthodoxy." Others have labeled it "mechanical jurisprudence," "classical legal thought," "liberal legal science," or "Langdellian formalism." Whatever term they have preferred, scholars have long agreed that Gilded Age legal thinkers viewed the common law as a rigidly logical, amoral system. Lewis A. Grossman, "Langdell Upside-Down: James Coolidge Carter and the Anticlassical Jurisprudence of Anticodification." *Yale J.L. & Human* 19 (2007): 149, 150.

62 Oliver Wendell Holmes, Jr., *The Common Law* (Mark DeWolfe Howe ed., Harvard University Press, 1963) (1881), p. 1. Holmes continued a sentence later, "[t]he form of continuity has been kept up by reasonings [*sic*] purporting to reduce every thing to a logical sequence; but that form is nothing but the evening dress which the newcomer puts on to make itself presentable according to conventional requirements. The important phenomenon is the man underneath it, not the coat; the justice and reasonableness of a decision, not its consistency with previously held views. … As a branch of anthropology, law is an object of science; the theory of legislation is a scientific study; but the effort to reduce the concrete details of an existing system to the merely logical consequences of simple postulates is always in

danger of becoming unscientific, and of leading to a misapprehension of the nature of the problem and the data." *Id.*

63 Roscoe Pound, "Mechanical Jurisprudence." *Columbia Law Review* 8 (1908): 605, 606.
64 Holmes, Privilege, Malice, and Intent, *Harv. Law Rev.* 8 (1894) 1, 7.
65 *Id.* at 7.
66 343 U.S. 579 (1952).
67 343 U.S. 579, 582–5 (1952).
68 343 U.S. 579, 585.
69 *Youngstown Sheet & Tube Co. v. Sawyer*, 343 U.S. 579, 588.
70 *Id.* at 579, 589.
71 *Id.* at 579, 588.
72 *Id.* at 579, 589.
73 *Id.* at 579, 647 (1952).
74 *Id.* at 579, 629 (1952).
75 *Chevron, U.S.A., Inc. v. NRDC, Inc.*, 467 U.S. 837, 844 (1984).
76 *Id.* at 837, 839–40.
77 *Id.* at 840.
78 *Id.*
79 *Id.*
80 *Id.* at 837, 843.
81 *Id.* at 843–4.
82 *Id.* at 837, 844.
83 *Id.*
84 Thomas W. Merrill, "Judicial Deference to Executive Precedent." *Yale L.J.* 101 (1992): 969.
85 *Id.* at 969–70.
86 Abbe R. Gluck, "Imperfect Statutes, Imperfect Courts: Understanding Congress's Plan in the Era of Unorthodox Lawmaking." *Harv. L. Rev.* 129 (2015): 62, 63.
87 Cristina Marcos and Sarah Ferris. "House Votes to Repeal ObamaCare | TheHill." Accessed May 19, 2021. https://thehill.com/policy/healthcare/231638-house-votes-to-repeal-obamacare.
88 *Id.*
89 Karlan, Pamela S. "Foreword: Democracy and Disdain, the Supreme Court 2011 Term." *Harv. L. Rev.* 126 (2012): 1–45, 5.
90 Carlos E. Gonzalez "Reinterpreting Statutory Interpretation." *NCL Rev.* 74 (1995): 585, 586.
91 "Methodological stare decisis—the practice of giving precedential effect to judicial statements about methodology—is generally absent from the jurisprudence of mainstream federal statutory interpretation, but appears to be a common feature of some states' statutory case law." Abbe R. Gluck "The States as

Laboratories of Statutory Interpretation: Methodological Consensus and the New Modified Textualism." *The Yale Law Journal* 119 (2010): 1750–1862, 1754.

92 Brian G. Slocum "Overlooked Temporal Issues in Statutory Interpretation." *Temp. L. Rev.* 81 (2008): 635, 637–8.

93 Glen Staszewski, "The Dumbing Down of Statuary." *B. U. L. Rev.* 95 (2015): 209, 217–19. (Staszweski argues against a uniform system of statutory interpretation throughout the article.)

94 Professor Gluck expands on the terms 'methodological' and 'formalistic'.

By "formalistic," I mean clearly defined, ex ante interpretive rules arranged to be applied in a consistent order. But the characteristics of the particular rules chosen (for instance, whether and when legislative history may be consulted) need not themselves be rigid. Cf. Cass R. Sunstein, *Must Formalism Be Defended Empirically?*, 66 U. Chi. L. Rev. 636, 638 (1999) ("Formalist strategies … entail three commitments: to promoting compliance with all applicable legal formalities (whether or not they make sense in the individual case), to ensuring rule-bound law … and to constraining the discretion of judges"). Abbe R. Gluck, "The States as Laboratories of Statutory Interpretation: Methodological Consensus and the New Modified Textualism." *The Yale Law Journal* 119 (2010): 1750–1862, 1754 fn. 8.

95 Sydney Foster, "Should Courts Give Stare Decisis Effect to Statutory Interpretation Methodology?" *Geo. L. J.* 96 (2008): 1863.

96 H. Robert, Robert's Rules of Order Newly Revised (1970). See generally Saul Levmore, Parliamentary Law, Majority Decisionmaking, and the Voting Paradox, 75 Va. L. Rev. 971 (1989): 971–1044.

97 Thomas Jefferson, Jefferson's Manual of Parliamentary Practice (1801), reprinted in Rules of the House of Representatives, H.R. Doc. No. 279, 99th Cong., 2d Sess. (1987).

98 A secondary account must be limited inherently to espouse the entire idea, but also to capture the rhetorical and poetic qualities inherent in Plato's writings. In some sense, this is a reflection or hyperreality simulacra of the "real" represented in Plato's corpus. See Jean Baudrillard, *The Precession of the Simulacra, in Simulacra and Simulation* (Sheila Faria Glaser trans., University of Michigan Press 1997) (1981).

See This is closely related to Zizek's assertion that "we lack the very language to articulate our unfreedom." Slavoj Žižek, Welcome to the Desert of the Real 2 (2002). See generally Sorajjakool, *infra* note 67 (It is extremely difficult to articulate conditions you refuse to believe or accept). Nick J. Scuillo, "Žižek/Questions/Failing." *Willamette L. Rev.* 47 (2011) 287, 325 n. 55.

99 Republic, 443c–e.

100 *Id*, at 441d12–e2.

101 *Id,* at 433a, where Socrates states, "And what we did lay down, and often said, you recall, was that each one man must perform one social service in the state for which his nature is best adapted." Likewise, if this does not happen, then there would be injustice (ἀδικία).

102 Etymologically speaking, The Liddell & Scott's *A Greek-English Lexicon* defines the word as, " λογιστικός from λογιστής 1 I. skilled or practised in calculating, Xen., Plat.:—ἡ λογιστική (sc. τέχνη), arithmetic, Plat. II. endued with reason, rational, Arist.:—τὸ λ. the reasoning faculty, Plat. 2.using one's reason, reasonable, Xen." Henry George Liddell, Robert Scott, "An Intermediate Greek-English Lexicon, Λογιστικός." Accessed May 19, 2021. http://www.perseus.tufts.edu/hopper/text?doc=Perseus%3Atext%3A1999.04.0058%3Aentry%3Dlogistiko%2Fs.

103 Republic, 435 e.

104 This can be compare to "*Crito* 46 B (one of the passages which the Christian apologists used to prove that Socrates knew the λόγος), *Theaetetus* 186 C ἀναλογίσματα πρός τε οὐσίαν καὶ ὠφέλειαν, and *Laws* 644 D. Aristotle *Eth.* 1139 a 12 somewhat differently."

"Plato, Republic, Book 4, Section 439d." Accessed May 19, 2021. http://www.perseus.tufts.edu/hopper/text?doc=Perseus%3Atext%3A1999.01.0167%3Abook%3D4%3Asection%3D439d.

105 Kenji Yoshino, *The City and the Poet*, 114 Yale L.J. 1835, 1841–1868 (2005).

106 Etymologically speaking, the Liddell & Scott's *A Greek-English Lexicon* defines the word as, "ἐπιθυμητικός from ἐπιθυμέω [select] desiring, coveting, lusting after a thing, c. gen., Plat., etc.:—adv., ἐπιθυμητικῶς ἔχειν τινός ˜ ἐπιθυμεῖν." Citing Liddell and Scott. *An Intermediate Greek-English Lexicon*. Oxford. Clarendon Press. 1889. "Henry George Liddell, Robert Scott, *An Intermediate Greek-English Lexicon*, Ἐπιθυμητικός." Accessed May 19, 2021. http://www.perseus.tufts.edu/hopper/text?doc=Perseus:text:1999.04.0058:entry=e)piqumhtiko/s.

See other references to Liddell & Scott's famous lexicon in legal secondary sources: Randall Baldwin Clark, "Platonic Love in a Colorado Courtroom: Martha Nussbaum, John Finnis, and Plato's Laws in Evans v. Romer." *Yale J. L. & Humanities* 12 (2000): 1, 5–6.

107 Republic, 439 d.

108 The Liddell & Scott's *A Greek-English Lexicon* defines the word as "θυμοειδής 1 εἶδος 1.high-spirited, courageous, Lat. animosus, Plat., Xen. 2.hot-tempered, restive, id=Xen." Henry George Liddell, Robert Scott, "An Intermediate Greek-English Lexicon, Θυμοειδής." Accessed May 19, 2021. http://www.perseus.tufts.

edu/hopper/text?doc=Perseus%3Atext%3A1999.04.0058%3Aentry%3Dqumoeid h%2Fs.

109 This spirit has been described in a distinctively Platonic sense of θυμόςas the power of noble wrath, which, unless perverted by a bad education, is naturally the ally of the reason, though as mere angry passion it might seem to belong to the irrational part of the soul, and so, as Glaucon suggets, be akin to appetite, with which it is associated in the mortal soul of the *Timaeus* 69 D. In Laws 731 BC Plato tells us again that the soul cannot combat injustice without the capacity for righteous indignation. The Stoics affected to deprecate anger always, and the difference remained a theme of controversy between them and the Platonists. *Cf.* Schmidt, Ethik der Griechen, ii. pp. 321 ff., Seneca, De ira, i. 9, and *passim*. Moralists are still divided on the point. *Cf.* Bagehot, Lord Brougham: "Another faculty of Brougham … is the faculty of easy anger. The supine placidity of civilization is not favorable to animosity [Bacon's word for θυμός]." Leslie Stephen, Science of Ethics, pp. 60 ff. and p. 62, seems to contradict Plato: "The supposed conflict between reason and passion is, as I hold, meaningless if it is taken to imply that the reason is a faculty separate from the emotions," etc. But this is only his metaphysics. On the practical ethical issue he is with Plato.

110 "James Adam, the Republic of Plato, Book 4, Section 439E." Accessed May 19, 2021. http://www.perseus.tufts.edu/hopper/text?doc=Perseus%3Atext%3A1999.04.0094%3Abook%3D4%3Asection%3D439e.

111 *Id.*

112 "Plato, Republic, Book 4, Section 439e." Accessed May 19, 2021. http://www.perseus.tufts.edu/hopper/text?doc=Perseus%3Atext%3A1999.01.0168%3Abook%3D4%3Asection%3D439e.

113 *Id.*

114 *Id.*

115 *Id.*

116 "The judicial Power of the United States, shall be vested in one supreme Court, and in such inferior Courts as the Congress may from time to time ordain and establish." U.S. Const. art. III, 1

Further, Chief Justice Marshall in *Marbury v. Madison* stated, "The particular phraseology of the constitution of the United States confirms and strengthens the principle, supposed to be essential to all written constitutions, that a law repugnant to the constitution is void; and that courts, as well as other departments, are bound by that instrument." 5 U.S. (1 Cranch) at 180.

117 W.K.C. Guthrie, *A History of Greek Philosophy* (Cambridge University Press, 1962), 419–34.

118 Republic, 550b.

119 *Id.*

120 Saikrishna Prakash and Steven D. Smith, "How to Remove a Federal Judge." *Yale LJ* 116 (2006): 72 87–8.

121 *Id*, at 136–7.

122 *Marbury v. Madison*, 5 U.S. (1 Cranch) 137, 177 (1803); accord *United States v. Nixon*, 418 U.S. 683, 703–5 (1974).

123 163 U.S. 537 (1896).

124 349 U.S. 294 (1955).

125 163 U.S. 537.

126 163 U.S. 537, 541 (1896).

127 349 U.S. 294.

128 *349* U.S. 294 (1955).

129 347 U.S. 483 (1954).

130 576 U.S. ___ (2015).

131 Kenji Yoshino, *The Supreme Court, 2014 Term—Comment: A New Birth of Freedom?: Obergefell v. Hodges*, 129 Harv. L. Rev. 147, 147. (2015).

Illustrating the differences of originalist and evolutionary document theories of interpreting the Constitution, Andrew W. Schwartz writes discussing the *Obergerfell* case, "[t]he majority and dissenting opinions in *Obergefell v. Hodges*, the Supreme Court's recent decision finding that same-sex marriage is a constitutional right, offer a lucid comparison of originalism with evolutionary document theories of interpretation. The majority point out that the institution of marriage 'has evolved over time.'" *Obergefell v. Hodges*, No. 14-556, slip op. at 6 (U.S. June 26, 2015). Finding that the right to marry the person of one's choice, regardless of their gender, was compelled by the due process clause of the Fourteenth Amendment, the majority described its task as interpreting a constitutional provision that sets forth broad principles rather than specific requirements. History and tradition guide and discipline this inquiry but do not set its outer boundaries. That method respects our history and learns from it without allowing the past alone to rule the present. The nature of injustice is that we may not always see it in our own times. The generations that wrote and ratified the Bill of Rights and the Fourteenth Amendment did not presume to know the extent of freedom in all of its dimensions, and so they entrusted to future generations a charter protecting the right of all person to enjoy liberty as we learn its meaning. When new insight reveals discord between the Constitution's central protections and a received legal stricture, a claim to liberty must be addressed. *Id.* at 10–11 (citations omitted). In sharp contrast, Chief Justice Roberts and Associate Justice Alito, in their dissenting opinions, refused to recognize contemporary views of marriage, asserting that the notion of marriage as solely between a man and a woman is "deeply rooted in this Nation's history and tradition." *Id.* at 14 (Roberts, C.J., dissenting); *id.* at 2 (Alito, J., dissenting) (quoting *Washington v. Glucksberg*, 521 U.S. 701, 720–1 [1997]). Justice Scalia, in a separate dissent, relied on the public understanding of the meaning of marriage at the time the due process clause was ratified in 1868, which, he argued, universally confined marriage to a man and a woman. *Id.* at 4 (Scalia, J., dissenting)." Andrew W. Schwartz, *No Competing Theory of Constitutional Interpretation Justifes Regulatory Takings Ideology*, 34 STAN. ENVTL. L.J. 247, 25. (2015).

132 Laurence Tribe, *Equal Dignity: Speaking Its Name*, 129 HARV. L. REV. F. 16, 16 (2015).

133 With its source of power from U.S. Const. art. II, § 1, cl. 1.

134 Plato, Phaedrus 248d–e. (Christopher J. Rowe trans., 1986) [hereinafter Phaedrus].

135 *Id.* at 247e–248e.

136 Republic, 550b.

137 *Id.*

138 National Archives. "Executive Orders Disposition Tables," August 15, 2016. https://www.archives.gov/federal-register/executive-orders.

139 "The Fifth Circuit Court of Appeals Rules against Obama's Executive Actions on Immigration—The Atlantic." Accessed May 19, 2021. https://www.theatlantic.com/politics/archive/2015/11/fifth-circuit-obama-immigration/415077/ and "Obama to Appeal Immigration Ruling to Supreme Court—The New York Times." Accessed May 19, 2021. https://www.nytimes.com/2015/11/11/us/politics/supreme-court-immigration-obama.html.

140 "Catastrophe" used here in the Ancient Greek sense of "cata" and "strophe," meaning under turned or overturning. Oxford English Dictionary (2d ed. 1989).

"Etymology: < Greek *καταστροφή* overturning, sudden turn, conclusion, < *κατα-στρέφειν* to overturn, etc., < *κατά* down + *στρέφειν* to turn." *Id.*

141 With its power generally emanating from U.S. Const. art. 1.

142 124 Stat. 119.

143 "Obama Signs Health Care Overhaul Into Law—*The New York Times*." Accessed May 19, 2021. https://www.nytimes.com/2010/03/24/health/policy/24health.html.

144 *Nat'l Fed'n of Indep. Bus. v. Sebelius*, 132 S. Ct. 2566, 2580.

145 The Federalist No. 47, at 301 (James Madison) (Clinton Rossiter ed., 1961).

4

Montesquieu and the French Government (Ancien Régime)

History furnishes no example of a free republic, anything like the extent of the United States. The Grecian republics were of small extent; so also was that of the Romans. Both of these, it is true, in process of time, extended their conquests over large territories of country; and the consequence was, that their governments were changed from that of free governments to those of the most tyrannical that ever existed in the world.

—Brutus, *Essay No. 1* (1787)

The latent causes of faction are thus sown in the nature of man; and we see them everywhere brought into different degrees of activity, according to the different circumstances of civil society.

—James Madison, *Federalist Paper No. 10* (1787)

Montesquieu remains one of the lasting and influential political philosophers of the Enlightenment. Montesquieu's full name was Charles Louis de Secondat, Baron de La Brède et de Montesquieu. He was born in 1689 and died in early 1755.[1] Montesquieu came to a Barony in early life through the death of his uncle.[2] Throughout his life, Montesquieu used his income to travel much of Europe.[3] He used his status to enter political circles of various countries from France, England, Austria, and Hungary.[4] With his knowledge and experience, he drew out political thought and structures of governments around the world in *The Spirit of the Laws* (French: *De l'esprit des lois*, originally spelled *De l'esprit des loix*) first published in 1748.

One of the enduring legacies of Montesquieu's *The Spirit of the Laws* is his profound impact on the thinking of the authors of the *Federalist Papers*. *The Federalist Papers* published in 1788 defended the structure of the Constitution. Moreover, it seems that Montesquieu formed the basis for key ideas debated and drafted at the 1787 Constitutional Convention. Thus, Montesquieu directly influenced the thinking of the Framers. As a result, Montesquieu's writings are one of the keys to interpreting the thoughts that led to the creation of the Constitution.

In Montesquieu's sweeping analysis of the many cultures and political structures of Europe in *The Spirit of the Laws*, he demonstrates an encyclopedic knowledge acquired from decades of research and travels throughout Europe. One of the central features of Montesquieu's thinking is his critique of despotism. Montesquieu lived in a time when monarchies ruled Europe and France. Thus, there is no explicit critique of the monarchy. But, one can find sentiments wrapped in deliberately esoteric words where Montesquieu critiques the French monarch and monarchy in general. One such instance where Montesquieu outlines the dangers of a monarchy appears in Book XI of *The Spirit of the Laws* in a pithy instance of a veiled and esoteric critique of monarchy, "When the legislative and executive powers are united in the same person, or in the same body of magistrates, there can be no liberty; because apprehensions may arise, *lest the same monarch or senate should enact tyrannical laws, to execute them in a tyrannical manner*."

The Spirit of the Laws is a dense book. It was written over a period of twenty years. To read *The Spirit of the Laws*, it would behoove a reader to read *The Persian Letters*, the book published before *The Spirit of the Laws. The Persian Letters* (French: *Lettres persanes*) can serve as an introduction to understanding *The Spirit of the Laws.*

The Persian Letters

In interpreting *The Spirit of the Laws*, one of Montesquieu's former books titled *The Persian Letters* (1721) echoes his later themes of republics, monarchies, and despotism. But his main and paramount theme is the critique and dangers of despotism. In reading Montesquieu's works, the reader should keep in mind the frequent and main objective of observing the problems of despotism.

The Persian Letters launched Montesquieu to fame in France. He employs the form of an epistolary novel between two Persians who are initially confused about the events occurring in Europe. The book at once invites a unique insight into European society and at the same time remains a book of comedy.

The comedy reveals itself frequently in the beginning. For example, one of the Persian authors named Rica remarks that the pope is a magician who can "make the king believe that three are only one, or else that the bread one eats is not bread, or that the wine one drinks is not wine, and a thousand other things of the same kind" (Letter 24). As the novel progresses, the writers become more incensed with insight into the world they view. They allow Montesquieu to critique and reflect Western political structures and society through their view.

The other interlocutor with Rica is Usbek. Usbek remarks that notions of honor "makes a Frenchman, willingly and with pleasure, do things that your Sultan can only get out of his subjects by ceaseless exhortation with rewards and punishments" (Letter 89).

Montesquieu's main concern is with despotism. Montesquieu sees despotism as the worst form of government. If the defects of Persia arise from the possibilities for despotism, Montesquieu shows the defects of Western society as arising through despotism as well in Europe.

Although the defects of Persia may lie in despotism, the flaws of Western society may lie in monarchy. Rica in Letter 24 describes the French king, not as one who collects money from gold mines, but by taxing his subjects. Specifically, Rica writes of Louis XIV, "The king of France is the most powerful of European potentates. He has no mines of gold like his neighbour, the King of Spain; but he is much wealthier than that prince; because his riches are drawn from a more inexhaustible source, the vanity of his subjects" (Letter 24). Indeed, taxation may produce more profits than mining gold, but it may not create a sustainable system. The French king maintains his power by diverting revenue to create marvelous works, such as statues, pay the army, and keep the country defended.

Concurrently, the extent of taxes may not be enough to create long-lasting revenue unless the taxpayers make money to pay the taxes. However, if there is only a cycle of taxes, paying the king, and then the king paying taxpayers, then there will never be an increase in revenue unless an extra state enterprise brings more money to the country.

Besides the tax system, a major problem for Western society at this time may emanate from the pope controlling the king. One prime example is the Constitution or the papal bull Unigenitus restricting the practice of Jansenists. Even though this was a religious dispute, Louis XIV's adherence to the papal bull shows how Western countries, at least France, were not entirely self-governing. Furthermore, this could lead them to a conflict of interests.

Next to a national government being controlled by the pope, the king is described, as having "invisible enemies" with the Jansenists who appeared friendly in the court, but wanted to create a schism in the church and break away from power.

Thus, the Western societies may have been found wanting in terms of accumulating enough revenues, adhering to the commands of the pope, and maintaining internal control.

The cause of despotism in both Persia and the West may be the ability to lack self-knowledge. Throughout the *Letters*, Rica and Usbek caricature and arguably lament how Westerners cannot see the despotism in which they live. But at the same time, Usbek who owns a harem—also called a seraglio—in Persia finds himself consumed with want of total control. In the harem, Usbek has supreme authority where he can kill and use any of his eunuchs or wives at will. But the further Usbek goes from Persia, the less control he has.

Ironically, Usbek acknowledges that he does not love his wives, but he wants to control them out of jealousy. As Usbek writes in *Letter 6*, "from my very lack of feeling has come a secret jealousy which is devouring me." Although Usbek writes to a eunuch to restore order in the harem, Usbek later finds out that his favorite wife Roxana whom he trusted the most betrays Usbek.[5] Usbek writes in *Letter 161*:

> How could you have thought me credulous enough to imagine that I was in the world only in order to worship your caprices? that while you allowed yourself everything, you had the right to thwart all my desires? No: I may have lived in servitude, but I have always been free. I have amended your laws according to the laws of nature, and my mind has always remained independent.

Ironically, the role of women in Persia is depicted as subservient while the role women have in Europe is juxtaposed as having more freedom. Montesquieu embeds the main view of Persian women in Usbek's harem. The women are not allowed to go out and are guarded by eunuchs. In this case, it seems that Usbek has four women. On the other hand, European women are depicted as monogamous. When Usbek arrives in Lehorn, Tuscany—as described in *Letter 23*—he is surprised to see women only wearing one veil while in Persia they are required to wear four. Moreover, unlike Persia, the women in Lehorn are free to move about the city on their own or with another woman.

In the seminal *Letter 24*, Usbek finds it pointless that women, described as Janesenists, oppose the king because they think his acceptance of the Papal

Bull inhibits their freedoms; because Usbek recalls from the Koran that women cannot ascend to heaven.

Letter 34 shows Usbek arguing that Persian women are more beautiful than French women, but French women are more open and spirited. The French women perhaps are more spirited because they have the ability to move about freely compared to the Persian women.

Letter 86 exposes the difference in legal standing that women have compared to Persian women. Usbek says when he visited the courts, or parliaments; he found it to be a dismal place where family affairs were exposed. A woman could file for dissolution of her marriage by accusing her husband of not upholding her "wifely" rights. Usbek does not comment on any similar system in Persia, presumably because it did not exist.

Before the scandal's eruption at the seraglio—the term for harem in the book—Usbek describes the difference in society in terms of values. Although this extends beyond just women, it has interesting implications. Usbek asserts in *Letter 100* that the French will admit you are wiser than they are if you admit they are better dressed. He says this sense of fashion pervades all aspects of French society. Indeed, according to Usbek, they do not have laws of their own, but rather import them from other places, such as Rome. Yet at the same time, the French detest foreign ways of doing things, such as cooking and fashion. This remains a fascinating contrast to their disregard for law.

Montesquieu's depiction of the harem erupting seems to mirror Odysseus's slaying of the slave girls in Homer's *Odyssey*.[6] Odysseus himself seems to fit into the category of a despot when he assumes the role of ruler of Ithaca. Likewise, Odysseus wants to maintain control of his kingdom and thus murders the slave girls who slept with the suitors. Both episodes in Montesquieu and Homer seem to inversely mirror each other.

Relevantly in Plato's *Republic*, Socrates critiques Homer as a bad influence. Socrates states that, in the ideal city following the ideal political structure, the poets and the artists must be controlled strictly. Likewise, Montesquieu may be drawing a direct allusion to Odysseus murdering his slave women in *The Persian Letters*. Such correlations are relevant considering the narrative nature of *The Persian Letters* and the role Plato's thought has had historically on Western conceptions of an ideal polity.

At the end of *The Persian Letters*, Montesquieu leaves the reader wondering about the difference between formalized law and natural law. Is the natural law how the French wear clothes and how they cook or is it the formalized law? Is it essential to create laws that follow human reason or should human reason follow laws? Should laws mirror nature in the same way that Newton's laws of gravity govern nature, or should laws set up a standard goal for a society to reach, even if it does not abide by those customs already?

Returning to theme of despotism, the major problem with Western societies for Montesquieu is creating a system of governance and laws that could sustain the continuance of nations. Montesquieu leaves us with a question of, how are the laws supposed to be formed? Are they to reflect a natural state of being or are people to learn how to behave depending on the laws? These questions find firmer answers in his *The Spirit of the Laws*. Thus, *The Persian Letters* functions as a reasonable introduction to *The Spirit of the Laws* representing over twenty years of research from the publication of 1721 of the former to 1748 of the latter.

The Spirit of the Laws

The Spirit of the Laws outlines three main types of governments: republican, monarchial, and despotic. In Book III, Chapter 9 Montesquieu briefly outlines the virtues or characteristics of citizens in each type of government. He writes that "[a]s virtue is necessary in a republic, and in a monarchy honour, so fear is necessary in a despotic government: with regard to virtue, there is no occasion for it, and honour would be extremely dangerous." But in Book III, Chapter 7, he indicates that honor plays a key role in these political systems because "honor sets all the parts of the body politic in motion, and by its very action connects them; thus each individual advances the public good, while he only thinks of promoting his own interest."

This reads similar to the eighteenth-century Scottish Enlightenment economist and philosopher Adam Smith's concept of the invisible hand. Smith writes in his *The Theory of Moral Sentiments* that the rich

> consume little more than the poor, and in spite of their natural selfishness and rapacity ... they divide with the poor the produce of all their improvements. They are led by an invisible hand to make nearly the same distribution of the necessaries of life, which would have been made, had the earth been divided into equal portions among all its inhabitants, and thus without intending it, without knowing it, advance the interest of the society, and afford means to the multiplication of the species.[7]

In short, the citizens of republics love virtue; the citizens of monarchies love honor; and the citizens of despots fear the ruler. Based on this premise, he shows that England could not form a republic after the Civil War of the 1642–51 because the populace lacked a love of virtue.[8]

As such, Montesquieu departs from Aristotle's view that governments depend on the virtue of the ruler. Instead, Montesquieu sees the virtue of the citizens as the key indication of the type of government.

Although Montesquieu's encyclopedic account of the various instances of history and different climates cause differing governments in his current world in *The Spirit of the Laws*, he identifies three key powers existing in every government. Those three aspects are the judiciary, the executive, and the legislative. Montesquieu explicitly states this in his discussion of what leads to liberty in Book XI: Of the Laws Which Establish Political Liberty, with Regard to the Constitution in Chapter 6 Of the Constitution of England, "In every government there are three sorts of power: the legislative; the executive in respect to things dependent on the law of nations; and the executive in regard to matters that depend on the civil law."[9]

Although these powers of government are divided into three parts, Montesquieu acknowledges that the powers can often be mixed together.

Montesquieu states that prior to the proper divisions of powers, the ruler of a country must

> By virtue of the first, the prince or magistrate enacts temporary or perpetual laws, and amends or abrogates those that have been already enacted. By the second, he makes peace or war, sends or receives embassies, establishes the public security, and provides against invasions. By the third, he punishes criminals, or determines the disputes that arise between individuals. The latter we shall call the judiciary power, and the other, simply, the executive power of the state.

A reader can find frequent references to the importance of virtue in the speeches of George Washington as well as in the *Federalist Papers*. Washington in his 1796 Farewell Address emphasizes the importance of virtue saying, "It is substantially true that virtue or morality is a necessary spring of popular government. The rule, indeed, extends with more or less force to every species of free government. Who that is a sincere friend to it can look with indifference upon attempts to shake the foundation of the fabric?"

Moreover, at the beginning of *Federalist Paper* No. 57, the author (either Hamilton or Madison) writes that "[t]he aim of every political constitution is, or ought to be, first to obtain for rulers men who possess most wisdom to discern, and most virtue to pursue, the common good of the society; and in the next place, to take the most effectual precautions for keeping them virtuous whilst they continue to hold their public trust."

In Madison's famous contention with Montesquieu in *Federalist Paper* No. 10 on whether a republic can successfully cover a large area. Montesquieu argued that only small geographic areas can constitute republics. In responding to such assertions, Madison appeals to virtuous citizens:

> Hence, it clearly appears, that the same advantage which a republic has over a democracy, in controlling the effects of faction, is enjoyed by a large over a small republic—is enjoyed by the Union over the States composing it. Does the advantage consist in the substitution of representatives whose enlightened views and virtuous sentiments render them superior to local prejudices and schemes of injustice? [10]

Montesquieu warns that when the powers of a country merge, the citizens lose liberty. He eloquently reasons that "[w]hen the legislative and executive powers are united in the same person, or in the same body of magistrates, there can be no liberty; because apprehensions may arise, lest the same monarch or senate should enact tyrannical laws, to execute them in a tyrannical manner."[11] In other words, when the powers that are meant for the creation of the laws and the powers that are meant for the execution of the laws come into one person or one body of people, then tyranny and despotism will arise.

Likewise, Montesquieu indicates that the two powers of government in the legislative and executive must be separated from the judiciary to avoid loss of liberty. Montesquieu reasons that "[a]gain, there is no liberty if the judiciary power be not separated from the legislative and executive. Were it joined with the legislative, the life and liberty of the subject would be exposed to arbitrary control; for the judge would be then the legislator. Were it joined to the executive power, the judge might behave with violence and oppression."[12] Again, if the power of the government tasked with judging and giving sentences or interpreting the laws were merged with the powers of the government charged with carrying out and creating the laws, then the citizenry would lose liberty.

Ultimately, the dangers of merging power leads to the logical conclusion that if all powers vest in one individual, then that individual would become a despot. He writes that such a despot would arise no matter what the citizenry and the nobles would try to do because "[t]here would be an end of every thing, were the same man, or the same body, whether of the nobles or of the people, to exercise those three powers, that of enacting laws, that of executing the public resolutions, and of trying the causes of individuals."[13]

Thus, based on Montesquieu's empirical analysis of various governments from the ancient Roman Republic, to the ancient Greek city states, to Gaul, to England, to Charlemagne's Holy Roman Empire, three powers of government exist. He identifies those powers at the executive, the judiciary, and the legislative. Montesquieu states that the temptation for avarice and despotism can be avoided if the three powers are held by different persons or different bodies.

Moreover, Montesquieu provided that three types of governments exist: republics governed by love of virtue among the citizenry; monarchies governed by the love of honor; and despotisms governed by a lust for power and through fears of the populace. Montesquieu's typology of government and its corresponding virtues and vulnerabilities is summarized in Table 4.1.

Montesquieu's division of government can be summarized in the following way:

Now that Montesquieu's theory of the three powers of government has been elucidated, next one must turn attention to the concept of the small geographic areas in which Montesquieu recommended republics exist in *The Spirit of the Laws*.

Small Republics?

One of the most-often cited portions of *The Spirit of the Laws* during the ratification debates of the US Constitution in 1788 focused on Montesquieu's critique

Table 4.1 Montesquieu's Typology of Government and Its Virtues and Vulnerabilities

Three Types of Government	Virtues of Citizens in Each Type of Government	Problems with Each Type of Government
Republican	Governed by love of virtue among the citizenry	Republics usually exist only in a small territory.
Monarchical	Governed by love of honor.	The branches of government exist in one person. This can lead to despotism.
Despotic	Governed by fear and lust for power.	Similar to a monarchial system, the branches of government can exist in one person. This can lead to tyranny.

of large republics. In short, Montesquieu argued that a republic cannot exist in a large geographic area. The Anti-Federalists leading the arguments against the ratification of the Constitution quoted the following from Montesquieu:

> It is natural to a republic to have only a small territory, otherwise it cannot long subsist. In a large republic there are men of large fortunes, and consequently of less moderation; there are trusts too great to be placed in any single subject; he has interest of his own; he soon begins to think that he may be happy, great and glorious, by oppressing his fellow citizens; and that he may raise himself to grandeur on the ruins of his country. In a large republic, the public good is sacrificed to a thousand views; it is subordinate to exceptions, and depends on accidents. In a small one, the interest of the public is easier perceived, better understood, and more within the reach of every citizen; abuses are of less extent, and of course are less protected.[14]

This quote is found in *Anti-Federalist Paper No. 1* written by an individual using the pseudonym Brutus. The author of the *Anti-Federalist Papers* is still undetermined by scholars. It is suspected that Brutus was Melancton Smith of Poughkeepsie and John Williams of Salem.[15] But even modern computational data of the grammatical styles of these two individuals leads to inconclusive results. This book assumes no specific author but refers to Brutus as the author.

Brutus lays out the argument that republics can only exist in small geographic areas, such as the Greek or Roman city states. Brutus uses the empirical data available to him writing:

> History furnishes no example of a free republic, any thing like the extent of the United States. The Grecian republics were of small extent; so also was that of the Romans. Both of these, it is true, in process of time, extended their conquests over large territories of country; and the consequence was, that their governments were changed from that of free governments to those of the most tyrannical that ever existed in the world.[16]

Brutus's main contention is that a slight majority in the United States would lead to a tyranny and would be unmanageable.[17]

James Madison writes a counter argument to Brutus in *The Utility of the Union as a Safeguard Against Domestic Faction and Insurrection* also known as *Federalist Paper No. 10*.

To counter Brutus's proposition, Madison writing as Publius in *Federalist Paper No. 10* argues that the tyranny of the majority in the United States could be superceded by factionalism. Madison sees these factions as inevitable. He writes that faction is caused in the nature of humanity where "[t]he latent causes of faction are thus sown in the nature of man."[18] Madison argues that the representative democracy will safeguard against the danger of a tyrannical majority. For example, Madison reasons that if the Episcopalians oppress the Presbyterians in Virginia, then the Presbyterians will oppress the Episcopalians in Pennsylvania.

Madison seems to acknowledge the development of proto-unions where "[t]he diversity in the faculties of men, from which the rights of property originate, is not less an insuperable obstacle to a uniformity of interests. The protection of these faculties is the first object of government."[19] Likewise, such unities of interest come in the form of fraternities and collegiate societies of professionals, such as bar associations for lawyers. In a way, Madison's argument is that the purpose of government is to ensure inequality of bargaining power.

Revisiting an Encomium on Deep Reading

Madison's *Federalist Paper No. 10* can be interpreted in two ways. Both ways are valid. However, the second way has an esoteric reading that Madison encapsulated in the text.

Esotericism is meant here in the context of holding heterodoxic views and hiding alternative readings within a text. German-Jewish twentieth-century philosopher Leo Strauss laid out the meaning of esotericism in his *Persecution and the Art of Writing* (1952). Strauss's simple argument that encapsulates esotericism is that some beliefs are not politically viable and thus must be represented in language that is not immediately apparent in a first or subsequent reading. A reader must endeavor to delve deeply into a text to understand it. Strauss shows a simple example is the Sephardic Jewish philosopher Maimonides, who lived in the Islamic Caliphate of Spain during the twelfth century in Medieval Europe. Strauss writes that Maimonides wrote in an esoteric way because "as a closet nonbeliever obfuscating his message for political reasons" this became necessary.

Strauss notes that moral, religious, and political philosophers in prior centuries had to hide their actual views from the public for fear of persecution of heterodox beliefs. However, Strauss indicates that writers use esoteric writing because "[p]ersecution cannot prevent even public expression of the heterodox truth, for a man of independent thought can utter his views in public and remain unharmed, provided he moves with circumspection. He can even utter them in print without danger, provided he can write between the lines." Thus, in Strauss's view, the most virtuous and in-depth texts require multiple readings with deep analysis. Strauss's view may be read as a variation of Plato's noble lie—where a political system must maintain a lie to maintain authority over the populace. Strauss suggested in his book *The City and Man* (1964) that a noble lie was necessary for political systems to exist.

The type of reading Strauss requires to discover esoteric meaning appears similar to the type of reading the German philosopher Friedrich Nietzsche requires of his readers outlined in his *On the Genealogy of Morals* (1887):

> If this writing be obscure to any individual, and jar on his ears, I do not think that it is necessarily I who am to blame. It is clear enough, on the hypothesis which I presuppose, namely, that the reader has first read my previous writings and has not grudged them a certain amount of trouble: it is not, indeed, a simple matter to get really at their essence. Take, for instance, my *Zarathustra*; I allow no one to pass muster as knowing that book, unless every single word therein has at some time wrought in him a profound wound, and at some time exercised on him a profound enchantment: then and not till then can he enjoy the privilege of participating reverently in the halcyon element, from which that work is born, in its sunny brilliance, its distance, its spaciousness, its certainty.

He tells the reader that no one can know Nietzsche's book *Thus Spoke Zarathustra* (1883–5) "unless every single word therein has at some time wrought in him a profound wound, and at some time exercised on him a profound enchantment." A reader must suffer and find enchantment in every word—as well as perhaps every syllable—to understand *Zarathustra*. Then, and only then will Nietzsche allow understanding. Such attentive reading represents the type of reading Leo Strauss urges a reader to discover in esoteric reading.

Thus, in summary, there are at least two ways to read a text. One is a simple and direct reading. Strauss would refer to this first type of reading as an exoteric understanding. It is not meant to be an incorrect reading. Such a reading starts a reader's interaction with a text. However, such a reading is an incomplete reading. The reader can only discover the second interpretation and reading of a text through intensive reading through training. Strauss would refer to this second type of reading as an esoteric understanding. Understanding the esoteric meaning of a text in this manner remains a difficult task to accomplish. Strauss reserves such reading for a select few members of society trained to read and write in esoteric ways.

The first interpretation of Madison's *Federalist Paper No. 10* is not an esoteric reading. It is an exoteric reading. This exoteric reading conveys to the reader that minority rights must be preserved over majority rights. Such preservation occurs through factionalism, where minorities in some states will support minorities in other states, or majorities in some states will support minorities in other states.

The second way to interpret James Madison's *Federalist Paper No. 10* is an esoteric reading. Esoterically, a reader could reasonably interpret Madison as writing that capitalists and businesses can exploit and create factions of whichever segments of society they would wish. In other words, according to Madison, the laws as structured in the Constitution would not restrain the monied interest and business owners from creating factionalism. This factionalism would prevent any attempts at achieving goals against the monied interests and property-owning class of society. Thus, people in the minority would find it incredibly difficult to change the law.

Likely none of the Founding Fathers read Adam Smith at the time of the Constitutional Convention debates in 1787. However, the ideas that Adam Smith is describing as existing in the world likely in the form of capitalism or a type of proto-capitalism. Indeed, in *The Wealth of Nations*, Smith argues that every individual naturally tries to use capital as near as home as possible to support domestic as long as they can get ordinary profits. Smith writes:

> First, every individual endeavours to employ his capital as near home as he can, and consequently as much as he can in the support of domestic industry; provided always that he can thereby obtain the ordinary, or not a great deal less than the ordinary profits of stock. Thus, upon equal or nearly equal profits, every wholesale merchant naturally prefers the home-trade to the foreign trade of consumption, and the foreign trade of consumption to the carrying trade.[20]

Furthermore, Smith indicates that using capital in domestic trade over foreign trade is bad for the individual and society. He writes:

> But a capital employed in the home-trade, it has already been shown, necessarily puts into motion a greater quantity of domestic industry, and gives revenue and employment to a greater number of the inhabitants of the country, than an equal capital employed in the foreign trade of consumption: and one employed in the foreign trade of consumption has the same advantage over an equal capital employed in the carrying trade. Upon equal, or only nearly equal profits, therefore, every individual naturally inclines to employ his capital in the manner in which it is likely to afford the greatest support to domestic industry, and to give revenue and employment to the greatest number of people of his own country.[21]

Smith concludes his argument and introduces the concept of the "invisible hand." Smith argues that every individual in society has a natural inclination toward increasing society's wealth by using capital to generate the greatest social benefits. Smith states:

> By preferring the support of domestic to that of foreign industry, he intends only his own security; and by directing that industry in such a manner as its produce may be of the greatest value, he intends only his own gain, and he is in this, as in many other cases, led by an invisible hand to promote an end which was no part of his intention. Nor is it always the worse for the society that it was no part of it. By pursuing his own interest he frequently promotes that of the society more effectually than when he really intends to promote it. I have never known much good done by those who affected to trade for the public good. It is an affectation, indeed, not very common among merchants, and very few words need be employed in dissuading them from it.[22]

Notes

1 Hilary Bok, *Baron de Montesquieu, Charles-Louis de Secondat*, The Stanford Encyclopedia of Philosophy (Edward Zalta ed., Winter 2018 ed. 2018), https://plato.stanford.edu/entries/montesquieu/.

2 *Id.*

3 *Id.*

4 *Id.*

5 Perhaps Montesquieu uses the name Roxane as a direct reference to Alexander the Great's wife also named Roxana. Alexander married a Persian.

6 Perhaps such a mirroring reflects Harold Bloom's theory of the anxiety of influence. Harold Bloom, *The Anxiety of Influence: A Theory of Poetry* (1973). Perhaps Homer influenced Montesquieu consciously or subconsciously. Such a connection between Homer and Montesquieu is not without merit. James Madison in *Federalist Paper No. 47* wrote:

> The British constitution was to Montesquieu, what Homer has been to the didactic writers on epic poetry. As the latter have considered the work of the immortal bard, as the perfect model from which the principles and rules of the epic art were to be drawn, and by which all similar works were to be judged; so this great political critic appears to have viewed the constitution of England as the standard, or to use his own expression, as the mirror of political liberty; and to have delivered in the form of elementary truths, the several characteristic principles of that particular system.

The Federalist Paper No. 47 (James Madison) (Clinton Rossiter ed., 1961).

7 Adam Smith, *The Theory of Moral Sentiments* (1759), Part IV, Chapter I, Paragraph 10.

8 As James Madison wrote in the in the National Gazette, February 18, 1792:

> Montesquieu has resolved the great operative principles of government into fear, honor, and virtue, applying the first to pure despotisms, the second to regular monarchies, and the third to republics. The portion of truth blended with the ingenuity of this system, sufficiently justifies the admiration bestowed on its author. Its accuracy however can never be defended against the criticisms which it has encountered. Montesquieu was in politics not a Newton or a Locke, who established immortal systems, the one in matter, the other in mind. He was in his particular science what Bacon was in universal science: He lifted the veil from the venerable errors which enslaved opinion, and pointed the way to those luminous truths of which he had but a glimpse himself.

James Madison, For the National Gazette, February 18, 1792, National Gazette, February 18, 1792, https://founders.archives.gov/documents/Madison/01-14-02-0203 (last visited August 26, 2023).

9 Book XI: Of the Laws Which Establish Political Liberty, with Regard to the Constitution in Chapter 6 Of the Constitution of England. *The Spirit of the Laws.*

10 *Id.*

11 *Id.*

12 *Id.*

13 *Id.*

14 Brutus, *Essay I, in* The Essential Antifederalist (W.B. Allen & Gordon Lloyd eds., 2d ed. 2002).

15 "The identity of the Anti-Federalist author Brutus remains a mystery. Recent scholarship favors the New York merchant Melancton Smith." Saul Cornell, *The People's Constitution vs. the Lawyer's Constitution: Popular Constitutionalism and the Original Debate over Originalism*, 23 YALE J.L. & HUMAN. 295, 311 (2011).

16 Brutus, 2002.

17 *Id.*

18 *The Federalist Paper No. 10*, at 78 (James Madison)(Clinton Rossiter ed., 1961).

19 *Id.*

20 Adam Smith, *An Inquiry Into the Nature and Causes of the Wealth of Nations 475–76* (Edwin Cannan ed., University of Chicago Press, 1976) (1776).

21 *Id.*

22 *Id.*

5

Polybius—The Constitution of the Roman Republic

A Counter Argument to the "Three Parts" of Government in the US Constitution

It is well known that in the Roman republic the legislative authority, in the last resort, resided for ages in two different political bodies not as branches of the same legislature, but as distinct and independent legislatures, in each of which an opposite interest prevailed: in one the patrician; in the other, the plebian.

—Alexander Hamilton, *Federalist Paper No. 34* (1788)

In republican government, the legislative authority necessarily predominates.

—James Madison, *Federalist Paper No. 51* (1788)

To these examples might be added that of Carthage, whose senate, according to the testimony of Polybius, instead of drawing all power into its vortex, had, at the commencement of the second Punic War, lost almost the whole of its original portion.

—Alexander Hamilton, *Federalist Paper No. 63* (1788)

A concrete counter argument to the theory of trifunctionalism that this chapter argues for comes from the Ancient Greek author Polybius (Greek: Πολύβιος). In short, this book argues that the US Constitution reflects a trifunctional nature mirrored in Dumézil's theory of trifunctionalism.[1] However, the counter argument emerges when examining Polybius's account of the Roman Republic in his *Histories* (Greek: *Ιστορίαι*).[2]

The authors of the Federalist Papers, writing under the pseudonym Publius,[3] frequently refer to Polybius in their letters and notes.[4] Such references explicitly indicate that the structure of the Roman Republic existed at the forefront of their thinking.[5] Moreover, the Federalist Papers frequently cited Polybius's writings and his three-part outline of the Roman Republic as being an ideal republic. For example, Madison in 1787 almost explicitly outlines a trifunctional structure of the Roman Republic in his *Additional Memorandums on Ancient and Modern Confederacies, [ante 30 November] 1787.* Madison writes:

> Suffetes—like Consuls—and annual does not appear by whom chosen—assembled Senate presiding—proposing & collecting the votes—presided also in Judgmts. of most important affairs—sometimes commanded armies—at going out were made Pretors
>
> Senate—composed of persons qualified by age—experience—birth—riches—were the Council of State—& the Soul of all public deliberation no. not known—must have been great since the 100 drawn out of it. Senate treated of great affrs—read letters of generals—recd. plaints of provinces—gave auds: to ambassrs—and decided peace and War† When Senate unanimous decided finally—in case of division people decided—Whilst Senate retained its authority says Polybius—wisdom & success marked every thing.
>
> People—at first gave way to Senate—at length intoxicated by wealth & conquests, they assumed all power—then cabals & factions prevailed & were one of the principal causes of the ruin of the State.[6]

Moreover, many of the Framers of the Constitution discuss Polybius in passing as an authority on the successes and failures of certain forms of government.[7] Alexander Hamilton, in *Federalist No. 63*, wrote in passing on Carthage's form of government that, "To these examples might be added that of Carthage, whose senate, according to the testimony of Polybius, instead of drawing all power into its vortex, had at the commencement of the second punic war, lost almost the whole of its original portion."[8]

Overall, there is evidence that the Framers of the 1787 Constitution referred to Polybius both in the context of what worked ideally for states and what did not.

In his *Histories*, Polybius outlined the Roman Republic as conforming in practice and theory to the Constitution of the Roman Republic in three parts: the Senate, consuls, and the people's assemblies.[9] Polybius argued that the success of the Roman Republic came from the structure of the Roman government and the structure of the Roman Constitution.[10]

The counter argument comes in the following form: it is not that the US Constitution, as it was envisioned in 1787, necessarily reflects the concept of Montesquieu's French Enlightenment thinking of the judiciary, the executive, and the legislative. Instead, the 1787 Constitution reflects the three parts of the Roman Republic's constitution laid out by Polybius. Polybius envisioned the Roman Republic as existing in three parts: the senate, the councils, and the People's assemblies. The Senate was composed of the patricians, the wealthy in Rome. The consuls were temporary leaders tasked with carrying out the military and executive functions of the Roman Republic. The People's assemblies represented the plebeians and the free citizens of Rome, who were less wealthy than the Senate.[11]

Likewise, compared with the Constitution, with the separation of powers envisioned in 1787, the Federalists wished to see a strong judiciary. Instead, those parts that existed started in 1789, when the new Constitution came into effect, were the House of Representatives, the Senate, and the Executive.

Again, Polybius viewed the Roman Republic's three parts without an explicit judicial function. Granted, outside the three parts of the Constitutional structure of the Roman Republic, tribunals could be set up for judges to hear cases.[12] However, those parts outlined by Polybius correlated to the three parts in the 1787 Constitution with no judiciary.

Polybius's formulation of the Roman Republic might bear more resemblance to the three branches of government—the Executive, the House of Representatives, and the Senate. This is the main counter argument: the US Constitution does not resemble the three parts of Plato's *Republic* or Montesquieu's idea of the three parts of government. Instead, the US Constitution of government reflects the Roman Republic's Constitution of classical antiquity.

Thus, the 1789 US Constitution could reflect the Roman Republic's Constitution.[13] The 1789 Constitution had the House of Representatives, the Senate, and the Executive. These correlate to Polybius's outline of the Roman Republic of the People's Assemblies, the Roman Senate, and the Consuls. The House of Representatives and People's assemblies had a larger body representing the less wealthy free citizens. The Senate represented the wealthy interests with a more petite body than the House and People's Assemblies. The Executive and the Consuls were responsible for carrying out the role and were never permanent positions, constitutionally.[14]

This counter argument fits in the following way, as summarized in Table 5.1, with no discussion of a judiciary.

As such, the critical key elements of the Roman Republic's constitutional framework lacked a judiciary. The US Constitution provides for a judiciary, but it was not clear in 1787 that it formed one of the critical parts of government or its functions.[15]

Table 5.1 Structural Parallels between the US Constitution and the Roman Republic (Excluding the Judiciary)

US Constitution of 1789	Roman Republic, outlined by Polybius	Key Characteristics
House of Representatives	People's Assemblies	A larger body representing less wealthy free citizens
Senate	Roman Senate	More petite bodies representing the wealthy interests of free citizens
Executive	Consuls	Temporary roles for carrying out specific duties

Regarding the judiciary, Alexander Hamilton, famously writing in *Federalist Paper No. 78*, explicitly calls for judicial review and a strong judiciary.[16] Regarding judicial review and the judiciary, Hamilton writes:

> If it be said that the legislative body is themselves the constitutional judges of their own powers and that the construction they put upon them is conclusive upon the other departments, it may be answered, that this cannot be the natural presumption, where it is not to be collected from any particular provisions in the Constitution. It is not otherwise to be supposed, that the Constitution could intend to enable the representatives of the people to substitute their will to that of their constituents. It is far more rational to suppose, that the courts were designed to be an intermediate body between the people and the legislature, in order, among other things, to keep the latter within the limits assigned to their authority.[17]

Hamilton further writes in *Federalist Paper No. 78* on the "weak" nature of the judiciary in comparison with the other branches:

> The Executive not only dispenses the honors but holds the sword of the community. The legislature not only commands the purse but prescribes the rules by which the duties and rights of every citizen are to be regulated. The judiciary, on the contrary, has no influence over either the sword or the purse; no direction either of the strength or of the wealth of the society; and can take no active resolution whatever. It may truly be said to have neither FORCE nor WILL, but merely judgment; and must ultimately depend upon the aid of the executive arm even for the efficacy of its judgments.[18]

However, there is no explicit textual reference to judicial review in the text of the Constitution, similar to what Hamilton outlines in *Federalist Paper No. 78*.[19]

Indeed, judicial review came about as a function of the midnight appointment of judges under the John Adams administration when there was a change of power from the Federalist Party in the 1800 election to Thomas Jefferson.[20] Among the appointments John Adams made was William Marbury as Justice of the Peace of the District of Columbia.[21] However, Marbury never had his commission delivered to him.[22] When Thomas Jefferson succeeded Adams as president, Jefferson did not want the commission delivered. Jefferson thought the commission to be void. Jefferson informed James Madison, now the Secretary of State, to withhold the commission from Marbury. Marbury sued Madison for the commission.[23]

Furthermore, John Adams appointed Federalist John Marshall Chief Justice of the Supreme Court.[24] In deciding the case of *Marbury v. Madison*, John Marshall argued from a staunchly Federalist perspective that judicial review was inherent in the Constitution.[25] However, no explicit text in the Judiciary Act of 1789 references calls for judicial review. It is difficult to prove a negative in a text to show what isn't there. But the text does not call for judicial review. Thus, the function of judicial review comes about more through a judicial creation than a constitutional provision or legislative implementation. Other than through a legislative grant or constitutional provision, where could the powers of judicial review have originated? Before answering that question, it is important to understand the arguments for and against judicial review and the problems that come about from judicial review.

However, there is a counter argument to the idea of judicial review. If the judiciary is tasked with interpreting the laws, which is not a far cry from interpreting such an idea from the Constitution, then how else would the Constitution be able to do this but by interpreting the laws and seeing what the law is as outlined in the case of *Marbury v. Madison*? This is a firm argument for the judicial branch inherently being part of the structure of any government. Paradoxically, almost any actor in government—whether executive or legislative—has some authority to "say what the law is," from a minor instance of a police officer implementing the law to a law clerk officiating a marriage. In some sense, all actors in the executive and legislative branches of government "say what the law is," not only in carrying out the law but as a type of interpretative role similar to what John Marshall articulated in *Marbury v. Madison*.

It is worth asking why the United States follows the idea of judicial review. Usually, courts do not critique or argue against judicial review. A rare instance of such critique arose in a dissenting opinion in 1825. The dissent in *Eakin v.*

Raub provides the most explicit critique of judicial review in American judicial history.[26] The case is known for establishing judicial review in Pennsylvania.[27] One of the judges opposed that determination—Judge John Bannister Gibson. When Gibson's serious critique emerged in 1825, the concept of judicial review was taken as truth. Judge Gibson wrote in his dissenting opinion in 1825:

> But I may premise, that it is not a little remarkable, that although the right in question has all along been claimed by the judiciary, no judge has ventured to discuss it, except Chief Justice Marshall (in *Marbury v. Madison*, 1 Cranch 176); and if the argument of a jurist so distinguished for the strength of his ratiocinative powers be found inconclusive, it may fairly be set down to the weakness of the position which he attempts to defend; *si Pergama dextra defendi potuit, etiam hac defensa fuisset*. In saying this, I do not overlook the opinion of Judge Patterson, in *Vanhorne v. Dorrance* (2 Dall. 307), which abounds with beautiful figures in illustration of his doctrine; but, without intending disrespect, I submit, that metaphorical illustration is one thing, and argument another. Now, in questions of this sort, precedents ought to go for absolutely nothing. The constitution is a collection of fundamental laws, not to be departed from in practice, nor altered by judicial decision, and in the construction of it, nothing would be so alarming as the doctrine of communis error, which affords a ready justification for every usurpation that has not been resisted in limine. Instead, therefore, of resting on the fact, that the right in question has universally been assumed by the American courts, the judge who asserts it ought to be prepared to maintain it on the principles of the constitution.[28]

Judge Gibson continues in his dissent that:

> It may be alleged that no such power is claimed, and that the judiciary does no positive act, but merely refuses to be instrumental in giving effect to an unconstitutional law. This is nothing more than a repetition, in a different form of the argument—that an unconstitutional law is ipso facto void; for a refusal to act under the law must be founded on a right in each branch to judge of the acts of all the others, before it is bound to exercise its functions to give those acts effect. No such right is recognised in the different branches of the national government, except the judiciary (and that, too, on account of the peculiar provisions of the constitution), for it is now universally held, whatever doubts may have once existed, that congress is bound to provide for carrying a treaty into effect, although it may disapprove of the exercise of the treaty-making power in the particular instance. A government constructed on any other principle, would be in perpetual danger of standing still; for the right to decide on the constitutionality of the laws, would not be peculiar to the

judiciary, but would equally reside in the person of every officer whose agency might be necessary to carry them into execution.[29]

The poignant challenge here to judicial review is the idea that the government would be in constant danger of standing still, trying to figure out what the laws are. Instead, every officer of the law needs to carry the laws out, requiring a modicum of analysis and interpretation. The person carrying out the law must interpret the law.[30] Gibson sees such a multitudinous interpretation of the law as an inevitable conclusion to Justice Marshall's pronouncement that "[t]hose who apply the rule to particular cases, must of necessity expound and interpret that rule. If two laws conflict with each other, the courts must decide on the operation of each."[31] But in this case, every agent of the law must interpret the law. Thus, there could be an infinite and limitless interpretation of law.

Judge Gibson argues that the logical conclusion for judicial review is that anyone holding any office—including those county clerks who grant routine activities as simple as marriage certificates—has the duty to interpret the law.[32] In other words, wouldn't every single person with authority in any branch of government in the United States have a duty to conduct some sort of "judicial review" or "review" of law? It would be their duty to decide whether a law is constitutional—or even just morally or legally correct. In short, "saying what the law is," according to John Marshall. In reading Judge Gibson's dissent, one wonders whether John Marshall would want the judiciary to accept legal concepts without questioning them.

Relevantly, Article III, Section 2, Clause 2 of the US Constitution provides that:

> In all Cases affecting Ambassadors, other public Ministers and Consuls, and those in which a State shall be a Party, the Supreme Court shall have original Jurisdiction. In all the other Cases before mentioned [within the judicial power of the United States], the supreme Court shall have appellate Jurisdiction, both as to Law and Fact, with such Exceptions, and under such Regulations as the Congress shall make.[33]

In this crucial provision regarding the judiciary's function, there is no explicit textual reference to the powers of judicial review. However, another act regarding the judiciary came from section 13 of the Judiciary Act of 1789:

> The Supreme Court shall also have appellate jurisdiction from the circuit courts and courts of the several states, in the cases herein after specially provided for; and shall have power to issue writs of prohibition to the district courts [...] and writs of mandamus [...] to any courts appointed, or persons holding office, under the authority of the United States.[34]

This passage also does not explicitly call for judicial review. However, if a court needs to hear a case and make a judicial decision, doesn't that imply that the court must "say what the law is" to decide the case?

On a related note, regarding constitutional powers, it is unclear whether the Judiciary Act of 1789 called for judicial review.[35] If that were so, could one branch of government give powers to another?[36] In other words, if three branches of government genuinely exist, could the executive give powers to the legislative?[37] Moreover, more specifically, in this case, could the legislature give powers to the judiciary?

The answer to the last question is that the legislature could give powers to the courts if the judiciary and the courts were indeed not a branch of government. In other words, if the US Constitution conformed to the three branches of Polybius's conception of the Constitution—with a House of Representatives, Senate, and Executive mirroring the Peoples' Assemblies, the Roman Senate, and the Consuls—then the legislature could delegate some authority it already has to a judiciary. This is because the judiciary follows from legislative power, not executive. That is to say, in the same way the executive can delegate authority to executive agencies, the legislative could delegate legislative powers to other bodies, such as a judiciary.[38] Whether the People of the united colonies delegated authority to the Convention that created the Constitution or whether the People delegated authority to the States that then delegated authority to the Convention that created the Constitution is likewise unclear. But depending on which formulation one accepts, the creation of judicial review could be seen as a necessity if the People directly delegated authority to the Convention that created the Constitution.

Alternatively, the creation of judicial review could be interpreted from the perspective of political practicalities. In 1800, Thomas Jefferson was elected President of the United States.[39] Jefferson represented the first change in political power from political parties.[40] The Federalist Party had power over the government from George Washington to John Adams.[41] Jefferson's electoral victory represented the first time a party peacefully came to power in the United States through elections.[42]

As a Federalist Party member and an operative of the losing party, Marshall could have been trying to maintain Federalist ideological control of the judiciary. Marbury, a Federalist, sought appointment and a writ of mandamus for support in the facts of the case *Marbury v. Madison*.[43] Marbury wished to be the Justice of the Peace of the District of Columbia.[44] In theory, John Adams had appointed Marbury through his so-called action of the "Midnight Judges Act," more formally known as the Judiciary Act of 1801.[45] In what is interpreted as a last effort to maintain Federalist Party control, John Adams and the Federalists appointed judges throughout the United States.[46] William Marbury was one of those judges appointed by the Adams administration in the last moments of the Adams Presidency.[47] Marbury was granted the commission of the Justice of Peace of the District of Columbia. However, that commission was never delivered. Ultimately, Marshall ruled against Marbury, denying him commission.[48] The Federalist Party lost the battle. However, Marshall won the war of "judicial review."[49]

In the sense of Marshall winning on "judicial review," Marshall won a Federalist Party policy. Hamilton, in Federalist No. 78, explicitly called for judicial review.[50] Thus, the Federalists lost the battle for the justice of the peace, but they won the war for judicial review—to "say what the law is" and effectively change the United States forever. Because of that case, the United States firmly had a third section of government recognized as a distinct branch.[51]

Whether such an action by Marshall was proper is up for debate. However, it did bring the US Constitution more in line with the concept of the three parts of government outlined in Montesquieu's *The Spirit of the Laws* (1748).[52] Whether what Marshall did was akin to seizing and expanding government power without a Constitutional Convention is debatable. However, history has generally accepted judicial review as a good move. And so does this author.

In conclusion, the counter argument against this chapter's trifunctional analysis is that the Constitution of 1787 came in the form of the President, the House of Representatives, and the Senate, similar to the form of the Roman Republic's Constitution that the framers cited frequently.[53] But this chapter does not assume that premise. This chapter assumes and comments on the form of the Constitution created after the firm introduction of judicial review by John Marshall in *Marbury v. Madison*.

A Counter Argument to the Counter Argument: This Is Not the Roman Republic's Constitution according to Polybius

Thus, this chapter does not analyze essentially what could be construed as the 1787 conception of the Constitution without a judiciary playing a key constitutional role through judicial review. Instead, this chapter focuses on a constitutional framework with the existence of judicial review. Judicial review now exists as the central role of a third branch of government, regardless of whether the Framers in 1787 intended such a branch to exist.

Granted, the Framers of the US Constitution could not have known of Dumézil—a twentieth-century figure—or anthropological studies of Indo-European society. Given that Dumézil began writing almost a century and a half later and the study of anthropology in its modern form occurred about a century and a quarter later, there is evidence of knowledge of a tripartite paradigm reflected in government.[54] Whether such a paradigm was discussed at the Constitutional Convention is unknown; it at least impliedly existed in their educations.[55] Indeed, James Madison's notes during the Constitutional Convention do not explicitly discuss Plato's *Republic*.

Even if the Framers did not have Plato's trifunctionalism in mind, the idea of Plato's Soul is arguably inherent in humans regardless of how it is defined.[56] Moreover, a structured approach to the philosophical underpinnings of a government can be assumed to have been in the framer's mind, whether consciously or subconsciously.[57] Dumézilian thought has similar methods of analysis.

Notes

1 A future article comparing Dumézil's theories to Polybius's account of Rome may prove fruitful because Dumézil wrote a book on the semi-legendary Marcus Furius Camillus that Polybius discusses in his *Histories* titled *Camillus: A Study of Indo-European Religion as Roman History. See generally* Georges Dumézil & Georges Edmond Raoul Dumézil, *Camillus: A Study of Indo-European Religion As Roman History* (University of California Press, 1980).

2 *See generally* Polybius, The Histories of Polybius (Evelyn S. Shuckburgh trans. 1962).

3 The authors of the Federalist Papers did not pick the name Publius randomly. It had a long history in the study of republics. It especially related to the post-revolutionary period of the Roman Republic to which the authors wished to draw attention. On the history of the Roman Republic and Publius, Professor Beardman of Emory University School of Law writes that:

> While modern historiography has suggested that the Roman Republic emerged gradually from a series of modest institutional and legal reforms, the Framing Generation would have believed that it came about as the result of a violent

revolution against the tyranny of the last king, Tarquinius Superbus. After the Roman nobility and people further repulsed an Etruscan attempt to reinstitute the monarchy, the Republic was on a firmer foundation. Indeed, the leading figure of the post-revolutionary period of the Roman Republic was the aristocrat Publius Valerius ("Poplicola"), a lawgiver as successful as Solon or Lycurgus, immortalized in Plutarch's Lives, and the pseudonym selected by Hamilton, Madison, and Jay for their Federalist Papers.

David J. Bederman, *The Classical Constitution: Roman Republican Origins of the Habeas Suspension Clause*, 17 S. Cal. Interdisc. L.J. 405, 412 (2008).

4 James Madison especially discusses Polybius in one document. *See Notes on Ancient and Modern Confederacies, [April–June?] 1786*, Nat'l Archives: Founders Online, https://founders.archives.gov/documents/Madison/01-09-02-0001 (last visited December 29, 2023).

5 As well as being a persuasive authority for their readers.

6 *Additional Memorandums on Ancient and Modern Confederacies, [ante 30 November] 1787*, Nat'l Archives: Founders Online, https://founders.archives.gov/documents/Madison/01-10-02-0183 (last visited December 29, 2023).

7 For a more comprehensive list of Federalist Papers that discuss Ancient Greek states and forms of government, see The Federalist No. 4, at 49 (John Jay) (referring to the history of ancient Greek states); The Federalist No. 6, at 54–5 (Alexander Hamilton) (discussing various Greek states); The Federalist No. 34, at 206 (Alexander Hamilton) (discussing the legislative system in the Roman Republic); The Federalist No. 38, at 231–3 (James Madison) (reviewing the foundation of Crete, the Locrians, Athens, Sparta, Rome, and the Achaean and Amphictyonic Leagues); The Federalist No. 41, at 257 (James Madison) (discussing Rome's expansion); The Federalist No. 63, at 385–9 (James Madison) (referring to the senates of Sparta, Rome, and Carthage and to putative representation in various ancient republics); The Federalist No. 70, at 423, 425 (Alexander Hamilton) (referring to Roman dictators and consuls); The Federalist No. 75, at 453 (Alexander Hamilton) (referring to the Roman tribuneship). This does not represent a complete list. *See also* Robert G. Natelson, *A Republic, Not a Democracy? Initiative, Referendum, and the Constitution's Guarantee Clause*, 80 Tex. L. Rev. 807, 817 n.51 (2002).

8 The Federalist No. 63 (James Madison). Compare with Professor Charles J. Reid of the University of Saint Thomas's discussion:

Hamilton looked to historical sources to justify this proposition. Drawing deeply from classical antecedents, Hamilton observed that even "commercial republics"—he gave the examples of Athens and Carthage—fought wars with their neighbors. He feared, he confessed, "an infinity of little jealous, clashing, tumultuous commonwealths, the wretched nurseries of unceasing discord, and the miserable objects of universal pity or contempt." Without a strong union committing them to larger objectives, the leaders of the various states and regions were at risk of descending into just such a cacophony of mayhem and strife.

Charles J. Reid, *America's First Great Constitutional Controversy: Alexander Hamilton's Bank of the United States*, 14 U. St. Thomas L.J. 105, 126 (2018).

9 Professor Ian Bartrum summarizes Polybius's analysis of Rome in the following way:

Several centuries later, the Greek historian Polybius would describe Roman efforts to put these principles into practice in his influential and enduring Histories. Indeed, Polybius went beyond Aristotle to argue that the best constitution is a mixture of monarchy, aristocracy, and the people. This happy circumstance he claimed for Rome:

The three kinds of government ... were all found united in the commonwealth of Rome. And so even was the balance between them all, and so regular the administration that resulted from their union, that it was no easy thing, even for the Romans themselves, to determine with assurance, whether the entire state was to be esteemed an aristocracy, a democracy, or a monarchy.

In the Consuls, Polybius saw elements of monarchy, and in the Senate the hallmarks of aristocracy. The People and their Tribunes, too, had such a "share ... in the administration of affairs" that one might consider the state democratic. Though he undoubtedly idealized the Roman constitution, Polybius's description of its structure, and the particular benefits thus derived, became mandatory reading for future theorists up to and including John Adams.

Ian Bartrum, *The People's Court: On the Intellectual Origins of American Judicial Power*, 125 Dick. L. Rev. 283, 303–4 (2021).

10 Polybius built off Aristotle's political philosophy. Professor Bartrum further writes:

In particular, Polybius explored, as Aristotle had not, the specific powers that each part of the Roman regime exercised in government. The Consuls—the absolute military leaders in the field—also enjoyed substantial civil authority while in Rome: "For all other magistrates, the Tribunes alone excepted, are subject to them and bound to obey their commands." They summoned the Senate and popular assemblies and carried out their decisions and decrees, and they could draw funds from the treasury to meet their personal needs. The Senate controlled all other spending, conducted criminal investigations, issued laws and decrees, and exercised extensive control in foreign policy matters. It also controlled the purse strings while the Consuls conducted war, and could terminate or continue a Consul's command on a yearly basis. Finally, the people exercised control of elections and the law courts, decided matters of war and peace, and had final approval over laws and peace treaties.

Id. at 304.

11 *See generally* Aditya Chakravarty, *What Role Did the Senate and Popular Assemblies Play in the Roman Republic?*, Hist. Hit (July 3, 2019), https://www.historyhit.com/what-role-did-the-senate-and-popular-assemblies-play-in-the-roman-republic/.

12 One example of such tribunals was the court of the centumviri:

The Roman jurists "held aloof from legal history"; "legal history remained a closed book"; "interest in legal history is shown only by two academic jurists, Pomponius and Gaius." The author is correct in stating that the extant writings on legal history per se are negligible and that the jurists were not interested in historical jurisprudence for itself. But when he offers the story told by Gellius of the jurist who has no idea of the meaning of a word in the Twelve Tables, that "as a practising lawyer he was not called upon to cumber himself with the antiquated lumber of the Twelve Tables, which had long been abandoned in practice," he is a little unfair. For Koschaker, who uses the story to point up exactly the contrary idea, gives us the rest of the passage: "and [since] all this antiquity of the Twelve Tables was put to sleep by the enactment of the lex Aebutia, except for cases tried by legis actio procedure before the court of the centumviri, I ought only be interested in the study and science of the law and the statutes and their words, which we use." In other words, where historical institutions were of practical value, the jurist perforce made them part and parcel of his intellectual equipment.

A. Arthur Schiller, Book Review, 57 Yale L.J. 324, 329 (1947) (reviewing Fritz Schulz, History of Roman Legal Science (Clarendon Press 1946)). For a literary extrapolation of the centumviri, see Laurent de Sutter, *Legal Shandeism: The Law in Laurence Sterne's Tristram Shandy*, 23 L. & Literature 224, 233 (2011).

13 Indeed, the Founders maintained a strong veneration for the Roman Republic. As Professor Timothy G. Kearley, Emeritus of Law, University of Wyoming, College of Law, wrote:

[T]he Founders' esteem for the ancient Rome sometimes approached veneration. Most of them saw the Roman Republic's mixed constitutional system as ideal and viewed themselves as creating a similar republic in the New World. As Mortimer Sellers succinctly states it, "The Roman example gave Americans heroes, the vocabulary, architecture, and constitution for their revolutionary experiment in governing without a king." General Washington demonstrated his own veneration of Roman heroes when, in the dire circumstances at Valley Forge, he staged a reenactment of Cato the Younger's resistance to Caesar and his death at Utica trying to save the Roman Republic.

Timothy G. Kearley, *From Rome to the Restatement: S.P. Scott, Fred Blume, Clyde Pharr, and Roman Law in Early Twentieth-Century America*, 108 L. Libr. J. 55, 57–8 (2016).

14 *See BRIA 8 4 b Democracy and Dictatorship in Ancient Rome*, Teach Democracy, https://www.crf-usa.org/bill-of-rights-in-action/bria-8-4-b-democracy-and-dictatorship-in-ancient-rome (last visited December 29, 2023) (consuls only held office for a year).

15 Some scholars such as Professor Charles J. Reid have referred to this as the "Pre-Marbury" Constitution:

> Throughout, this Article will be sensitive to historical context. And that means chiefly that attention must be paid to the ways in which members of Congress and the executive branch viewed themselves as constitutional interpreters. It must be borne in mind that the debate over the Bank of the United States occurred twelve years before the US Supreme Court handed down Marbury v. Madison. If we view the debate as the participants would have seen it, we must acknowledge that they could not have known whether a subsequent Supreme Court would claim for itself the implied power of judicial review. In that context, Congress was defining for itself what it meant to behave constitutionally, and the debate over the Bank was very much a part of that self-definition.

Reid, *supra* note 42, at 108.

16 The Federalist No. 78 (Alexander Hamilton).

17 *Id.*

18 *Id.*

19 Judicial review did not explicitly exist, and thus the Supreme Court in *Marbury v. Madison* had to establish judicial review. *See Marbury v. Madison*, 5 U.S. (1 Cranch 137), 173–4 (1803); *see also* The Federalist No. 78 (Alexander Hamilton).

20 Jed Glickstein, *After Midnight: The Circuit Judges and the Repeal of the Judiciary Act of 1801*, 24 Yale J.L. & Humans. 543, 543–4 (2012).

21 Indeed, "[a]s the familiar story goes, right before the end of his term, President John Adams, together with the Senate, made a series of last-minute appointments, including naming William Marbury a justice of the peace for the District of Columbia." Jane Manners & Lev Menand, *The Three Permissions: Presidential Removal and the Statutory Limits of Agency Independence*, 121 Colum. L. Rev. 1, 25 (2021).

22 As the story continues:

> Unfortunately for Marbury, Adams's Secretary of State—who was none other than John Marshall, already doubling as Chief Justice—failed to deliver Marbury's commission, and the new Secretary, James Madison, refused. After a ten-month wait, Marbury sought a writ of mandamus from the Supreme Court ordering Madison to deliver his commission. Under the act that created the office, Marbury's lawyer explained, the position was for a term of five years, full stop. The act gave the President no authority to remove justices of the peace in the middle of their terms, and thus none existed.

Id.

23 This is the historically:

[C]elebrated application of William Marbury, then pending before the Supreme Court, for a mandamus to compel the delivery to him by Secretary Madison, of the commission which had been signed by President Adams and sealed by Chief Justice Marshall as acting Secretary of State, appointing Marbury a justice of the peace for Washington County in the District of Columbia, and which commission had been by order of President Jefferson, who took office the day succeeding that on which the commission was sealed, retained in the Secretary's office.

Gordon E. Sherman, *The Case of John Chandler v. the Secretary of War*, 14 Yale L.J. 431, 436 (1905).

24 John Marshall, as one of the "Midnight Judges," a label properly applied only to those appointed to the sixteen circuit judgeships, newly created by the Second Judiciary Act, which became law on February 13, 1801, and the judges and justices of the peace (of which Marbury was one) appointed under the statute establishing the District of Columbia, enacted February 27, 1801, less than a week before the end of President Adams's term of office. Marshall was nominated as Chief Justice (to succeed Oliver Ellsworth) on January 20 and took the oath of office on February 4, 1801. Telford Taylor, Book Review, 79 Colum. L. Rev. 1209, 1221–2 n.61 (1979) (reviewing Laurence H. Tribe, American Constitutional Law (1978)).

25 5 U.S. (1 Cranch) 137, 174–5 (1803).

26 12 Serg. & Rawle 330 (Pa. 1825).

27 *Id.* at 339 (Gibson, J., dissenting).

28 *Id.* at 346 (Gibson, J., dissenting).

29 *Id.* at 351 (Gibson, J., dissenting).

30 *Marbury*, 5 U.S. (1 Cranch) at 178. One is reminded of the Roman satirist's quote, "Quis custodiet ipsos custodes?" If those tasked with carrying out the laws need to interpret the law, then who and what theories guide their interpretation of the law? Juvenal, *Satire VI*, *in* The Satires ll. 347–8 (Niall Rudd trans., Clarendon Press 1991).

31 *Eakins*, 12 Serg. & Rawle at 346, 350 (Gibson, J., dissenting); *Marbury*, 5 U.S. (1 Cranch) at 177.

32 *Eakins*, 12 Serg. & Rawle at 353 (Gibson, J., dissenting).

33 us Const. art. III, § 3, cl. 2.

34 Judiciary Act of 1789, ch. 20, § 13, 1 Stat. 73 (1789).

35 *Cf.* Wallace Mendelson, *The Judiciary Act of 1789: The Formal Origin of Federal Judicial Review*, 76 Judicature 133, 135 (1992). Consider alternate positions that argue perhaps judicial review was recognized by the Federalist-controlled Congress prior to the Marbury Congress. Professor Wallace Mendelson of the University of Texas wrote in 1992 that of the question of judicial review that:

At least two pre-Marbury Congresses—in the Judiciary Acts of 1789 and 1801—and the pre-Marbury Supreme Court, recognized judicial review as a constitutionally authorized power of the federal courts. What makes *Marbury v. Madison* outstanding is that in the classic age of American constitutional law it alone sought to rationalize and justify what all the other decisions and Congress had taken for granted. This is why it—an otherwise quite forgettable case—appears in so much of the literature. The Court went out of its way to rationalize and justify because it was a crucial ploy in the complex and vicious contest between the Jeffersonians and the Federalists following the "revolution at the polls" in 1800.

Id.

Nonetheless, the fact that such a question of judicial review existed suggests the idea of judicial review was not firmly embedded in the constitutional framework of the nascent and fledgling republic.

36 This has been a hotly contested issue historically, for example, as Professor Ronald A. Cass Dean Emeritus of Boston University School of Law, wrote:

The American Constitution designed structures intended to limit discretionary government power, checking assignments of discretionary power necessary for effective government (something the new Constitution was supposed to improve) by dividing them among different entities and different officials. The national government was granted limited powers; the states retained plenary powers not at odds with national powers; and the "vesting clauses" of Articles I, II, and III grant the entirety of the legislative, executive, and judicial powers of the national government to specific bodies and officers. That set of assignments has long been understood to preclude reassignment of those powers to others. Congress cannot, for example, claim for itself part of the President's power to appoint officers of the United States or to execute the laws, nor can it assign to non-Article III officers the judicial power of the United States.

Ronald A. Cass, *Delegation Reconsidered: A Delegation Doctrine for the Modern Administrative State*, 40 Harv. J.L. & Pub. Pol'y 147, 148–9 (2017).

37 *Cf.* Ilan Wurman, *Nondelegation at the Founding*, 130 Yale L.J. 1490, 1493 (2021). As Ilan Wurman, Associate Professor of Law at the Sandra Day O'Connor College of Law at Arizona State University, wrote recently in a 2021 *Yale Law Journal* article concerning this question:

In a series of recent articles, scholars have cast doubt on originalist efforts to revive a robust nondelegation doctrine. In the most provocative of these, Julian Mortenson and Nicholas Bagley argue that there was no nondelegation doctrine at the Founding at all. According to their argument, the Founders agreed that although the legislative branch could not alienate its power—it could not give away its power for good—the legislative branch could delegate its power, so long as it had the ultimate authority to reclaim any legislative power that it had so delegated. Additionally, the Founding generation recognized governmental power to be "nonexclusive" to one particular branch; so long as Congress has authorized the Executive to take some action, that action could be characterized as executive and therefore permissible for the Executive to undertake. Turning away from Founding-era thought to legislative practice after 1789, Mortenson and Bagley argue that the legislation of the First Congress demonstrates that the Founding generation had no problem delegating vast, presumably legislative powers to the Executive. Summarizing their findings, they write, "There was no nondelegation doctrine at the Founding, and the question isn't close."

Id.

38 *See* discussion *infra* Section II.B.

39 Amy Tikkanen, *US Presidential Election of 1800*, Britannica, https://www.britannica.com/event/United-States-presidential-election-of-1800 (November 15, 2023).

40 *Federalist Party*, History (June 21, 2023) https://www.history.com/topics/early-us/federalist-party.

41 *Id.*

42 Sarah Pruitt, *How John Adams Established the Peaceful Transfer of Power*, History, (January 14, 2021) https://www.history.com/news/peaceful-transfer-power-adams-jefferson.

43 5 US (1 Cranch) 137, 154 (1803).

44 *Id.*

45 Melvin I. Urofsky, *Judiciary Act of 1801*, Britannica, https://www.britannica.com/topic/Judiciary-Act-of-1801 (February 19, 2018).

46 *Id.*

47 *Id.*

48 *Marbury*, 5 US at 180.

49 Melvin I. Urofsky, *Marbury v. Madison*, Britannica, https://www.britannica.com/event/Marbury-v-Madison (November 6, 2023).

50 The Federalist No. 78 (Alexander Hamilton).

51 *See Marbury*, 5 US at 173–4.

52 Matthew P. Bergman, *Montesquieu's Theory of Government and the Framing of the American Constitution*, 18 Pepp. L. Rev. 1, 25 (1991). Moreover, James Madison in Federalist No. 47 discusses the nature of separation of power in the three branches of government. *See also* The Federalist No. 47 (James Madison).

53 Indeed, a future article could analyze the Roman Republic's Constitution laid out in Polybius's *Histories* from a Dumézilian perspective.

54 *Module 6: Separation of Powers and Federalism*, Nat'l Const. Ctr., https://constitutioncenter.org/education/constitution-101-curriculum/6-separation-of-powers-and-federalism (last visited December 29, 2023).

55 *Signers of the Constitution: Biographical Sketches*, NAT'L PARK SERV., (July 29, 2004), https://www.nps.gov/parkhistory/online_books/constitution/bio.htm; Gordon Lloyd & Jeff Sammon, *The Educational Background of the Framers*, TEACHING AM. HIST., https://teachingamericanhistory.org/resource/convention/delegates/education/ (last visited December 29, 2023); *See generally* Thomas E. Ricks, *First Principles: What America's Founders Learned from the Greeks and Romans and How That Shaped Our Country* (2020). Ricks explores the latest documentary evidence of the education of the main framers of the United States, focusing on George Washington, Thomas Jefferson, John Adams, and James Madison. The book explores Greek and Roman ideals of virtue as well as classical republicanism. Rick's presents a compelling image of classically educated Framers and Founders of the US Republic. He suggests that the value of classics and education waned after the 1790s. But the importance of such thoughts still exists in the structure and form of the US government.

56 *See* Lincoln, *supra* note 1.

57 *Id.*

6

A Freudian Psychoanalytic Etiology of the US Constitution

Another Paradigm to Interpret the US Constitution

The magistrate in whom the whole executive power resides cannot of himself make a law, though he can put a negative on every law; nor administer justice in person, though he has the appointment of those who do administer it. The judges can exercise no executive prerogative, though they are shoots from the executive stock; nor any legislative function, though they may be advised with by the legislative councils. The entire legislature can perform no judiciary act, though by the joint act of two of its branches the judges may be removed from their offices, and though one of its branches is possessed of the judicial power in the last resort. The entire legislature, again, can exercise no executive prerogative, though one of its branches constitutes the supreme executive magistracy, and another, on the impeachment of a third, can try and condemn all the subordinate officers in the executive department. The reasons on which Montesquieu grounds his maxim are a further demonstration of his meaning. "When the legislative and executive powers are united in the same person or body," says he, "there can be no liberty, because apprehensions may arise lest THE SAME monarch or senate should ENACT tyrannical laws to EXECUTE them in a tyrannical manner." Again: "Were the power of judging joined with the legislative, the life and liberty of the subject would be exposed to arbitrary control, for THE JUDGE would then be THE LEGISLATOR. Were it joined to the executive power, THE JUDGE might behave with all the violence of AN OPPRESSOR." Some of these reasons are more fully explained in other passages; but briefly stated as they are here, they sufficiently establish the meaning which we have put on this celebrated maxim of this celebrated author.

—*Federalist Paper No. 47*, James Madison, February 1, 1788—discussing the separation of powers in the proposed federal government in the US Constitution

Summary of Chapter

This chapter offers an interpretation of the eventual teleological goal of the US structure of government outlined in the Constitution. Simultaneously, it seeks to analyze and explain the continued three-part structure of the US federal government as outlined in the Constitution. Subsequently, this chapter defines the three parts of the federal government—judiciary, executive, and legislative—as explained through the lens of the Freudian psychoanalytic paradigm of *id*, *ego*, and *super-ego*, whereby the *id* represents the legislative function, the *super-ego* represents the executive function, and the *ego* represents the judicial functions of government in the US system of government. This chapter picks off from a previous article by this author titled *A Structural Etiology of the US Constitution*.[1] That article also provided a tripartite analysis of the US Constitution. However, the analysis occurred through the lens of Plato's tripartite conception of the soul, where logos (word = law), thumos (external driving spirit = executive), and eros (general welfare = legislative) were extrapolated from Plato's dialogues.

First, this chapter establishes the Freudian model of the psyche in three parts. This is the major premise—as in a syllogism. Second, the chapter lays out the generally accepted division of the US Constitution of 1789 as laying out three parts to the federal government—the legislative, as described in Article I, the executive as described in Article II, and the judicial, as described in Article III. This second part represents the minor premise. Third, the syllogism completes by weaving in the major premise of Freud's conception of the psyche into the three parts of the US federal government.

This chapter fits into the wider issue of the functionally efficient and naturally adaptive structure of the US federal government. Providing a historical, literary, and philosophical context to this structural analysis will serve as a framework for future research on the operation of the federal government. When the branches of the federal government step out of their roles, then the balance of the structure of the federal government becomes disrupted, occurring in liminal periods of paradigmatic change. Moreover, this chapter fits into the greater research of tripartite structures and analysis in relation to the US Constitution and federal government.

Introduction to Freudian Psychoanalysis

This chapter argues that the tripartite system of government in the United States can be viewed through the Freudian psychoanalytic theory of the psyche.[2] The major premise of this chapter is the definition and elements of the Freudian structure of the psyche as outlined by the Austrian psychoanalyst Sigmund Freud. The minor premise is that the US federal government has three major parts: the judiciary, the executive, and the legislative. The syllogism and argument of this chapter is that the three federal parts of government represent the Freudian psyche: the judiciary being the *ego*, the executive being the *super-ego*, and the legislative being the *id*. This chapter will explore these concepts in greater depth. As a corollary, when the psyche of the polity—arguably in a Jungian sense of the psychoanalytic tradition—becomes unbalanced, then people become dissatisfied with the government because the government does not fulfill its function administratively—as in acting in opposition to the laws—and in promoting justice. However, sometimes overstepping a role in the Freudian psyche of the polity is a necessary change.

Premises and Structures of Analysis

Assumed throughout this chapter is the acceptance of the premises Sigmund Freud wrote about in his research into the psyche. Indeed, much of his psychoanalytic writings have been critiqued—to the author's satisfaction. This chapter's primary interest is in the accessible and readable style Freud writes and the tripartite system Freud employs. This chapter will rely primarily on primary source written material by Sigmund Freud, specifically, *The Origin and Development of Psychoanalysis* (1910), *Beyond the Pleasure Principle* (1920), *Neurosis and Psychosis* (1923), and *The Ego and the Id* (1923), while also attempting to avoid secondary literature interpreting Freud.

Fundamentally, the validity of Freud's assertions is less attractive than the results that can come about from utilizing his paradigm of the psyche. Given that Freudian psychoanalysis is not necessarily valid for its scientific accuracy but instead for its literary value, this chapter is more an interpretation of the literary devices present in Freud. The paradigm Freud can apply to the structure of the US Constitution—much in the same way literary analysis interprets legal principles. Thus, Freudian psychoanalytic thought provided by Freud provides a way to read the US Constitution. Likewise, it is just as important to focus on the primary sources of Freud's own writings to apply Freudian thought as a literary device. Thus, there is an even more critical need to focus on the primary texts. Indeed, given that literature and stories can represent mythological constructs, such an analysis can ultimately itself inversely have implications for the psyche—not through the validity of Freud's claims but through the literary value it has.[3]

Furthermore, this chapter assumes that reason and order is reflected in nature.[4] In the Platonic dialogue named *Timaeus*, Plato's interlocutor suggests that nature and the world is organized.[5] The corollary of this assumption is that the world can be interpreted logically.[6] The inverse of this assumption is that no order exists in the universe and instead humans attempt to *a priori* impose order to the world.[7] In *On the Nature of the Universe*, Lucretius introduced such a view.[8] Likewise, law can be represented in the structure of law—especially in the law of the United States.[9]

A Philosophical-Psychoanalytic Explanation for Such an Approach

To understand why it is appropriate to analyze and compare the US government with the Freudian conception of the psyche, it is helpful to have some understanding of the context of philosophical-psychoanalytic thought related to such thought.

Claude Lévi-Strauss's theory of structuralism provides an anthropological basis for interpreting society and the rules governing societies.[10] Alternatively, Michel Foucault wrote that the incentives and impetus for a government is to allocate power to those already in power.[11] A twentieth-century anthropologist named Marvin Harris wrote on how rules that are unwritten can frequently govern society, such as the gift-giving incentives that can exist in multiple societies' structures—where reciprocity and reciprocal gifts are.[12] Likewise, more explicitly, the conception of tripartite societies comes from the French anthropologist George S. Dumézil.[13] Supporting the universal nature outside of Indo-European cultures, the Dumézilian approach has been applied to Pre-Columbian Mayan Yucatán societies.[14] Furthermore, poetically, in the Homeric Ancient Greek account of the causes of the Trojan War, Paris was initially given a tripartite choice indicating the various features of humanity during a beauty contest among three goddesses—namely, Athena for wisdom, Hera for agricultural production, and Aphrodite for social replication—as referenced in Homer's *Iliad*.[15] Freud too posited trifunctionality conceptions of humans—but by correlation, some of these ideas could be taken to interpret society as a whole.[16] Thus, there is ample evidence to support such a trifunctional approach.

The French philosopher and political theorist Montesquieu wrote that a government balanced through the separation of powers would help avoid a tyrannical government whereby a government "that of enacting laws, that of executing the public resolutions, and of trying the causes of individuals."[17] Indeed, James Madison echoed Montesquieu's assertion "[i]n The Federalist No. 47, Madison explained that while Montesquieu was correct in saying that the separation of the legislative, executive, and judicial powers was essential to liberty, that conclusion did not purport to tell us how strict the resultant separation had to be."[18] This author suggested in a previous article that the Framers had an education that almost certainly had them engage with Plato's conception of the Soul and could have discussed such a concept during the closed-door Constitutional Convention.[19] Granted, the Framers of the Constitution could not have known of Freud, given that Freud began writing almost a century later, there is evidence of knowledge of a tripartite paradigm reflected in government. Whether such a paradigm was discussed at the Constitutional Convention is unknown; it at least subconsciously existed in part of their educations. Even if the Framers did not consciously discuss Plato, Plato provides a uniquely appealing literary perspective to interpret the human condition.[20] Likewise, Freudian thought has similar undertones as reflecting the human condition in a literary way.

Why Should Freud's Tripartite Conception of the Soul Be Used to Interpret the US Constitution?

If a reader finds the premise of a structured approach, then why should Freud's approach be used?

The idea of comparing a tripartite conception of the human mind—or mode of existence—is not original. Indeed, this author has written how the idea of comparing the Platonic soul to the US federal system of government has previously been written about by Akiba Covitz in *The Soul of the Polity*.[21] Covitz argued the syllogism as judiciary is the thumos, the executive is the logos, and the legislative is the eros. This author and chapter greatly appreciate Covitz's theory and writing. The predecessor to this chapter by this author on the Platonic interpretation of the US Constitution switched correspondences from thumos to logos for judiciary, logos to thumos for executive, and maintains Covitz's conception of legislative as eros.[22] Indeed, Covitz used a different terminology of (a) artifice (Ancient Greek: τέχνη);(b) nature (Ancient Greek: φύσις); and (c) history/divinity/myth (Ancient Greek: ἱστορία/οὐσία/μῦθος) in lieu logos, eros, and thumos, respectively.[23] In reading Covitz, it seems reasonable to interpret that Covitz argues that within the constitution existed a psychoanalytic dimension and that the Platonic soul as outlined in *The Republic* and *Phaedrus* represented this psychoanalysis.[24] This author continues to garner inspiration from Covtiz's inquiry.

The inquiry here in this chapter is what psychoanalytic characteristics can we extrapolate from the US Constitution using the Freudian paradigm of the human psyche. Ultimately, this is an experimental test that could lead to insights as to the etiology or cause of the US Constitution from a teleological perspective—but not direct practical inquiries. Much in the same way that in classical Graeco-Roman studies, myths frequently are used as an interpretation for why a specific custom existed in Ancient Greece or Roman antiquity.

In his *Myth and History in Ancient Greece: The Symbolic Creation of a Colony* (2003), Claude Calame drew on work by George Dumézil, arguing that the Ancient Greeks would not have viewed what we consider to be their mythology as a fiction but rather the historical archeological basis of their society.[25] Likewise, the enshrining of the US Constitution carries some mythological status through its interpretation in popular culture—despite a more abundant aggregation of resources compared to Ancient Greece. However, regardless of whether such an event is fictional or not, its representation as an etiology for the subsequent events in US history is reasonable. Thus, analyzing the Constitution much like a literary document makes sense following the classical Graeco-Roman tradition of archeological analysis.

This author gained much inspiration from such inquiries. It seems reasonable and in the spirit of Covitz's analysis to pursue the Freudian paradigm. This analysis will extend beyond the works available to the Framers of the Constitution from 1789, specifically into the Freudian psychoanalytic tradition.

Freud's Psychoanalytic Theory

A Layout of the Freudian Psyche

Before understanding how the Freudian psyche functions within the US federal government, a brief outline of Freudian conception of the psyche is required.

Freud wrote that the psyche (deriving from the Ancient Greek word for soul: ψυχή) consists of three parts: the ego (the more logical and self-sustaining force), the super-ego (the force often pressing down as a sort of moral force), and the id (more emotional and erotically chaotic part of the psyche). A person has all three parts within themselves concurrently and acts justly if each part of the psyche acts as it is supposed to act. If each part of the psyche and each part of the city conducts their activities according to their mode of existence, then the person can reach some psychological stability.

Ego

In Freud's *The Ego and the Id*, he writes that "[t]he functional importance of the ego is manifested in the fact that normally control over the approaches to motility devolves upon it."[26] This represents the idea that the ego's manifestation controls the state of existence of the person and that it is a key driver coordinating the focus on the mind. Freud continues, "thus, in its relation to the id, [the ego] is like a man on horseback, who has to hold in check the superior strength of the horse; with this difference, that the rider tries to do so with his own strength, while the ego uses borrowed forces," taking a type of control by driving the direction of the mind.[27] Specifically, the ego controls the id and tries to hold it back from getting out of control. This makes sense; the ego is our rational self "telling" us not to partake in chaotic tendencies. Indeed, this is a powerful analogy Freud presents and he takes it further by stating, "[o]ften, a rider, if he is not to be parted from his horse, is obliged to guide [the horse] where it wants to go; so, in the same way, the ego is in the habit of transforming the id's will into action, as if it were its own."[28] Thus, the rider controlling the horse cannot leave the horse—the rider is inevitably never directly separated from it.

So much seems clear—arguably the ego is the most accessible portion of Freud's paradigm because one can more consciously relate to it. Indeed, in our conscious lives, the ego is generally considered, in Freudian terms, to be a more active agent. Furthermore, Freud's classical knowledge shines—either consciously or unconsciously—because the image of the horseman guiding a horse also appears in Plato's theory of the soul.[29] Plato's theory of the soul frequently appears to parallel the Freudian tripartite conception of the soul.

Specifically in relation to the ego, the l*ogos* (λογιστικόν)[30] in the Platonic sense represents the part of the soul that loves knowledge and the search for knowledge.[31] It emphasizes the moral calculation of consequences, as opposed to "blind passions."[32] This idea can be compared to the section in the Platonic dialogue *Phaedrus* where "Socrates compares the soul to a charioteer who controls two horses—one white and docile, the other black and intemperate. These three figures echo the division of the soul into reason, emotion, and appetite in Book IV of the Republic."[33] The charioteer is *logos* keeping control of the two horses. Likewise, the logos and ego seem to be related—and it is possible Freud even wanted to make this direct analogy without explicitly referring to Plato's theory.

Id

The id is a slightly more difficult concept to fully understand because, in Freudian terms, the id is not directly evident to us. It is more closely associated with the unconscious aspects of our psyche. Freud writes in his *New Introductory Lectures on Psychoanalysis* (1933) that the id "is the dark, inaccessible part of our personality; what little we know of it we have learnt from our study of the dream-work, and, of the construction of neurotic symptoms, and most of that is of a negative character and can be described only as a contrast to the ego."[34] Essentially, Freud is stating that the id is generally inaccessible because it is part of our subconscious. Here, it may make more sense to draw the contrast between the conscious and subconscious; the id more closely associates itself with the subconscious, while the ego associates itself with the conscious. Indeed, it may be more accurate to state that the ego is the conscious existence guiding our actions, while the id represents unconscious motives we may have.

Freud continues his exposition of the id in his *New Introductory Lectures on Psychoanalysis* (1933) by extrapolating how "[w]e approach the id with analogies: we call it a chaos, a cauldron full of seething excitations. … It is filled with energy reaching it from the instincts, but it has no organization, produces no collective will, but only a striving to bring about the satisfaction of the instinctual needs subject to the observance of the pleasure principle."[35] Indeed, these analogies are helpful because the unconscious dimension of the psyche is difficult to interpret and delineate. Moreover, the id frequently tries to satiate its needs and desires, but the cause—or etiology—is difficult to identify. However, the instinctual need to seek pleasure guides the id through what Freud calls the "pleasure principle."

The pleasure principle is key to Freud's interpretation of the id.[36] However, the reality principle functions as a part of the ego trying to achieve the id's desires in realistic ways.[37] Freud states that in relation to the id, "an ego thus educated has become 'reasonable'; it no longer lets itself be governed by the pleasure principle, but obeys the reality principle, which also at bottom seeks to obtain pleasure, but pleasure which is assured through taking account of reality, even though it is pleasure postponed and diminished."[38] In other words, the ego—as educated through social interactions—becomes "reasonable" and cannot be governed by the pleasure principle. Thus, the psyche keeps the constant demand of the pleasure principle in check. However, instead of seeking pleasure instantaneously, Freud posits that the reality principle itself also seeks pleasure, but only in realistic and guided terms.

Further separating the id from the ego, Freud explains that the "contrary impulses exist side by side, without cancelling each other. … There is nothing in the id that could be compared with negation … [or] which corresponds to the idea of time."[39] Therefore, the id is difficult to identify, and even if certain impulses are identified, there is likely a contradictory impulse leading to a different result. Moreover, enigmatically, Freud suggests that the id does not correspond to time. This lack of correspondence with time could either mean that these impulses are usually better suited for another time or that the id lacks a conception of tracking regular motions. The former may be a more likely answer because impulses can arise without causes or incentives if they lack a system of control, which is what the ego does.

Compared to the Platonic paradigm, there is eros. Eros represents what Socrates says is "that with which it [soul] loves, hungers, thirsts, and feels the flutter and titillation of other desires, the irrational and appetitive—companion of various repletions [*sic*] and pleasures."[40] This, too, seems akin to Freud's conception of the id. Thus, it gives further credence to the theory that the Platonic conception of the soul and Freud's structure of the psyche run in tandem. Discussion of the parallel nature of the Platonic and Freudian systems has occurred previously. [41]

Super Ego

Finally, the third part of the Freudian paradigm is the super-ego. Freud describes the super-ego at times as an almost societal force, reinforcing historical tradition. Freud specifically writes of the moral force of the super-ego, "a child's super-ego is in fact constructed on the model not of its parents but of its parents' super-ego; the contents which fill it are the same and it becomes the vehicle of tradition and of all the time-resisting judgments of value which have propagated themselves in this manner from generation to generation."[42] Here, Freud suggests that children do not gain this type of moral guidance from their parents, but rather from their parents' super-ego. This moral guidance comes from societal traditions that will continue from generation to generation. In a sense, Freud posits a type of conservativism in this sense whereby the super-ego constrains activity as a sort of social norm. In this sense, investigating the nature of the super-ego is almost an anthropological discourse into the social values of the society in which one resides.

In the Platonic conception of the soul, the Freudian super-ego compares most closely with *thumos*, which represents a "principle of high spirit" or righteous anger[43] that unifies with the *logos* while resisting the erotic part of the soul.[44]

Again, Freud's conception of the super-ego is something that is passed down from a person's parents. Thus, it represents a societal force brought down to an individual level into the psyche.

The Freudian Psyche Overall

Essentially, the Freudian psyche overall consists of three parts: the ego, id, and super-ego. For Freud, each part represents a key part of the human mind, each part works in conjunction with the other parts, and each part is essential for the psyche's healthy functioning. In a sense, a balance must exist between all three parts.

Likewise, in parallel, the Platonic soul (ψυχή) consists of three parts: the λογιστικόν (logical, or logos), the θυμοειδές (thumotic/spirit, or thumos), and the ἐπιθυμητικόν (appetitive/erotic, or eros). Each part represents an integral part of how a human functions. However, there must exist a balance between the parts for justice to exist.

Regarding the overall functioning of the psyche, Freud wrote, "The ego is not sharply separated from the id; its lower portion merges into it." Here, Freud means that the ego and id are deeply connected. The id seeks the pleasure principle of constant, immediate gratification. However, the ego relies on the reality principle that also seeks to fulfil desires, but in a more coordinated way based on realistic outcomes. Freud incorporates "the repressed"—meaning the super-ego—into the schema by outlining, "the repressed merges into the id as well, and is merely a part of it. The repressed is only cut off sharply from the ego by the resistances of repression; it can communicate with the ego through the id." Here, there is a deep connection between the id and super-ego. The repressed attempts to suppress the ego, but the ego pushes off this repression to ensure the super-ego can only communicate with the id through the mediating force of the ego.

Such a mediation between the super-ego and id could be read as Freud suggesting that the ego wants to meet the desires of the id, but only to the extent that it conforms to the societal pressures pushing down on it. That is to say, the ego wishes to meet its desires based on the reality principle while still maintaining part of the pleasure principle's id. The super-ego is constantly trying to suppress the id, but in perhaps an ironic or unexpected way, the ego preserves the desires of the id.

Arguably, the best and clearest artistic representation of Freud's paradigm comes from the philosopher and psychoanalytic social critic Slavoj Žižek. In his documentary titled *The Pervert's Guide to Cinema* (2009), he engages in a psychoanalytic interpretation of the three layers of the house in Alfred Hitchcock's *Psycho* (1960).[45] Žižek observes that the main house in *Psycho* has three levels. He contends that each level represents a part of the human psyche postulated by Freudian psychoanalysis. In Žižek's conception, the top floor represents the super-ego, where Norman Bates' mother presumably resides throughout the movie; the ground floor represents the Freudian ego where all the normal, seemingly pedestrian activity of the movie occurs; and the basement/fruit cellar represents the id, where the mother's corpse is finally discovered at the end of the film. Žižek describes the id as the reservoir of emotions and chaos. Moreover, in the movie, Bates moves his mother's corpse from the top floor to the cellar. Žižek suggests this represents a deep connection in Freudian psychoanalysis between the id and super-ego. He suggests this connection exists because the super-ego often achieves a pressing and controlling force upon the psyche through terms of "obscenity." He supports this proposition by observing the somewhat "obscene" language the mother uses to command Bates.[46] Žižek's psychoanalytic interpretation of *Psycho* (1960) and its Freudian structure is summarized in Table 6.1.

Thus, the three levels of the Bates house in Alfred Hitchcock's *Psycho* (1960) arguably represent the most accurate depiction of the Freudian paradigm of the psyche in the human mind.

This section shows how the Freudian theory of psychoanalysis can be applied to another field—in this case cinema. There is no indication that Hitchcock had Freud in mind making these movies. But whether Hitchcock had such an idea in mind does not matter if one takes Freud's theories seriously. If Freud's

Table 6.1 Žižek's Psychoanalytic Interpretation of *Psycho* (1960) and the Freudian Psyche

Freudian Psyche Component	Psychological Function	Spatial Representation in *Psycho*	Žižek's Interpretation
Super-ego	Internalized authority, moral pressure, oppressive commands	Top Floor (Mother's Room)	Site of haunting moral judgment; mother's voice symbolizes overbearing, obscene moral authority
Ego	Rational self, mediator of reality and desire	Ground Floor (Living Space)	Represents the apparent "normalcy" of Norman's life—the realm of polite appearances and social negotiation
Id	Unconscious drives, repressed chaos and desire	Basement (Fruit Cellar)	Site of primal emotion and horror; mother's corpse hidden here signifies the buried core of violent impulse

theories actually represent the psyche, then Hitchcock's movies could simply represent the human condition. If Freud's theories do not represent the psyche, there still exists a heuristic value in interpreting cinema. Likewise, using Freud as a heuristic to interpret the Constitution could be helpful. The comparison to Hitchcock movies provides a unique viewpoint and hopefully this chapter will also provide a unique view point on the US Constitution.

Comparing the Structure of the Federal Government to the Freudian Tripartite Conception of the Psyche

Judiciary as Ego

The judiciary[47] in this chapter's paradigm represents the ego. Article III judges—as intended by the Framers of the Constitution—are not politicians seeking re-election.[48] Rather, they are aloof from the political system in seeking to interpret and apply the law. Impartial logical analysis—although it can be informed by the other elements of the soul—is the guiding principle of the judiciary. The judiciary represents *ego*.

Cases and Examples Showing Why the Judiciary Represents the Freudian Ego

Freud regarded the ego as a rider controlling his horse: the id. Similarly, Chief Justice Marshall once said, "it is emphatically the province and duty of the judicial department to say what the law is."[49] The Supreme Court uses judicial review to interpret the Constitution and statutes passed by the legislature to keep the legislature in check—much like in the analogy of the rider.

When the constituent parts of the psyche become imbalanced, then unjust results arise, such as *Plessy v. Ferguson*.[50] However, imbalance and the blurring of separation of powers may occasionally lead to more just and fair results, such as *Brown v. Board of Education*.[51]

As discussed previously in this book, *Plessy*,[52] the Supreme Court stepped out of its judicial authority and took on a legislative function, but with an unjust result. The Court upheld as constitutional a Louisiana law declaring that a "State, shall provide equal but separate accommodations" for members of different races.[53]

Moreover, as discussed previously in this book, *Brown v. Board of Education*,[54] the Supreme Court stepped out of its judicial authority and took on a legislative function, but this time with a just result. In *Brown v. Board of Education*,[55] the Court noted that "[t]he doctrine of 'separate but equal' did not make its appearance in this Court until 1896 in the case of *Plessy v. Ferguson* … involving not education but transportation," thus highlighting that the *Plessy* Court had strayed from its mode of *stare decisis* and made law based on no previous law.[56]

Most recently, in *Obergefell v. Hodges*,[57] many in the United States appreciated the decision, but public perception saw it as a violation of natural law.[58] The public perception itself could inform law.[59]

Professor Tribe does not assert that the Court overstepped its boundary. Tribe's article does not explicitly make clear who the "glib detractors" are. However, Tribe offers clues by stating, "among those who emphatically agree with Justice Kennedy that the Constitution affords same-sex couples the right to marry, many are quick to claim that his sweeping opinion was heavy on rhetoric and light on legal reasoning—a political masterstroke but a doctrinal dud." In other words, the "glib detractors" are likely those who support legal formalism and originalism. This is an assumption based on the circumstantial evidence in the article. Although not the focus of this chapter, Tribe calling the detractors "glib" perhaps originates from the idea that several legal academic scholars—such as Richard Fallon[60] and Charles Fried[61]—have written that originalism and legal formalism did not exist in the early republic, and as such, courts do not need to necessarily rely on such legal reasoning.[62]

Over time, society may come to a consensus on whether the Court decided the case correctly. Currently, *Obergefell* serves as an example of the Court stepping outside of its judicial role and acting in a legislative capacity, with an unclear result on justice.

Although the Court and judiciary as a whole, in the Freudian conception of the US division of government, should act as an ego mediating force focused on reality and mediating the desires of the id. As Freud wrote:

> The ego is that part of the id which has been modified by the direct influence of the external world. … The ego represents what may be called reason and common sense, in contrast to the id, which contains the passions … in its relation to the id it is like a tug of war, which the ego has to hold in check the id to not let it loose; with the difference, that the teams fought against one other in equality, while the ego was against the much stronger 'id.'[63]

Thus, the Supreme Court, as the mediating ego force in the US Constitutional framework, must come to logical and necessary decisions that provide justice. This means balancing out the potential will of Congress—that could represent immediate desires—with the restrictions of the Constitution. Likewise, the Supreme Court must balance the legal actions of the president as well.

However, at the same time, the Supreme Court is composed of individual humans who each have three parts of the Freudian psychoanalytic framework. Each member of the judiciary and the Supreme Court has more forces than the pure ego on acting on them, because each member is a human with the tripartite psyche constitution operating within them.

While the idea of a three-part psyche can be applied to understand the basic functions of an aspect of government, each individual member has an entire psyche governing their own mind. This leads to more nuanced decisions, not only in the judiciary but in all three branches of the government. Like the id can lead individuals to seek immediate gratification so too can members of the judiciary seek immediate gratification for an innumerable number of reasons. Likewise, an individual could be governed by the notions of the super-ego. The super ego acts moral authority imposing morals down on the individual—frequently coming from parental authority figures.[64] Frequently the super ego can manifest as the morals of society where according to Freud, "super-ego retains the character of the father ... the stricter will be the domination of the super-ego over the ego later on—in the form of conscience or perhaps of an unconscious sense of guilt."[65]

In terms of the judiciary, straying from the principle of separation of powers or its designated role in the soul of the polity can have bad and good outcomes.

Justice from the judiciary could come in various forms. In this case, the ego likely guides to just results by keeping emotional forces, as represented through the id, and repressive forces, as represented through the super-ego, in check. It is not clear whether a certain case, such as *Obergefell*, would fit into the narrow category of just the judiciary carrying out the ego of itself or the ego ideal of the ideal of what the Supreme Court would like to be.

At first, this swerve from purely *a priori* logic and analysis toward using "experience" may seem like a contradiction of the purely non-emotional and non-pleasure-seeking aspect of the *ego* in the Freudian psyche.

Arguably, the judiciary is a mix of all the three-part Freudian constituent elements operating with each other. It is unclear how or which ones are most effective. However, the notion of the ego ideal, where "the individual's conscious and unconscious images of what he would like to be, patterned after certain people whom ... he regards as ideal"[66] drives action, likely explains the Supreme Court activity. In a sense, the ultimate ego ideal of an individual working toward a desired goal, seeming as if it is promoting justice, is what the judiciary likely functions as.

Executive as the Super-ego

In this chapter, the Executive[67] represents super-ego. Super-ego, in the Freudian structure, represents a societal force that represses the desires of the id through the mediation of the ego.

This indicates that a person will likely turn to politics while in the tension of the ego and *id*, because the *id* drives an individual to pursue the pleasure principle. The *id* becomes more prevalent when the super-ego can no longer mediate between the ego and the *id*. Likewise, in this specific instance, humans who find excessive pleasure in politics likely find this pleasure from pursuing the pleasure principle, where the pleasure derives from their successes.[68] Indeed, the praise and acceptance a successful politician receives likely fulfill the basic human instinct of wanting acceptance. This likely provides a deeper understanding of why politicians engage in politics.

In other words, when a tension exists between the ego[69]—the part of the mind that deals with interpreting reality[70]—and the unconscious—the part of the mind that deals with more primitive impulses and desires as a driving force—those individuals can turn to politics as a means of reconciling such a tension.[71]

This ties into Freud's short statement, "The id wants what it wants when it wants it," which reaffirms that the id pursues the pleasures that it seeks without reference to other potential issues, such as delayed gratification for greater pleasure later. In his 1920 *Introductory Lectures*, Freud asserted that: "an ego thus educated has become 'reasonable'; it no longer lets itself be governed by the pleasure principle, but obeys the reality principle, which also, at bottom, seeks to obtain pleasure, but pleasure which is assured through taking account of reality, even though it is pleasure postponed and diminished."[72] In other words, the ego usually mediates the pleasure principle to ensure that the pleasure principle does not govern the individual entirely. But in the context of a politician pursuing politics, the impulse to pursue politics seems to engage in a risky activity that could ruin a person's psyche in case of loss and ruin one's employment potential thereafter.[73] Thus, the urge to pursue politics surpasses the ego's regulatory force to take a safer course.

This is more akin to the president—rather than a member of the judiciary—who likely is in search of honors and recognition, much like other politicians. Given that federal judges do not need to seek re-election, their incentive to seek recognition does not exist—unless such judges seek to be appointed to circuit courts up the appellate ladder.[74] Alternatively, a president,[75] political appointees,[76] and politicians regularly seek re-election or reappointment.[77] Such a recognition of a politician's psyche is not a negative aspect of the executive, necessarily. Indeed, addressing criticism and political concerns could feed into a politician's need for recognition while also serving the needs of a democracy.[78] Because if the executive of the country did not seek honor or maintain some "haughtiness" other politicians and world leaders would take advantage of us.

As president, she must be a decisive president, not merely following the Freudian ego. Yet, ego—as well as id—may and must exist within her, but she must, as president have a prevailing super-ego element. As president, crucial decision-making skills must exist that align with the dominant super-ego structure of where the executive fits into the US Constitution. However, at the same time, the id and the ego forces subject the president—like all human beings—to their functions in the human mind. The id represents primitive instincts focusing on immediate gratification, while the ego seeks to balance such urges with the demands of existing in the world external to the mind.

Analogously, the president must find a way to balance the competing demands of the id, ego, and superego to act as a more effective leader. Moreover, analogously, the president must find a way to balance the demands of the legislative functions and the judicial functions in the United States.[79] The president cannot act contrary to the will of Congress.[80] Because of the Constitution's tripartite framework, the President must act within statutory and constitutional limits and cannot act contrary to Congress or binding Supreme Court precedent.[81] Furthermore, the president cannot act contrary to a Supreme Court opinion.[82] In line with taking into consideration judicial decisions, the president or the president's staff often predict how courts may react to presidential actions.[83] As such, to function as a more effective leader, the president must understand her own psyche and the broader societal and political institutions that affect the executive branch of government.

In this way, the Freudian framework provides a useful tool for understanding the complexities between the individual psyche and the Constitutional layout in the United States.

Cases and Examples Showing Why the Executive Represents the Super-ego

Here, the super-ego manifests itself where a part of the executive branch of government, such as through executive agencies. Such executive agencies interpret a statute from the legislature and implement it. This occurs through the rules laid out by the Supreme Court and the judiciary, as seen in the *Chevron* case.

Frequently, the president issues executive orders. Moreover, federal courts often declare executive orders unconstitutional. Regardless of whether the executive orders are eventually upheld as constitutional or not, such executive actions represent the executive branch of government conducting actions in an attempt to solve problems in society that the executive sees as existing.[84] In this sense, such executive orders act as a super-ego. If the orders are upheld to be constitutional after all, then the judiciary or the legislature will deem them to have been the most effective approach at the time to avoid a greater disaster later. If not, then the judiciary or the legislature will have deemed them to be an ineffective approach at the time.

Because the executive branch and the legislature as well are charged with carrying out the daily activities of the nation, international relations appear to be of paramount importance with spirited leadership that represses immediate instincts of pleasure—as represented by the Freudian id.

Thus, because the leadership and individuals themselves are humans, each of the three parts of the Freudian psyche exists within them. Therefore, such action may not necessarily reflect merely the super-ego idea of government. The leadership and executive actions that may not or may be based in *ego* and *id*, but through the regulating force of the super-ego, which this chapter argues fits into the paradigm of the executive branch of government in the US Constitution.

The Legislature as the Freudian Id

In this chapter, the legislature[85] represents *id*. The id represents the basic instincts and desires of the subconscious and of preconscious. Freud breaks down the unconscious into two different types: the "preconscious" and the "unconscious." Freud explains that there exist:

> two kinds of unconscious—one which is easily, under frequently occurring circumstances, transformed into something conscious, and another with which this transformation is difficult and takes place only subject to a considerable expenditure of effort or possibly never at all. [. . .] We call the unconscious which is only latent, and thus easily becomes conscious, the "preconscious," and retain the term "unconscious" for the other.[86]

Here, Freud says that individuals can easily access "preconscious" and transform it into the conscious mind.[87] This occurs under normal circumstances. Memories,[88] thoughts, feelings, desires exist immediately below the surface of the consciousness. Thus, because of their proximate closeness with the consciousness, they can come to the consciousness.

The second type of unconscious Freud calls the "unconscious."[89] For individuals, this second type exists deeper than the "preconscious." Thus, because the "preconscious" is much deeper, the conscious awareness cannot easily access it. Repressed memories, traumas, and desires that one finds difficult to acknowledge—such as taboos—exist in the unconscious.[90] Indeed, in Freudian terms, these unconscious thoughts may operate as the source of psychological problems.

Congress, in theory, enacts the will of the people and is the closest interaction most of the population can have with the three main branches of government.

Thus, many proposals in Congress can represent more emotional responses to issues—even if some of the laws that are passed are eventually thwarted by the other branches of government.

As such, the desires and pleasures of the Congress may seem contradictory—indeed, they often are—but over time, they may become more or less clear. Indeed, one of the most difficult things to divine is the legislative intent of a congressional act. Much like the Freudian id, an act of Congress can exhibit contradictory aims at the same time.

Conclusion

To reiterate, this chapter has used the Freudian tripartite constitution of the psyche to interpret the US federal government's three-part system of government outlined in the Constitution of 1787. Such an analysis does not prove that the Freudian conception is represented in the US Constitution. Such a proof may be impossible—or unfalsifiable. It is likely unfalsifiable because such a proposition cannot be tested, proven, or shown false through empirical evidence.[91] Because such a proposition is unfalsifiable, such a theory likely rests in the realm of nonempirical philosophy and literature in law. Such a reading takes inspiration from interpreting Freud from a literary perspective.[92] As the luminary Yale University literature professor as Harold Bloom wrote, "I favor a Shakespearean reading of Freud, and not a Freudian reading of Shakespeare."[93] Likewise, this chapter hopes to favor of a legal reading of Freud not a Freudian reading of the US Constitution. Thus, this chapter does not hope to fit in with the category of psychology and law but rather law and literature. Freud's tripartite model of the psyche and its analogous functions in the US federal government are summarized in Table 6.2.

This chapter attempted to show that the lens of the Freudian paradigm of the id, ego, and super-ego could be seen as existing and superimposed onto the US Constitution.

If the reader accepts the premises of such an unfalsifiable argument, the major premise of the paper is Freud's tripartite psyche. The minor premise is the three-part structure of the US government. The syllogism is the analysis in the article that attempts to show how each part of the Freudian psyche represents itself in the three parts of the judiciary for *ego*, executive for *super-ego*, and legislature for *id*.

Table 6.2 Freud's Tripartite Psyche and Its Analogous Functions in the US Federal Government

Freudian Psyche Component	Psychological Function	US Constitutional Branch	Governmental Function
Super-ego	Moral oversight, internalized norms, inherited authority	Executive	Executes laws with the authority and restraint of societal and moral expectations
Ego	Mediator, rational decision-maker, balances competing forces	Judiciary	Interprets laws rationally, balancing power and resolving conflicts
Id	Instincts, desires, drives (especially *eros* and *thanatos*)	Legislative	Responds to the people's desires, impulses, and material needs via representative action

Overall, this Freudian psychoanalysis of the Constitution's structure and function could add to the dialogue of constitutional analysis by providing a different perspective for how to discuss the functions of the three parts of the federal government. Indeed, there are arguments for living constitution, purposivism, and political process theory, but there also seems to be a basis for a Freudian interpretation of the Constitution based on the suggestion in this chapter.

In line with a balanced soul of the polity and a balanced government, each part of government would not reach into another's duties in line with the outline of Federalist No. 47.[94]

As Freud outlined his theory, each person has three parts of the psyche. Although an individual may act in one part of the federal government, each person has all three parts of the Freudian structure operating within their psyche. Thus, it is to be expected that different parts of the psyche would manifest in different parts of the federal government from various individuals.

Plato's paradigm of a long-lasting government archetype, which Freud likely explored in a different way through his psychoanalytic theory at the individual level, seems suitable regardless of the correct Freudian application to the three-part structure of the US government.[95] From a Freudian perspective, is it fair to say that the best government, at least in part, represents the individual or the psyche of the individual? Likewise, it seems fair to say that an anthropological archetype of government could exist based on the psychology of humans. The topic of such a connection of the psychological archetype of government would fall into the scope of a different article and further research.

Notes

1 Charles Lincoln, *A Structural Etiology of the US Constitution*, 43 J. LEGIS. 122 (2016).

2 Sigmund Freud, *The Ego and the Id* (1923), The Standard Edition of the Complete Psychological Works of Sigmund Freud 3, 25 (James Strachey ed. & trans., 1961).

3 See for further analysis of legal principles of law through literary traditions, such as J.R.R. Tolkien's writings. Lincoln, Charles Edward Andrew IV (2020) "A Literary Lens into Constitutional Interpretation and a Possible Synthesis of Natural and Positive Law: The Silmarillion," *Mitchell Hamline L. J. of Pub. Pol. & Prac.*: Vol. 41: Iss. 1, Article 4.

4 Cicero, *De Republica* (Loeb Classical Library, Cambridge, MA, 1928), 3.22.33.

5 Plato, *Timaeus* (Oxford University Press, Oxford, trans., Robin Waterfield, 2008) at 30a–31b. The page numbers used throughout this chapter to refer to Platonic texts are in accord with the Stephanus pagination.

Substantively, are randomness or patterns provable or real? How do we even decide what is random if not through statistical or other mathematical analysis? Philosophically speaking, there could be a discrepancy between a series following a mathematical rule or being truly random. Ludwig Wittgenstein, in his *Philosophical Investigations*, explained how randomness *can* really be explained in terms of increasing complexity of following a rule, but paradoxically, if everything can be shown to be following a rule, it can also at the same time be shown to not follow a rule.

201 This was our paradox: no course of action could be determined by a rule, because every course of action can be made out to accord with the rule. The answer was: if everything can be made out to accord with the rule, then it can also be made out to conflict with it. And so there would be neither accord nor conflict here. It can be seen that there is a misunderstanding here from the mere fact that in the course of our argument we give one interpretation after another, as if each one contented us at least for a moment, until we thought of yet another standing behind it. What this shows is that there is a way of grasping a rule which is not an interpretation but which is exhibited in what we call "obeying the rule" and "going against it" in actual cases. Hence, there is an inclination to say: every action according to the rule is an interpretation. But we ought to restrict the term

"interpretation" to the substitution of one expression of the rule for another. Ludwig Wittgenstein, Philosophical Investigations § 201 (G.E.M. Anscombe & R. Rhees eds., G.E.M. Anscombe trans., 1972).

This makes one question whether randomness really exists or does everything follow a set rule. See e.g., Ahilan T. Arulanantham, *Breaking the Rules?: Wittgenstein and Legal Realism*, 107 Yale L.J. 1853, 1869–1871 (1998). Dennis Patterson, *Wittgenstein and Constitutional Theory*, 72 Tex. L. Rev. 1837, 1851 (1994). Scott Hershovitz, *Wittgenstein on Rules: The Phantom Menace*, 22 Oxford J. of Leg. Stud. 619, 639–40 (2002).

6 *Id.*

7 Such an example can be seen in literature,

> Borges's *The Library of Babel* implicitly undercuts all the written structures—religion, science, art—through which human beings strive to impose order on an unruly world. It consists of a fantastic monologue in which a Librarian, who lives in a Library which is also the universe, tries unsuccessfully to describe the chaotic infinity (or near infinity) that surrounds him. According to the Librarian, the Library may or may not be endless; but it is certainly meaningless, being made up of numberless books in a Babel of tongues. Because it contains all the possible combinations of letters in all languages, many of the books contain only an intelligible word or two, or are only partially true copies of books contained in their proper form elsewhere in the Library. The Librarians spend their time, among other ways, searching for the true catalogue that would bring order and meaning to their incomprehensible collection.

Susan Mann, *The Universe and the Library: A Critique of James Boyd White as Writer and Reader*, 41 Stan. L. Rev. 959, 965 (1989).

8 *Lucretius: On the Nature of Things* (H. A. J. Munro trans.), reprinted in 12 *Great Books of the Western World* 1, 12 (Robert Maynard Hutchins ed., 1952).

Concurrently, directly contrasting the Platonic theory of order in the universe,

> The contrary materialist view characterizes archetypes as speculative constructs. Aristotle and Plato had their ancient Greek materialist counterparts in Epicurus, Democritus, and Lucretius, who in his *On the Nature of the Universe* wrote that all things began from "the purposeless congregation and coalescence of atoms." There are uniform and entirely natural causes in a closed system not ordered or otherwise affected by the presence of a higher mind capable of recognizing and ordering information. Thus Epicurus could hold that morality was merely a sensual matter of seeking pleasure and avoiding pain, not a sensitivity issue to any particular purpose or design. Aristotle's teleological universe was rejected for an atomistic universe without purpose or form in which biological forms and the

ordered universe in which they exist were not the fixed product of information, intelligence, or design but of random accretion. Nobel Prize–winning biologist George Wald, physicist Freeman Dyson, and astronomer George Greenstein explain the improbability of the universe's remarkable order by suggesting either that the universe did not exist until humans observed it and (in Wald's words) that "[t]he universe wants to be known."

Marion Hilligan, Nelson P. Miller, Don Petersen & Chris Hastings, *Symposium Issue: World Views Collide: A Dialogue on State-Authored Embryonic Stem-Cell Research, Human Enhancements, Physician-Assisted Suicide and the Value of Life: Superhuman-Biotechnology's Emerging Impact on the Law*, 24 T.M. Cooley L. Rev. 1, 25–6 (2007).

9 As the interlocutor suggests, nature represented itself in Athens. *Timaeus* 90b–c. See Recent work suggests there is an order to the world's structure. "About fifty years ago a physicist called Paul Dirac asked himself why the number ten to the fortieth power keeps occurring. The square of this number, ten to the eightieth power, is the mass of the visible universe, measured in terms of the mass of the proton. The number itself, ten to the fortieth, is the present age of the universe, expressed in units of time it takes light to travel across a proton. And, get this, the constant that measures the strength of gravity in terms of the electrical force between two protons is ten to the fortieth times weaker! Also, ten to the fortieth to the one-fourth, or ten to the tenth, just about equals the number of stars in a galaxy, the number of galaxies in the universe, and the inverse of the weakfine structure constant! John Updike, Roger's Version 23–4 (1986); George Johnson, A Fire in the Mind: Science, Faith, and the Search for Order 308–16 (1996)." Robert Birmingham, *Proving Miracles and the First Amendment*, 5 Geo. Mason L. Rev. 45, 60 (1996).

10 "To illustrate the nature of structuralist theory, this discussion will concentrate on the work of Claude Levi-Strauss. Levi-Strauss has made the search for the fundamental properties of human thought the focus of his work. His basic objective is uncovering the universal, basic structure of human thought, which is deep below the surface but is manfested [*sic*] in myth, language, cooking, table manners, and the general structures of social life. This basic structure, which is termed 'deep structure,' will identify cross-cultural similarities." Donald H. J. Hermann, *Phenomenology, Structuralism, Hermeneutics, and Legal Study: Applications of Contemporary Continental Thought to Legal Phenomena*, 36 U. Miami L. Rev. 379, 390–1. (1982).

11 "Michel Foucault's compelling and poetic methodological manifesto describes the nature of 'critique' and, thereby, the proper role of the critic. For Foucault,

'critique' was more than a means to an end; criticism was itself an act of resistance and refusal. Toward this end, Foucault sought to decouple criticism from positive programs for social and political change. Criticism is, according to this view, a negative operation—'essays in refusal'—resisting and rejecting 'what is' without regard for 'what needs to be done.' For this reason, Foucault's views have occasionally been labeled 'rejectionist.' Such 'rejectionist' claims, in turn, exemplify the most feared aspects of a new challenge to traditional legal thought: postmodernism." Derek P. Jinks, *Essays in Refusal: Pre-Theoretical Commitments in Postmodern Anthropology and Critical Race Theory*, 107 YALE L.J. 499, 499–500. (1997). *See also* For a discussion on Foucault's ideas on law and sovereignty: Tom Frost, "Agamben's Sovereign Legalization of Foucault." *Oxford J Legal Studies* 30, 3 (2010): 545.

12 Marvin Harris, The Rise of Anthropological Theory (1968). See Perry Dane, Jurisdictionality, Time, and the Legal Imagination, 23 HOFSTRA L. REV. 1, 94. (1994). See "The reciprocity concept justifies the assumption that one who gives will receive in return, though there are no hard promises as to timing, quality, or quantity." John W. Ragsdale, Jr., *The Rise and Fall of the Chacoan State*, 64 UMKC L. REV. 485, 528. See Perry Dane, *Jurisdictionality, Time, and the Legal Imagination*, 23 HOFSTRA L. REV. 1, 94. (1994). *See* in regard to gift giving cultures. Bronislaw Malinowski, Argonauts of the Western Pacific 72–6 (Routledge 1961) (1922).

13 According to Dumézil, the division of society—government—into three parts was inherent in all Indo-European societies. The trifunctional pattern (and implicit political separation of powers) is manifest among the Hindus in the original castes: Brahmana (teachers, priests, keepers of the law), Ksatriya (warrior kings), and Vaisya (farmers, producers, merchants and doctors). "For classic development of this so-called 'tripartite hypothesis' concerning the division of social roles in Proto-Indo-European societies, see generally Georges Dumézil, *Flamen-Brahman* (1935); Georges Dumézil, *Mitra-Varuna: An Essay on Two Indo-European Representations of Sovereignty* (Derek Coltman trans., 2nd ed. 1988)." Robin Bradley Kar, *Western Legal Prehistory: Reconstructing the Hidden Origins of Western Law and Civilization*, 2012 U. ILL. L. REV. 1499, 1525 n. 71. (2012). See Georges Dumézil, *Archaic Roman Religion* 585 (1966). *See also* For critiques of the Trifunctional Hypothesis: Wouter W. Belier, Decayed Gods: Origin and Development of Georges Dumézil's "Ideologie Tripartie" 17–20 (1991).

14 Lincoln, Charles E., *Ethnicity and Social Organization at Chichen Itza, Yucatan, Mexico* (1990) (Ph.D. dissertation, Department of Anthropology, Harv. Univ. Advisors Mathews, Peter, and Gordon R. Willey). *See* Charles E. Lincoln, *The Chronology of Chichen Itza: A Review of the Literature*. In Late Lowland Maya Civilization: Classic to Postclassic (ed., Jeremy A. Sabloff and E. Wyllys Andrews V, University of New Mexico Press, Albuquerque, 1986), 141–56.

15 Homer, *The Iliad of Homer* 295 (Richmond Lattimore trans., 25th report. ed. 1976) (1951). *See* "[T]he well known Judgment of Paris, which Homer apparently knew. Although it is not directly recounted in the Iliad, there is a clear reference to it in Book 14, where Hera's displeasure with the other gods (i.e., gods who were urging Achilles to treat Hector's corpse with respect) was attributed to the Judgment of Paris: 'because of the delusion of Paris / who insulted the goddesses when they came to him in his courtyard / and favoured her who supplied the lust that led to disaster.' The myth of the Judgment of Paris began when Peleus and Thetis did not invite Eris, the goddess of discord, to their wedding. Eris, feeling snubbed, concocted one of literary history's most evil schemes. She procured a golden apple and inscribed it "For the fairest." She then crashed the wedding feast and tossed the apple onto the table. Three goddesses, Hera, Athena, and Aphrodite, each argued that it should be her's. They asked Zeus to decide. He refused because he feared his wife's anger in the event that he did not choose her. He passed the buck and suggested that the Trojan prince Paris, the son of Priam, act as arbiter." Russ VerSteeg, *A Contract Analysis of the Trojan War*, 40 ARIZ. L. REV. 173, 192 (1998).

16 David S. Caudill, *Freud and Critical Legal Studies: Contours of a Radical Socio-Legal Psychoanalysis*, 66 IND. L.J. 651, 658–9. (1991). *See* Sigmund Freud, *The Standard Edition of the Complete Psychological Works Sigmund Freud* 19 (J. Strachey ed. 1953).

17 Montesquieu, *The Spirit of the Laws* bk. XI, ch. 6, at 152 (Hafner Pub, trans., Thomas Nugent, 1949) (1748).

18 John F. Manning, "Separation of Powers as Ordinary Interpretation." 124 HARV. L. REV. 1939, 2004 (2010).

19 Charles Lincoln, *A Structural Etiology of the U.S. Constitution*, 43 J. LEGIS. 122 (2016). James J. Walsh, *Education of the Founding Fathers of the Republic: Scholasticism in the Colonial Colleges*, 104–5 (1935).

20 Jean-Francois Pradeau, Plato and the City 129 (Janet Llyod trans.) (2002).

21 Akiba J. Covitz, Dissertation, *The Soul of the Polity: Beginnings of American Constitutional Thought*, UMI, x (1999). As far as the author knows, Akiba Covitz is the only person to have written on this subject. See Charles Lincoln, A Structural Etiology of the US Constitution, 43 J. LEGIS. 122 (2016).

22 Charles Lincoln, *A Structural Etiology of the U.S. Constitution*, 43 J. LEGIS. 122 (2016).

23 Covitz, *supra* note 22, at xxii–xxv. Charles Lincoln, A Structural Etiology of the US Constitution, 43 J. LEGIS. 122 (2016).

24 *Id.* at xviii–xx. Charles Lincoln, A Structural Etiology of the US Constitution, 43 J. LEGIS. 122 (2016).

25 Claude Calame, *Myth and History in Ancient Greece: The Symbolic Creation of a Colony* (Daniel W. Berman trans.) (2003). Charles Lincoln, A Structural Etiology of the US Constitution, 43 J. LEGIS. 122 (2016).

26 Freud, *supra* note 4, at 30.

27 *Id.*

28 *Id.*

29 The Freudian and Platonic paradigms seem to closely resemble each other. Buckley, Peter. "Freud's term, *popular distinction*, can be used as a denial of the Platonic origins of this metaphor. Notwithstanding Freud's abjuration of any debt to Plato, it is clear that this ancient Greek philosopher anticipated the creator of modern psychodynamic theory when he articulated in *The Republic* a conflict model for the psyche in which instinctual drives represent a constant threat to rational behavior." "Ancient templates: The classical origins of psychoanalysis." *American Journal of Psychotherapy*, 55, no. 4 (2001): 451–9.

30 Etymologically speaking, "λογιστικός" is defined as "I. skilled or practised in calculating, Xen., Plat.:—ἡ λογιστική (sc. τέχνη), arithmetic, Plat. II. endued with reason, rational, Arist.:—τὸ λ. the reasoning faculty, Plat. 2. using one's reason, reasonable, Xen." Henry Liddell & Robert Scott, *An Intermediate Greek-English Lexicon* 476 (1889), http://www.perseus.tufts.edu/hopper/text?doc=Perseus%3Atext%3A1999.04.0058%3Aentry%3Dlogistiko%2Fs. http://www.perseus.tufts.edu/hopper/text?doc=Perseus%3Atext%3A1999.04.0058%3Aentry%3Dlogistiko%2Fshttp://www.perseus.tufts.edu/hopper/text?doc=Perseus%3Atext%3A1999.04.0058%3Aentry%3Dlogistiko%2Fs

31 Plato indicates that each class of the soul has a love representative affiliated with its class. For example, the love of knowledge and wisdom comes from the class ruled by logos. In the Jowett translation, this is explicitly clear, "And that is why we say that the primary classes of men also are three, the philosopher or lover of wisdom, the lover of victory and the lover of gain." "Precisely so." "And also that there are three forms of pleasure, corresponding respectively to each?" "By all means." "Are you aware, then," said I, "that if you should choose to ask men of these three classes, each in turn, which is the most pleasurable of these lives, each will chiefly commend his own?" See Plat. Rep. 9.581c. http://www.perseus.tufts.edu/hopper/text?doc=Perseus%3Atext%3A1999.01.0168%3Abook%3D9%3Asection%3D581c *See also.* PLATO, PLATO IN TWELVE VOLUMES, VOLUMES 5 & 6 (Paul Shorey trans., Harvard University Press 1969), Perseus Digital Library 4.435e, https://www.perseus.tufts.edu/hopper/text?doc=Perseus%3Atext%3A1999.01.0168%3Abook%3D4%3Asection%3D435e#note2.

32 This can be compared to "*Crito* 46 B (one of the passages which the Christian apologists used to prove that Socrates knew the λόγος), *Theaetetus* 186 C ἀναλογίσματα πρός τε οὐσίαν καὶ ὠφέλειαν, and *Laws* 644 D. Aristotle *Eth.* 1139 a 12 somewhat differently." *Id.* at 4.439 n. 8, http://www.perseus.tufts.edu/hopper/text?doc=Perseus%3Atext%3A1999.01.0167%3Abook%3D4%3Asection%3D439d.

http://www.perseus.tufts.edu/hopper/text?doc=Perseus%3Atext%3A1999.01.0167%3Abook%3D4%3Asection%3D439d

33 Kenji Yoshino, *The City and the Poet*, 114 Yale L.J. 1835, 1856 (2005).

34 Sigmund Freud, *New Introductory Lectures on Psycho-Analysis 91* (James Strachey ed., James Strachey trans., W.W. Norton & Company 1964) (1933).

35 *Id.* at 91–2.

36 Sigmund Freud, *Introductory Lectures on Psycho-analysis* 443 (James Strachey ed., James Strachey trans., W.W. Norton & Company 1966) (1917).

37 *Id.* at 444.

38 *Id.*

39 Freud, *supra* note 81, at 92.

40 Plato, *supra* note 78, at 439d, https://www.perseus.tufts.edu/hopper/text?doc=Perseus%3Atext%3A1999.01.0168%3Abook%3D4%3Asection%3D439d.

41 *See* Robert C. Bordone et al., *The Negotiation Within: The Impact of Internal Conflict Over Identity and Role on Across-the-Table Negotiations*, 2014 J. Disp. Resol. 175, 180 (2014).

42 Sigmund Freud, *New Introductory Lectures on Psychoanalysis*. 4676 (1933), Internet Archive, https://ia802907.us.archive.org/17/items/SigmundFreud/Sigmund%20Freud%20%5B1933%5D%20New%20Introductory%20Lectures%20On%20Psychoanalysis%20%28James%20Strachey%20translation%2C%201961%29.pdf.

43 This spirit has been described as in a distinctively Platonic sense of θυμός as the power of noble wrath, which, unless perverted by a bad education, is naturally the ally of the reason, though as mere angry passion it might seem to belong to the irrational part of the soul, and so, as Glaucon suggests, be akin to appetite, with which it is associated in the mortal soul of the *Timaeus* 69 D. In Laws 731 BC Plato tells us again that the soul cannot combat injustice without the capacity for righteous indignation. The Stoics affected to deprecate anger always, and the difference remained a theme of controversy between them and the Platonists. *Cf.* Schmidt, Ethik der Griechen, ii. pp. 321 ff., Seneca, De ira, i. 9, and passim. Moralists are still divided on the point. *Cf.* Bagehot, Lord Brougham: "Another faculty of Brougham … is the faculty of easy anger. The supine placidity of civilization is not favorable to animosity [Bacon's word for θυμός]." Leslie Stephen, Science of Ethics, pp. 60 ff. and p. 62, seems to contradict Plato: "The supposed conflict between reason and passion is, as I hold, meaningless if it is taken to imply that the reason is a faculty separate from the emotions," etc. But this is only his metaphysics. On the practical ethical issue, he is with Plato. Plato, *Republic*, *in* Plato in Twelve Volumes, Vol. 5–6 439e n.11 (Paul Shorey trans., Harvard University Press 1969).

44 Available at http://www.perseus.tufts.edu/hopper/text?doc=Perseus%3Atext%3A1999.04.0094%3Abook%3D4%3Asection%3D439e

45 The Pervert's Guide to Cinema (Amoeba Film & Mischief Films 2006).

46 *Id.*

47 "The judicial Power of the United States, shall be vested in one supreme Court, and in such inferior Courts as the Congress may from time to time ordain and establish." US Const. art. III, § 1.

Further, Chief Justice Marshall in *Marbury v. Madison* stated, "the particular phraseology of the constitution of the United States confirms and strengthens the principle, supposed to be essential to all written constitutions, that a law repugnant to the constitution is void; and that courts, as well as other departments, are bound by that instrument." 5 US 137, 180 (1803).

48 "Federal judges in the United States, and many judges throughout the rest of the world, have life tenure because of the effect of a set of empirical beliefs about the consequences to judicial behavior of certain kinds of incentives. The Framers of the Constitution, for example, believed that judges who were freed of the desire for re-election would be in important ways independent." Frederick Schauer, *Incentives, Reputation, and the Inglorious Determinants of Judicial Behavior*, 68 U. Cin. L. Rev. 615, 636 (2000).

49 *Marbury*, 5 U.S. at 177.

50 163 U.S. 537 (1896).

51 349 U.S. 294 (1955).

52 163 U.S. 537.

53 163 U.S. at 537.

54 349 U.S. at 294.

55 347 U.S. 483 (1954).

56 347 U.S. 483, 491 (1954).

57 576 U.S. 644 (2015).

58 "See Erwin Chemerinsky, Rethinking State Action, 80 Nw. U. L. Rev. 503, 527–31 (1985) (discussing 'natural law' that 'predate[s] the creation of the state'); see also Obergefell v. Hodges, 135 S. Ct. 2584, 2594 (2015) (recalling the 'centrality of marriage to the human condition' that has existed for millennia)." Sonu Bedi, *An Illiberal Union*, 26 Wm. & Mary Bill Rts. J. 1081, 1153 (2018). See "The nine-page introduction to Senate Bill 752 makes mention of 'natural' marriage or law approximately twenty-five times. In the bill's framing, naturality is invoked as a means to challenge the Obergefell v. Hodges US Supreme Court decision, such as stating, 'WHEREAS, the decision in Obergefell purporting to overturn natural marriage flies in the face of reality, the created order, and the law of nature, just as if the Court were to claim authority to strike down the law of gravity or other natural laws.'" Antron D. Mahoney & Heather Brydie Harris, *When the Spirit Says Dance: A Queer of Color Critique of Black Justice Discourse in Anti-Transgender Policy Rhetoric*, 19 U. Md. L.J. Race Religion Gender & Class 7, 16 (2019).

59 James Boyd White, "What's an Opinion for?" *The University of Chicago Law Review* 62, 4 (1995): 1363–9. See Lawrence M. Friedman, "The Law and Society Movement." *Stanford Law Review* 38, no. 3 (February 1986): 763–80.

60 Richard Fallon, *The Dynamic Constitution* (2013).

61 Charles Fried, *Saying What The Law Is: The Constitution in the Supreme Court* (2004).

62 For a comparison of the two authors, "another, more conservative member of Rawls's posse, Fallon's colleague Charles Fried ... both Fried and Fallon believe that reasoning about constitutional doctrine is important in constitutional adjudication. For Fallon, doctrinal and precedential reasoning explicates the meaning of the constitutional text; for Fried, precedent shapes and determines constitutional doctrine and decision." André LeDuc, Book Review: Law and Legitimacy in the Supreme Court, Richard H. Fallon, Jr., 92 *S. Cal. L. Rev. Postscript* 39, 63 (2018).

63 Freud, *The Ego and the Id*, On Metapsychology pp. 363–4.

64 Sigmund Freud, *New Introductory Lectures on Psychoanalysis*. 4676 (1933), Internet Archive, https://ia802907.us.archive.org/17/items/SigmundFreud/Sigmund%20Freud%20%5B1933%5D%20New%20Introductory%20Lectures%20On%20Psychoanalysis%20%28James%20Strachey%20translation%2C%201961%29.pdf.

65 Freud, *The Ego and the Id*.

66 Eric Berne, A Layman's Guide to Psychiatry and Psychoanalysis (Penguin 1976) p. 96.

67 With its source of power from U.S. Const. art. II, § 1, cl. 1.

68 This chapter argues that the drive to engage in politics likely comes from the Freudian pleasure principle. "Existing theories struggle when political engagement is an end in itself. To explain intrinsically motivated engagement in politics, this study synthesizes psychological theories to deduce a need-based theory of political motivation. It posits that intrinsic political motivation has roots in seemingly apolitical processes of need satisfaction that are universal and deeply ingrained in the human psyche." Alexander Wuttke, "The Pleasure Principle: Why (some) People Develop a Taste for Politics: Evidence from a Preregistered Experiment." *Politics and the Life Sciences* 40, 1 (2021): 19–39.

69 Jacques Lacan describes such a tension as "different forms according to the way the subject deals with it. ... The aggressiveness involved in the ego's fundamental ... but upon the intrá-psychic tension we sense in the warning of the ascetic that 'a blow at your enemy is a blow at yourself.' This is true in all the forms of that process of negation." Jacques Lacan. "Some Reflections on the Ego." *The International Journal of Psycho-Analysis* 34 (1953): 11.

70 Jacques Lacan defines the ego in such a way in his Lacan, Jacques. *The Ego in Freud's Theory and in the Technique of Psychoanalysis, 1954–1955*. Vol. 2. WW Norton & Company, 1991.

71 *Cf.* John Freeman in his introduction to Carl Jung's *Man and his Symbols* writes that Jung's reinterpretation of Freud where Jung's "overwhelming contribution to psychological understanding is his concept of the unconscious—not (like the unconscious of Freud) merely a sort of glory-hole of repressed desires, but a world that is just as much a vital and real part of the life of an individual as the conscious, 'cogitating' world of the ego, and infinitely wider and richer. The language and the 'people' of the unconscious are symbols, and the means of communications dreams." Jung, Carl G. *Man and His Symbols.* Vol. 5183. Dell, 1968.

72 Sigmund Freud, *Introductory Lectures* 16.357. https://eduardolbm.files.wordpress.com/2014/10/a-general-introduction-to-psychoanalysis-sigmund-freud.pdf

73 Compare this with the concept of "Avoidance of value trade-offs. For an array of cognitive, emotional and social reasons, politicians find value trade-offs unpleasant and frequently define issues in ways that bypass the need for such judgments." Philip E. Tetlock, "Social Psychology and World Politics." *Handbook of Social Psychology* 2 (1998): 868–912.

74 Ryan C. Black and Ryan J. Owens, "Courting the President: How Circuit Court Judges Alter Their Behavior for Promotion to the Supreme Court." *American Journal of Political Science* 60, 1 (2016): 30–43.

75 Kathryn Dunn Tenpas, "Campaigning to Govern: Presidents Seeking Reelection." *PS: Political Science & Politics* 36, 2 (2003): 199–202.

76 David E. Lewis, "The Politics of Presidential Appointments." In *The Politics of Presidential Appointments.* Princeton University Press, 2010.

77 Sean Gailmard and John W. Patty, *Learning While Governing: Expertise and Accountability in the Executive Branch.* University of Chicago Press, 2012.

78 D. Theodore Rave, "Politicians as Fiduciaries." *Harvard Law Review* 126 (2013): 671–739.

79 Neal Kumar Katyal, "Internal Separation of Powers: Checking Today's Most Dangerous Branch from Within." *Yale Law Journal* 115 (2005): 2314.

80 G. Lawson, "The Rise and Rise of the Administrative State." *Harvard Law Review* 107, 6 (1994): 1231–54.

81 Louis Fisher, "The Korean War: On What Legal Basis Did Truman Act?" *American Journal of International Law* 89, 1 (1995): 21–39.

82 Either the President's power is diminished or canceled by a Supreme Court judicial opinion. Grand, Cara J. "Zivotofsky v. Kerry: Of Passports, Politics, and Foreign Policy Powers." Duke J. Const. L. & Pub. Pol'y Sidebar 10 (2014): 39.

83 Terry M. Moe and William G. Howell, "Unilateral Action and Presidential Power: A Theory." *Presidential Studies Quarterly* 29, 4 (1999): 850–73. See generally. James David Barber. *The Presidential Character: Predicting Performance in the White House.* Routledge, 2017.

84 Margaret R. Ferguson and Cynthia J. Bowling, "Executive Orders and Administrative Control." *Public Administration Review* 68 (2008): S20–S28. See Driesen, David M. "*President Trump's Executive Orders and the Rule of Law*." UMKC L. Rev. 87 (2018): 489.

85 With its power generally emanating from U.S. Const. art. 1, § 1.

86 Sigmund Freud, *New Introductory Lectures on Psychoanalysis* (PFL 2) p. 103.

87 James Strachey's introduction to *The Ego and the Id* provides "What is latent and only temporarily unconscious received the name of 'preconscious' and, from the systematic point of view, was brought into close proximity to the conscious." https://www.sas.upenn.edu/~cavitch/pdf-library/Freud_SE_Ego_Id_complete.pdf

88 Sigmund Freud, *On Metapsychology* pp. 192–207.

89 Indeed, this double meaning of the term unconsciousness could be confusing. As Starchy writes, "The double meaning of the term 'unconscious' undoubtedly involved disadvantages, though they were of little significance and were difficult to avoid. It has turned out, however, that it is not practicable to regard the repressed as coinciding with the unconscious and the ego with the preconscious and conscious. The speaker discussed the two facts which show that in the ego too there is an unconscious, which behaves dynamically like the repressed unconscious: the two facts of a resistance proceeding from the ego during analysis and of an unconscious sense of guilt." https://www.sas.upenn.edu/~cavitch/pdf-library/Freud_SE_Ego_Id_complete.pdf

90 In other words, "If consciousness is then the sum total of everything of which we are aware, preconsciousness is the reservoir of everything we can remember, all that is accessible to voluntary recall: the storehouse of memory. This leaves the unconscious area of mental life to contain all the more primitive drives and impulses influencing our actions without our necessarily ever becoming fully aware of them, together with every important constellation of ideas or memories with a strong emotional charge, which have at one time been present in consciousness but have since been repressed so that they are no longer available to it, even through introspection or attempts at memory." David Stafford-Clark, *What Freud Really Said* (1965).

91 The idea of whether a concept is unfalsifiable comes from Karl Popper's writing. Karl Popper, *The Logic of Scientific Discovery* 57–61 (Routledge 2002) (1935).

92 Bloom, Harold. *The Western Canon: The Books and School of the Ages*. Houghton Mifflin Harcourt, 2014.

93 *Id.*

94 The Federalist No. 47, at 301 (James Madison) (Clinton Rossiter ed., 1961).

95 Charles Lincoln, *The Dialectical Path of Law*, viii (2021).

7

A Dumézilian Trifunctionalist Analysis of the US Constitution

This chapter offers an interpretation of the US' structure of government outlined in the Constitution of 1789 from an anthropological perspective. Simultaneously this chapter seeks to analyze and explain the continued three-part structure of the US federal government as outlined in the Constitution. Subsequently, this chapter defines the three parts of the federal government—judiciary, executive, and legislative—as explained through the lens of the anthropologist Georges Dumézil's trifunctional hypothesis of the Proto-Indo-European paradigm of society. Dumézil's trifunctional hypothesis is broken into the following three functions: productivity, military, and sovereignty. This chapter aims to demonstrate that the productivity represents the legislative function, the military represents the executive function, and the sovereignty represents the judicial function in the US system of government. This chapter draws from a previous article by this author titled A Structural Etiology of the US Constitution.[1] *That article also provided a tripartite analysis of the US Constitution. However, the analysis in that article occurred through the lens of the Ancient Greek philosopher Plato's tripartite conception of the soul where (logos = word = law), (thumos = external driving spirit = executive), and (eros = general welfare = legislative) extrapolated from Plato's dialogues—primarily the* Republic *and* Phaedrus. *This chapter swerves from that interpretation on Plato's* Republic.

The structure of this chapter is as follows: First, this chapter establishes a working understanding of the French anthropologist Georges Dumézil's (1898–1986) trifunctional hypothesis of prehistoric Proto-Indo-European society that applied to Indo-European society universally. Dumézil's trifunctional theory is the major premise, as in a syllogism. Second, the chapter lays out the generally accepted division of the US Constitution of 1789 by laying out three parts to the federal government: the legislative as described in Article I, the executive as described in Article II, and the judicial as described in Article III. This second part represents the minor premise syllogistically. Third, the syllogism completes by weaving in the major premise of Dumézil's conception of the trifunctional hypothesis into the minor premise of the three parts of the US federal government. This third step of analysis suggests possible future evolution of the structure of the US federal government.

This chapter fits into the broader issue of the functionally efficient and naturally adaptive structure of the US federal government. Providing a historical and anthropological context to this structural analysis will serve as a framework for future research on the operation of the federal government. When the branches of the federal government step out of their roles, then the balance of the structure of the federal government becomes disrupted, occurring in liminal periods of paradigmatic change.

> Ambition must be made to counteract ambition. The interest of the man must be connected with the constitutional rights of the place. It may be a reflection on human nature, that such devices should be necessary to control the abuses of government. But what is government itself, but the greatest of all reflections on human nature? If men were angels, no government would be necessary. If angels were to govern men, neither external nor internal controls on government would be necessary. In framing a government which is to be administered by men over men, the great difficulty lies in this: you must first enable the government to control the governed; and in the next place oblige it to control itself.
>
> —James Madison or Alexander Hamilton, *Federalist Paper No. 51* (1788)

Introduction to Dumézilian Thought

This chapter argues that the tripartite system of government in the United States can be viewed through the Dumézilian trifunctional hypothesis. The major premise of this chapter is the definition and elements of the Dumézilian structure of the prehistoric Proto-Indo-European society as outlined in Georges Dumézil's anthropological hypothesis of a tripartite society found in Indo-European cultures. The minor premise of this chapter is that the US federal government has three major parts: the judiciary, the executive, and the legislative. The syllogism and argument of this chapter is that the three federal parts of US government represent the Dumézilian structure of anthropological prehistoric Proto-Indo-European society: the judiciary as the sovereignty, the executive as the military, and the legislative as the productivity. This chapter will explore these concepts in greater depth. As a corollary, when the anthropological etiology of the polity—arguably archetypal structure—becomes unbalanced, then people become dissatisfied with the government. This occurs because the government does not fulfill its function administratively—as in acting in opposition to the laws—and in promoting justice. However, sometimes overstepping a role in the Dumézilian structure of the polity is a necessary change.

Premises and Structures of Analysis

Assumed throughout this chapter is the acceptance of the premises Georges Dumézil wrote about and analyzed in his anthropological investigation into Proto-Indo-European society. Much of his anthropological writings have been critiqued to the satisfaction of the author.[2] Dumézil's accessible and readable style, along with his employment of the tripartite system, is the primary shared interest of this chapter. This chapter will rely significantly on secondary source written material by Covington Scott Littleton to interpret the primary material written by Dumézil. Specifically, it relies on *The New Comparative Mythology: An Anthropological Assessment of the Theories of Georges Dumézil* (1973),[3] as well as Claude Calame's *Myth and History in Ancient Greece: The Symbolic Creation of a Colony* (2003).[4]

Fundamentally, the validity of Dumézil's assertions is less interesting than the results that can come about from utilizing his paradigm of the tripartite system of society. Given that Dumézil's trifunctional hypothesis is not necessarily valid for its scientific accuracy but rather its interpretative value, this chapter is more an interpretation of the anthropological devices present in Dumézil's writings and analysis. The paradigm Dumézil provides in application to the structure of the US Constitution uses literary analysis to interpret legal principles.[5] Thus, Dumézilian anthropological analysis and thought provide one possible way to read the US Constitution. There may be many mutually exclusive ways to read the Constitution that are equally valid.[6] Likewise, it is just as important to focus on the primary sources of Dumézil's own writings to apply Dumézilian thought as an interpretative device. Thus, there is an even more important need to focus on the primary texts. Given that literature and stories can represent mythological constructs, such an analysis can ultimately have inverse implications for society and anthropology, not through the validity of Dumézil's claims but through the interpretative value it has.[7]

Furthermore, presumed throughout this chapter is that the world has an order based on a reason that reflects nature.[8] In connection with this foundational idea of an orderly and rational reflection of nature, Plato's *Timaeus* introduces the idea that nature is organized and thus comprehensible.[9] Relevant to Plato's substantive inquiry in the *Timaeus* order of nature, Plato inquires whether randomness or patterns are provable or real.[10] How do we even decide randomness exists if not through statistical or other mathematical analysis—namely, through inductive or deductive analysis?[11] Philosophically speaking, there could be a discrepancy between a series following a mathematical rule or being truly random. Ludwig Wittgenstein (an Austrian-born British philosopher)[12] in his *Philosophical Investigations* explained how randomness can really be explained in terms of the increasing complexity of following a rule.[13] But paradoxically, according to Mr. Wittgenstein,[14] if everything can be shown to be following a rule, it can also, at the same time, be shown not to follow a rule.[15] Wittgenstein says as much in the following way:

> This was our paradox: no course of action could be determined by a rule, because every course of action can be made out to accord with the rule. The answer was: if everything can be made out to accord with the rule, then it can also be made out to conflict with it. And so there would be neither accord nor conflict here. It can be seen that there is a misunderstanding here from the mere fact that in the course of our argument we give one interpretation after another; as if each one contented us at least for a moment, until we thought of yet another standing behind it. What this shews is that there is a way of grasping a rule which is not an interpretation, but which is exhibited in what we call "obeying the rule" and "going against it" in actual cases. Hence there is an inclination to say: every action according to the rule is an interpretation. But we ought to restrict the term "interpretation" to the substitution of one expression of the rule for another.[16]

The alternative to this presumption is that there is no order to the universe or world, and humans try to impose order onto it.[17] Lucretius in his *On the Nature of Things* introduced such a view.[18] Consequently, nature can represent itself in the structure of law, specifically the law of the United States.[19]

Why a Structured Approach at All? A Philosophical-Anthropological Explanation

To understand why it is appropriate to analyze and compare the US government with the anthropological Dumézilian conception of Proto-Indo-European society, it is helpful to have some understanding of the context of philosophical-anthropological thought related to such conception. The following paragraph is a brief overview of relevant historical analysis to provide context related to structural and "trifunctionalist" analysis.

Many philosophical-anthropological theories exist for understanding the basic structures of societies and governments, from Claude Lévi-Strauss[20] on structuralism theories,[21] to Michel Foucault[22] on the impetus behind government function,[23] and Marvin Harris[24] on the materialist gift-giving incentives in a society's structure.[25] Concurrently, the idea of a "tripartite" structure of society being inherent to human cultures is not new, having been written about extensively by Dumézil,[26] and discussed in Plato's dialogues regarding the soul.[27] Indicative of the universal nature of the "trifunctionalist" Dumézilian approach, it has even been applied to Pre-Columbian Yucatán Mayan societies.[28] Such an analysis of Mayan societies takes the universalist approach in Claude Lévi-Strauss's anthropological analysis and applies it, here, to Mayan society.[29] Poetically, in the Homeric Greek account of the Judgment of Paris, prior to the beginning of the Trojan War in Homer's *Iliad*, Paris of Troy is given a Dumézilian "choice." This choice takes the form of a beauty contest among three goddesses—Hera, Athena, and Aphrodite.[30] It seems fitting to apply the Ancient Greek concept of the Platonic Soul to governmental structure, because the "trifunctionalist" approach has origins in Ancient Greece but can also be identified in non-Western civilizations as well.[31]

A balanced view of government may exist in the separation of powers as Montesquieu laid out: "that of enacting laws, that of executing the public resolutions, and of trying the causes of individuals."[32] Exploring this thought "[i]n The Federalist No. 47, Madison explained that while Montesquieu was correct in saying that the separation of the legislative, executive, and judicial powers was essential to liberty, that conclusion did not purport to tell us how strict the resultant separation had to be."[33] This author suggested in a previous article that "[b]ased on their education, the framers of the Constitution may have even had Plato's Soul in mind when they framed the Constitution."[34]

Why Dumézil?

If one accepts the premises that structured and anthropological approaches are a reasonable mode of analysis of law, then why should one use Dumézil's approach specifically?

The idea of comparing a tripartite conception of the human society or mode of existence is not original. The idea of comparing the Platonic soul to the US federal system of government has previously been written about by Akiba Covitz in *The Soul of the Polity*.[35] With the executive as logos and the legislature as eros, Covitz argued that the judiciary is thumos.[36] This chapter greatly appreciates Covitz's theory and writing. The predecessor to this chapter on the Platonic interpretation of the US Constitution switched correspondences from thumos to logos for judiciary and logos to thumos for executive and maintains Covitz's conception of legislative as eros.[37] Covitz used a different terminology of (1) artifice; (2) nature; and (3) history/divinity/myth in lieu of logos, eros, and thumos, respectively.[38] Covitz argues that the Constitution had a psychoanalytic dimension, and these Platonic elements largely represented this psychoanalysis.[39]

Professor Covitz sincerely wanted to explore what a constitution is. He asked "*ti esti*" or "what is?" translated from Greek.[40] This is a classic question that drove the Ancient Greeks in their purely innocent love of searching for knowledge.[41] This chapter has sourced inspiration from such an inquiry.

The inquiry here is what anthropological characteristics can be extrapolated from the US Constitution using the Dumézilian paradigm of the human psyche. Ultimately, this is an experimental test that could lead to insights into the etiology or cause of the US Constitution from a teleological perspective, but not direct practical inquiries, much in the same way that in classical Graeco-Roman studies, myths frequently are used as an interpretation for why a specific custom existed in Ancient Greece or Roman antiquity.

In his *Myth and History in Ancient Greece: The Symbolic Creation of a Colony* (2003), Claude Calame drew on work by Georges Dumézil, arguing that the Ancient Greeks would not have viewed what we consider to be their mythology as fiction but rather the historical archeological basis of their society.[42] Likewise, the enshrining of the US Constitution carries some mythological status through its interpretation in popular culture.[43] The Framers of the Constitution and the Constitution carry a cult following despite a more abundant aggregation of resources reflecting the actual nature of the Constitutional Convention of 1787, compared to events in Ancient Greece.[44] However, regardless of whether such an event is fictional, its representation as an etiology for the subsequent events in US history is reasonable. Thus, analyzing the Constitution is much like investigating a myth brought down from antiquity. Additionally, it makes sense following the classical Graeco-Roman tradition of archeological analysis.

In returning to Covitz's initial inquiries of "what a constitution is," Covitz suggests an easy answer to these questions would be to "choose the Constitution of the United States and a more contemporary and more straightforward text (at least in terms of form) such as Locke's *Second Treatise on Government*, or Montesquieu's *Spirit of the Laws*."[45] But Professor Covitz sought "more than a deeper understanding of the American Constitution; [he sought] its beginnings."[46]

Covitz followed the path of answering these questions through Platonic dialogues because if one is to understand the beginning of the US Constitution, one must be familiar with not only the circumstances that gave its birth but also the great books that the authors of the Constitution read.[47] Covitz supports this point by writing, "[I]f one is to search out the theoretical beginnings of American constitutional thought, one must come to grips with the textual beginnings of the Western constitutional thought in which the American experience is itself framed."[48] This statement can be interpreted as the books and laws with which the Framers were most familiar. "[R]egardless of our views of Plato's tyrannical or democratic qualities [, i]mportant, underlying aspects of this broader realm of Western constitutional thought began in the dialogic pages and the constitutional theory of Plato's Republic."[49]

This chapter gained much inspiration from such inquiries. It seems reasonable, and in the spirit of Covitz's analysis, to pursue the Dumézilian paradigm. This analysis will extend beyond the works available to the Framers of the Constitution from 1789, specifically into the Dumézil trifunctionalist tradition.

Three Parts of the Federal Government

The Judiciary

The role of judiciary, in large part, is to follow syllogistic and logical application of the law as found in the idea of *stare decisis et non quieta movere*[50] to provide a system of legitimacy and predictability.[51] As the Ninth Circuit Court of Appeals stated, "Stare decisis is the policy of the court to stand by precedent; the term is but an abbreviation of stare decisis et non quieta movere—'to stand by and adhere to decisions and not disturb what is settled.'"[52]

However, pure syllogistic thinking manifested in stare decisis does not always occur. Justice Rehnquist, writing for the majority in *Payne v. Tennessee*, admits,

"*Stare decisis* is the preferred course because it promotes the evenhanded, predictable, and consistent development of legal principles, fosters reliance on judicial decisions, and contributes to the actual and perceived integrity of the judicial process."[53] Moreover, regarding policy, Rehnquist writes, "Adhering to precedent 'is usually the wise policy, because in most matters it is more important that the applicable rule of law be settled than it be settled right.'"[54] However, he claims "when governing decisions are unworkable or are badly reasoned, 'this Court has never felt constrained to follow precedent,'" meaning, in other words, "[*s*]*tare decisis* is not an inexorable command; rather, it 'is a principle of policy and not a mechanical formula of adherence to the latest decision.'"[55] He further indicates that not using *stare decisis* is "true in constitutional cases, because in such cases 'correction through legislative action is practically impossible.'"[56]

Rehnquist's opinion on *stare decisis* has been affirmed and restated in several Supreme Court opinions. Recently in *Johnson v. United States*, Justice Scalia wrote in the majority opinion, "The doctrine of stare decisis allows us to revisit an earlier decision where experience with its application reveals that it is unworkable," showing how experience can inform application of *stare decisis*.[57]

At first, this move away from purely logical application toward using "experience" may seem like a contradiction of the purely non-emotional and non-pleasure-seeking aspect of the ego in the Freudian psyche.[58] This move away from logical application is not akin to the *elegantia juris* using pure logic in law as envisioned by the Romans.[59] Rather, this move is more similar to Oliver Wendell Holmes's legal realism, where he writes in his book *The Common Law*, "The life of the law has not been logic: it has been experience."[60] In a separate article, Holmes critiqued Christopher Columbus Langdell's purely scientific and logical approach, suggesting that such a method eschews the emotional aspects of law.[61] Holmes suggested that Langdell:

> [C]ould be suspected of [not] ever having troubled himself about Hegel, [but] we might call him a Hegelian in disguise, [because] so entirely is he interested in the formal connection of things, or logic, as distinguished from the feelings which make the content of logic, and which have actually shaped the substance of the law.[62]

This mode of realism could come into action in judicial decisions, specifically with "sociological jurisprudence" proposed by Roscoe Pound, whereby courts could consider social factors in decision making.[63] Furthermore, Holmes wrote that even when decisions appear to be grounded in pure logical deductions, such decisions are just forms of policy; Holmes succinctly wrote:

> Perhaps one of the reasons why judges do not like to discuss questions of policy, or to put a decision in terms upon their views as law-makers, is that the moment you leave the path of merely logical deduction you lose the illusion of certainty which makes legal reasoning seem like mathematics.[64]

However, when one picks policy as a premise for making a logical argument, and then uses logic, the legal reasoning still mirrors or can pretend to be based purely in logic—even if such a decision reflects a chosen policy. Hence, the perceived "certainty is only an illusion, nevertheless," as Holmes stated.[65]

The Executive

A prime example of the outline of the definition of the executive branch's power is seen in *Youngstown Sheet & Tube Co. v. Sawyer*.[66] The case arose as a result of the steel strikes during the Korean War in the Truman administration.[67] President Truman sought to take executive control over the steel producers under the inherent powers doctrine.[68]

Writing for the majority opinion, Justice Black stated the presidential and executive power "must stem either from an act of Congress or from the Constitution itself."[69] The Court's majority opinion stated that the Court could not:

> [W]ith faithfulness to our constitutional system hold that the Commander in Chief of the Armed Forces has the ultimate power as such to take possession of private property in order to keep labor disputes from stopping production. This is a job for the Nation's lawmakers, not for its military authorities.[70]

Furthermore, the Court declared that "[i]n the framework of our Constitution, the President's power to see that the laws are faithfully executed refutes the idea that he is to be a lawmaker."[71] This holding's assertion means that the Constitution limits the executive's rulemaking force. Instead, the Court continues interpreting the Constitution so as to give power to the legislature to make rules:

> "All legislative Powers herein granted shall be vested in a Congress of the United States ..." After granting many powers to the Congress, Article I goes on to provide that Congress may "make all Laws which shall be necessary and proper for carrying into Execution the foregoing Powers, and all other Powers vested by

this Constitution in the Government of the United States, or in any Department or Officer thereof."[72]

Specifically in terms of the taking of private property for public use, the Court stated only Congress is authorized for "the taking of private property for public use."[73]

Finally—perhaps in originalist interpretation fashion—the Court declared:

> The Founders of this Nation entrusted the lawmaking power to the Congress alone in both good and bad times. It would do no good to recall the historical events, the fears of power and the hopes for freedom that lay behind their choice. Such a review would but confirm our holding that this seizure order cannot stand.[74]

In the concurring opinion, Justice Frankfurter wrote, "Loose and irresponsible use of adjectives colors all nonlegal and much legal discussion of presidential powers. 'Inherent' powers, 'implied' powers, 'incidental' powers, 'plenary' powers, 'war' powers and 'emergency' powers are used, often interchangeably and without fixed or ascertainable meanings."[75]

Discussing the separation of powers, Justice Frankfurter stated:

> The doctrine of the separation of powers was adopted by the Convention of 1787, not to promote efficiency but to preclude the exercise of arbitrary power. The purpose was, not to avoid friction, but, by means of the inevitable friction incident to the distribution of the governmental powers among three departments, to save the people from autocracy.[76]

In relation to the thumos, *Youngstown Sheet & Tube Co.* represents how the executive branch is limited in its functions of making laws, but it carries out these laws. The executive may resolve conflicts through agencies.[77]

Through the *Chevron* deference doctrine, the Supreme Court decided that "considerable weight should be accorded to an executive department's construction of a statutory scheme it is entrusted to administer, and the principle of deference to administrative interpretations."[78]

Justice Stevens wrote, "In the Clean Air Act Amendments of 1977 ... Congress enacted certain requirements applicable to States that had not achieved the national air quality standards established by the Environmental Protection Agency (EPA) pursuant to earlier legislation."[79] He continued, stating that, "[t]he amended Clean Air Act required these 'nonattainment' States to establish a permit program regulating 'new or modified major stationary sources' of air pollution."[80] Furthermore, the EPA required that plants comply with a certain level of conditions.[81] The issue of the case was "whether EPA's decision to allow States to treat all of the pollution-emitting devices within the same industrial grouping as though they were encased within a single 'bubble' is based on a reasonable construction of the statutory term 'stationary source.'"[82]

The Court reasoned that when reviewing an agency's construction of a statute, it must ask two questions.[83] The first question is "whether Congress has directly spoken to the precise question at issue. If the intent of Congress is clear, that is the end of the matter; for the court, as well as the agency, must give effect to the unambiguously expressed intent of Congress."[84] The second question arises if "Congress has not directly addressed the precise question at issue … the question for the court is whether the agency's answer is based on a permissible construction of the statute," meaning the court defers to an agency's interpretation.[85] If the agency does not have an interpretation, then the court would interpret the statute.[86]

The Court reasoned and "justified this new general rule of deference by positing that Congress has implicitly delegated interpretive authority to all agencies charged with enforcing federal law."[87] Indeed, "the decision [made] administrative actors the primary interpreters of federal statutes and relegated courts to the largely inert role of enforcing unambiguous statutory terms."[88]

The Legislative

With the example of the Eighteenth Amendment, Congress passed a law representing the *will* of portions of the country to not allow alcohol.[89] But it took the Twenty-First Amendment to realize that the Eighteenth Amendment did not accurately represent what people desired.[90] In a sense, the Eighteenth Amendment represented the soul of the polity going out of control.[91] This amendment was an unjust result, although deemed just at the time. Then Congress repealed it by deciding the Twenty-First Amendment was just and the Eighteenth unjust.[92]

The need to have rules of statutory interpretation indicates that there is a need to interpret often difficult-to-understand laws.[93] This need could be the effect of many things, such as quick drafting or the function of political maneuvering to gain enough votes.[94] Professor Gluck has pointed out that a large part of the problem with public outcry against the courts and the legislature is that the public does not have a clear idea of what the judiciary and the legislature should be doing:

> These moves have been grounded in a spectacular lack of theory about the role that courts should play in the legislative process itself—which is, after all, the fundamental constitutional question of the Court-Congress relationship

> in statutory cases. Should courts try to understand how Congress works, or is Congress too complex to understand? Should courts be "tough" on Congress, perhaps to incentivize Congress to draft better the next time, or should courts cut Congress some slack, and even correct enacted imperfections? Perhaps courts are best conceived as guardians of the US Code, obligated to shape increasingly imperfect statutes into a more coherent product for the public, no matter how disconnected that result may be from Congress's own intentions. The Court has long resisted definitively answering these basic questions, even as the most difficult statutory cases turn on them.[95]

The problem with the legislature not conforming to its theoretical role within the three branches of government has occurred in other branches as well, including the judiciary with the Supreme Court. Even "[t]he Warren Court understood the problems and the promises of politics from its own experience. The Court numbered among its members former senators, representatives, and state legislators, a former governor and a former mayor, and former cabinet members."[96]

Moreover, there does not seem to be a uniform system of interpreting statutes, despite its large importance for courts upholding the rules.[97] Others argue for adopting a uniform system of statutory interpretation.[98] There could be problems using different types of statutory analysis within courts because one method may work in one case, but not in another case; yet, the subsequent courts would be urged to use precedent from the former case.[99] Alternatively, others argue against a uniform system of statutory interpretation because such a system could lead to a rigid system of *stare decisis* for interpreting statutes.[100] However, despite several states having adopted "methodological" and "formalistic" *stare decisis*,[101] it is unclear whether the method produces equitable results.[102]

Although the legislatures have utmost formality, such as with Robert's *Rules of Order*[103] or Thomas Jefferson's *Manual of Parliamentary Practice*,[104] statutes that come from Congress are often unclear.

Dumézilian Trifunctionalist Theory

Welcome to the Dumézilian Trifunctionalist Anthropological Theory of Proto-Indo-European Society

Before understanding how the Dumézilian trifunctionalist theory functions within the United States federal government, a brief outline of Dumézilian conception of Proto-Indo-European society is required.

Dumézil originated this theory as a formulation in the field of anthropology, specifically within the study of comparative mythology.[105] Dumézil's key formulation is that Indo-European societies, starting with Proto-Indo-European societies, organize the realm of human social interaction into three functions.[106] Those three functions correspond to the religious, the warlike, and economic duties key for social organization.[107] Each of these functions operates separately.[108] This organization of human activity leads to a hierarchy.[109] The first function is the priestly function, which relates to the notions of the sacred but also relates to aspects of custom, law, and order.[110] The second function is the warlike function related to military activity and defense of society.[111] The third function is the productive function related to agricultural productivity.[112]

Mythological Examples of Dumézil's Trifunctional Hypothesis

Dumézil identifies the earliest manifestation of the tripartite distinction in Proto-Indo-European mythological constructs.[113] Each portion of society had a link to a god to represent that social group's function.[114] Dumézil identifies these functions in cross-mythological schemes.[115] Dumézil analyzes the myths as representations of the values in society, stating:

> These myths may be of diverse types. With respect to their origin, some are drawn from authentic events and actions in a more or less stylized fashion, embellished, and set forth as examples to imitate; others are literary fictions incarnating important concepts of the ideology in certain personages and translating the relations between these concepts into the connections between various figures. With respect to their settings and to the cosmic dimensions of the scenes, some are located outside the narrow confines and the few centuries of national experience; they adorn a remote past or future and inaccessible zones where gods, giants, monsters, and demons have their sport; others are content with ordinary men, with familiar places, and with plausible eras. But all these narratives have one and the same vital function.[116]

Such an idea is not unique to Dumézil.[117] Dumézil admits, "The comparative investigation of the oldest Indo-European civilizations which has been going on for about thirty years has had to take into account both this functional unity of the myths and this variety of mythic types." Interpreting myths or religion as a way to justify society relates to a long tradition of societal and anthropological analysis.

Dumézil writes on the importance of poetry and myth to justify the functions of society in the following way:

> "A land that has no more legends," says the poet, "is condemned to die of cold." This may well be true. But a people without myths is already dead. The function of that particular class of legends known as myths is to express dramatically the ideology under which a society lives; not only to hold out to its conscience the values it recognizes and the ideals it pursues from generation to generation, but above all to express its very being and structure, the elements, the connections, the balances, the tensions that constitute it; to justify the rules and traditional practices without which everything within a society would disintegrate.[118]

For the first function of the priestly activities, Dumézil identifies gods linked to Vedic India, the Mahābhārata, Norse Mythology, and Roman mythology. Dumézil compares all these Indo-European myths with each other, where "[t]he oldest son representing sovereignty and moral virtue as they are connected with … the Indo-European first function, is Yudhisthira, the son of … myth and epic: for instance, in Rome, Greece, and India."[119] Respectively, in Vedic India, the gods Mitra and Varuna relate to the priestly function of sovereignty relating to notions of sacred and magical activities.[120] Dumézil writes, "[a]t the first level of Vedic theology, the two principal sovereign gods, Varuna, the all-powerful magician, and Mitra, the contract personified, have created and organized the worlds, with their plan and their overall mechanisms."[121]

Professor C. Scott Littleton expands on Dumézil's idea, writing that at "[t]he first or most important function (i.e., the priestly stratum) … appear the sovereign gods, Mitra and Varuna."[122] The priestly function also relates to justice and notions of law as outlined in contracts.[123] Likewise, in the Mahābhārata, the hero Yudhishthira relates to the priestly function.[124] In the Norse mythological tradition, Odin and Týr relate to the priestly function of law and a connection to the notion of the mystical or magical.[125]

Roman mythology directly reinforces the idea of a tripartite system of the Archaic Triad of the divine Roman mythology, consisting of Jupiter, Mars, and Quirinus. Of the gods in the Archaic Triad, Jupiter is most closely associated with the sovereign function relating to law, justice, and the idea of the sacred.[126]

The second function deals with the military and defense of people relating to notions of physical activity and the idea of nobility. Dumézil notes that in Vedic India, the gods associated with this function are Indra and Vāyu.[127] Dumézil identifies the heroes Arjuna and Bhima as related to nobility and physical defense.[128] In Norse mythology, Dumézil identifies the god Thor as most closely related to the physical activity of warlike functions.[129] Finally, in the Roman pantheon, Mars in the Archaic Triad represents the warlike function.[130]

The third function relates to the idea of fertility in social activity. Specifically, this fertility function relates to farmers and agricultural activity[131] as well as to craftsmen and merchants. Likewise, in Vedic India, the two Ashvins relate to the fertility function.[132] In the Mahābhārata, the heroes Nakula and Sahadeva relate to the fertility function.[133] In Norse mythology, Dumézil identifies several gods related to the function of fertility. Those gods in the Norse mythological construct are Frey, Freyja,[134] Njord, and the gods Vanir.[135] In the Roman Archaic Triad, the god Quirinus relates to the fertility function.[136]

Ancient Rome as an Example of Dumézil's Trifunctional Hypothesis

Dumézil argues that Ancient Roman society provides a unique insight into the trifunctional hypothesis.[137] In Ancient Roman society, Dumézil identified three classes: the flamen, the Roman citizens, and the residents and slaves.[138]

In outlining the structure of Roman society from a Dumézilian anthropological perspective, the Italian historian and professor of Classical Antiquity, Arnaldo Momigliano, provides a unique insight into Dumézil's description of Ancient Rome and the three classes.[139] Donald Kagan, Sterling Professor of Classics and History Professor of Yale University, described Momigliano as "the world's leading student of the writing of history in the ancient world."[140] Momigliano's outline is particularly insightful because the goal of his work overall aims to critique Dumézil's theories.[141] Therefore, such an accurate reflection of Dumézil's writings is even more compelling before Momigliano criticizes them.

Dumézil identifies the flamen as the priests of the Ancient Roman religion.[142] The flamen did not have explicit political power.[143] In relation to the nature of the flamen's political authority, Professor Momigliano writes that "[i]n Ouranos-Varuna Dumézil studies the god of sovereignty, and in Flamen-Brahman he tackles the relation between priest and sacrifice at that precise point in which the priest acts in support of sovereignty." Historian Charles Goldeberg writes that the flamen's "duties severely curtailed or prohibited outright the ability of these priests to hold political office."[144] Yet at the same time, the flamen were those who managed and regulated the state-sponsored religion in Rome that helped legitimize the current regime of political power.[145] The emperors, including Octavian, would ask the priestly class to provide legitimacy to the new emperor's regime.[146]

Dumézil describes the Roman citizens as consisting of the second class.[147] Professor Momigliano discusses Dumézil's interpretation of the legends of Camillus and Coriolanus as preserving the trifunctionalist mentality.[148] The absence of the second function is deliberate because Coriolanus himself represents the second function.[149] Discussing the second class in Ancient Rome, Momigliano writes:

> [I]n his latest stage Dumézil attributes more importance to the legends of Camillus and Coriolanus, in both of which he recognizes the preservation of the trifunctional Indo-European mentality. Camillus and Coriolanus would be antithetic heroes: Camillus saves Rome, Coriolanus betrays Rome. In the episode of the siege of Rome by the Gauls, in which Camillus is ultimately involved as the savior, three episodes discourage the Gauls and give courage to the Romans. The geese repel the Gauls; the Romans throw bread from the besieged Capitol to show that they have plenty to eat; and a member of the Fabian gens goes down from the Capitol to fulfill religious duties and is not molested, which may be a miracle. In the attempt to persuade Coriolanus not to attack Rome, there is a sequence of three embassies: the first by Roman notables; the second by priests; the third by ladies, including Coriolanus's mother: needless to say, the success is with the Roman ladies, "matronae." Dumézil has no particular difficulty in showing that in the Camillus story the geese may represent the military function, the bread is evidently third function, and the godly Fabius who performs a sacrifice is first function par excellence. Things are not so simple for Dumézil in the story of Coriolanus because Dumézil is not prepared to admit that the first embassy of the notables represents the Roman army, that is the second function, while of course the priests and women of the other delegations easily fit the roles of the first and of the third function. Dumézil prefers to believe that both the first and the second embassy represent the first function in its bipartition of magic and law. Why then is the second function missing? Dumézil has a wonderful solution to his own difficulty. If the second function does not appear in the embassies it is because the second function was embodied in Coriolanus, and Coriolanus is now, so to speak, on the other side. Those who composed the legend of Coriolanus knew so much about the three functions that they could intentionally eliminate the second function from the embassies.[150]

However, the citizens of Rome did not mean residents of Rome.[151] To become a senator or an emperor in Ancient Rome, a person had to be a citizen.[152] Regarding eligibility of Roman citizenship, the American historian Bruce Bartlett writes that distinctions existed within Rome for government benefits and namely that "[e]ligibility consisted mainly of Roman citizenship, actual residence in

Rome, and was restricted to males over the age of fourteen. Senators and other government employees generally were prohibited from receiving grain."[153] A citizen in Ancient Rome meant a free man.[154] As Jane F. Gardner wrote, "[s]ome Roman citizens were in fact born free, but not as citizens, and these included not only free foreigners granted citizenship, but also freed slaves."[155]

Finally, the residents and noncitizens—often consisting of Roman slaves—were the third class.[156] In analyzing Dumézil's writings, Momigliano writes of the third class of Rome:

> [T]he recent views of Dumézil on Roman Law, contained in his book on *Mariages indo-europeiens*. In this work Dumézil partly depends on the late Lucien Gerschel, but has also received help at various stages from specialists of Roman Law of the eminence of the late Pierre Noailles and of Andre Magdelain. Dumézil argues that the three Roman forms of marriage (by *confarreatio*, by *usus*, and by *coemptio*), the three forms of testament (before the *comitia curiata*, *in procinctu*, and *per aes et libram*) and finally the three forms of manumission of slaves (*vindicta*, *censu*, and *testament*) reflect the trifunctional structure of Roman society with its Indo-European roots. Taken literally, this statement would mean that Roman society was divided into priests, warriors, and peasants and that each group had its own peculiar form of marriage, of testament, and of manumission of slaves. Thus the priests would marry by *confarreatio*, by sharing a sort of cake. They would make their testament at stated dates (perhaps twice a year) before the whole assembly of the *comitia curiata*, and would liberate their slaves by the complex and symbolic ceremony of the *vindicta*. The soldiers in their turn would marry informally by simple cohabitation (*usus*), would make their own testament in the presence of their own comrades just before a battle (*in procinctu*), and would free their slaves by inserting their names into the lists of Roman citizens during a *census*. The workers would buy their wives (*coemptio*), would make their testament in the form of a fictitious sale of their own property (*per aes et libram*), and would free their slaves by testament only. Of course, none of this is true, or almost none. It is possible that the marriage by *confarreatio* was originally confined to patricians; it was certainly not confined to priests. All the rest was anarchically left to individual choice. It was for the individual citizen to choose what form of testament he preferred. It is also obvious that the testament on the battlefield was an emergency measure for those who had not made a testament either before the *comitia curiata* or in the complex form of a fictitious sale. In later periods there were in fact even more than three forms of testament. Societies are apt to provide alternative forms of doing the same thing.[157]

Bartlett describes the conditions of this separate class by stating that "grain was available only to adult male Roman citizens, thus excluding the large number of women, children, slaves, foreigners, and other noncitizens living in Rome."[158] Here, Bartlett indicates that those who were not Roman citizens did not have as many rights as Roman citizens.[159] For this specific analysis of Roman history, Dumézil received criticism.[160] For example, Momigliano argued that such an understanding of Ancient Roman society was incorrect.[161] Such criticisms seem thorough, well thought out, concise, and germane. Again, this chapter does not argue that Dumézil's analysis is true or factually accurate.[162] Rather, this chapter hopes to deploy it as a useful heuristic in analyzing law, namely the US Constitution.

The End of Indo-European Trifunctionalism

Dumézil argued that the three functions of Indo-European society lasted naturally from the Middle Ages until 1789, when the French Revolution led to the abolishment of the tripartite Ancien Régime.[163] The Estates General had three formal class distinctions in the French kingdom at the time.[164] The clergy made up the First Estate.[165] The nobility consisted of the Second Estate.[166] The commoners formed the Third Estate.[167] These three Estates aligned perfectly with Dumézil's trifunctionalist hypothesis.[168] Dumézil argues that the Estates General of 1789 led to the end of the tripartite system.[169]

More recently, Thomas Piketty, the French economist,[170] adopted Dumézil's trifunctional approach in his *Capital and Ideology* (2019) book on wealth and income inequality in the modern world.[171] Piketty writes:

> In 1939, the anthropologist and linguist Georges Dumézil published *Mythes et dieux des Germains* (*Myths and Gods of the Germans*), an "essay of comparative interpretation," in which he analyzes the relationship of ancient German mythology to Indo-European religious concepts and representations. In the 1980s Dumézil was caught up in a nasty polemic in which he was accused of conniving with Nazis or at the very least participating in an anthropological justification of the warrior spirit said to have come from the East. In reality, he was a French conservative of monarchical leanings who could not really be accused of Hitlerist sympathies or Germanophilia. In his book on trifunctional ideology he sought to show that ancient Germanic myths were structurally unbalanced by hypertrophy of the warrior class and an absence of a true sacerdotal or intellectual class (in contrast to the Indian case, for example, where the Brahmins generally dominated the Kshatriyas).

> These references to trifunctional logics in the interwar years may seem surprising. Once again, they illustrate the need to make sense of structures of inequality and the way they evolve, in this case, through the emergence of a new warrior order in Europe. They also remind us that proprietarian ideology never really stopped trying to justify inequality in the trifunctional key. Europe's economic takeoff owed little to its virtuous and peaceful proprietarian institutions. … It owed much more to the ability of European states to maintain order to their advantage at the international level as they relied both on military domination and on their supposed intellectual and civilizational superiority.[172]

Reviewing Piketty's work in *The New Yorker* magazine, Idrees Kahloon writes, "[a]dopting a theory of the French philologist Georges Dumézil, Piketty writes that early societies were 'trifunctional'—in ways largely determined by birth, you were a member of the clergy, the warrior-nobility, or the peasantry."[173] Piketty further summarizes Dumézil's:

> [G]eneral thesis (founded on the analysis of ancient myths, a method that, as we saw in the case of India, is not always well suited to analyzing sociohistorical change and that tends to petrify supposed civilizational differences) was that Germano-Scandinavian myths and religions were excessively focused on the warrior cult and neglected the trifunctional equilibrium that one finds in both the Italo-Celtic and Indo-Iranian worlds.[174]

Kahloon points out that Piketty compares the notion of Dumézilian trifunctionalism as "similar, he notes, [as that which] can be seen in 'Planet of the Apes' and 'Star Wars.'"[175] Kahloon further identifies that Piketty notes that "[d]uring this period of limited mobility, inequality was justified by the notion that the castes were interdependent—like the limbs of the body."[176] Piketty's serious treatment of Dumézil's theories shows that such analysis is warranted and makes sense within the conception of constitutional interpretation.

Concurrently, a society has all three parts within itself. One might expect that such a society acts justly if all the parts of the society act as each is meant to act. This is not always so.

Summary of Dumézil's Theory of Trifunctionalism

The following is this author's summary of the structure of Dumézil's trifunctionalist hypothesis. Dumézil's trifunctional hypothesis across cultures is summarized in Table 7.1.

Table 7.1 Summary of Dumézil's Trifunctional Hypothesis across Cultures

	First	Second	Third
	Priestly—Sovereign Function	Warlike—Military Function	Productivity—Fertility Function
Vedic India	Mitra & Varuna	Indra & Vāyu	The two Ashvins
Mahābārata	Yudhishthira	Arjuna & Bhima	Nakula & Sahadeva
Norse Mythology	Odin & Týr	Thor	Freyr, Freyja, Njord, & the gods Vanir
Roman Mythology—focusing on the Archaic Triad	Jupiter	Mars	Quirinus
Estates of the *Ancien Régime*	First Estate (clergy)	Second Estate (nobility)	Third Estate (commoners)
Ancient Rome	Flamen	Roman citizens	Roman residents

Freudian Psychoanalysis as an Example of Dumézil's Trifunctional Hypothesis

Sigmund Freud was an Austrian neurologist known as the founder of psychoanalysis.[177] Freud developed a paradigm that divides the human psyche into three parts.[178] Winfried Brugger, the Professor of Public Law, Philosophy of Law and Theory of State at Heidelberg University in Germany, outlined the Freudian psyche and its philosophical basis in the following way:

> According to Kant, humans are influenced but not necessarily determined by their urges and inclinations, which is why they can and should be responsive to social and legal norms that can be scrutinized and approved of by everyone concerned, using the categorical imperative. Thus, according to Kant, humans have the task to discipline, cultivate, civilize, and moralize their empirical inclinations. Psychoanalysis is one of the disciplines that has systematized the main drift of these ideas. Sigmund Freud speaks of the configuration of the human psyche in the categories of Id, Ego, and Super-Ego. The Id is our animalistic nature pressuring the ego "from below," representing our most basic human needs and their desire for satisfaction. The norms and ideals of what is beautiful, good, just, and transcendent, herald "from above," visually and metaphorically speaking.

These highest ideals—fostered in all individuals through their socialization and enculturation—expand or delimit the basic needs "from below" and turn the human eye "forward" toward the future.[179]

Freud wrote that the psyche (ψυχή) consists of three parts: the ego (the more logical and self-sustaining force),[180] the super-ego (the force often pressing down as a sort of moral force),[181] and the id (the more emotional and erotically chaotic part of the psyche).[182] Regarding the super-ego, Freud wrote:

> [A] child's super-ego is in fact constructed on the model not of its parents but of its parents' super-ego; the contents which fill it are the same and it becomes the vehicle of tradition and of all the time-resisting judgments of value which have propagated themselves in this manner from generation to generation.[183]

Concurrently, a person has all three parts within themselves and acts justly if all the parts of the psyche act as they are supposed to act.[184] If each part of the psyche and each part of the polity or political union conduct their activities according to their mode of existence, then the person could reach some psychological stability in their mind.[185]

Essentially, the Freudian psyche overall consists of three parts: the ego, id, and super-ego. Each part represents a key part of the human mind's psyche for Freud, and each part works in conjunction with the other parts and is essential for their healthy functioning. In a sense, a balance must exist between all three parts.

Arguably, the most vivid and compelling artistic representation of Freud's paradigm comes from the philosopher and psychoanalytic social critic Slavoj Žižek's interpretation from his 2009 documentary titled *The Pervert's Guide to Cinema*.[186] Of the three layers of the house in Alfred Hitchcock's 1960 movie from golden age classic Hollywood cinema, *Psycho*,[187] he observes that the main house in *Psycho* has three levels and contends that each level corresponds a part of the human psyche postulated by Freudian psychoanalysis.[188] According to Žižek, the top floor represents the super-ego, where Norman Bates' mother resides entirely in the movie; the ground floor represents the Freudian ego, where all the normal-seeming activity of the movie occurs; and the basement/fruit cellar represents the id, where the mother's corpse is finally discovered in the film.[189] Žižek describes the id as the reservoir of emotions and chaos.[190] In the movie, Bates moves his mother's corpse from the top floor to the cellar.[191] He further suggests this represents a deep connection in Freudian psychoanalysis between the id and super-ego.[192] Then, he proposes this connection exists because the super-ego usually represents a pressing and controlling force on the psyche but often in terms of "obscenity."[193] Žižek supports this connection of the super-ego and the id by observing the somewhat "obscene" language the mother uses to command Bates to act in a way that fulfills the needs of the id.[194] Thus, the three levels of the Bates house in Hitchcock's *Psycho* as described by Žižek in *The Pervert's Guide to Cinema* arguably represent the most accurate depiction of the Freudian paradigm of the psyche in the human mind.

Fundamentally, the validity of Freud's assertions is less interesting than the results that can come about from utilizing his paradigm of the psyche. Given that Freudian psychoanalysis is not necessarily valid for its scientific accuracy but rather its literary value, this chapter is more an interpretation of the literary devices present in Freud.

Moreover, it is clear that Dumézil himself did not see the trifunctional analysis as going beyond Indo-European society. On the other hand, Freud wrote of his psyche as applying universally to all individuals regardless of society.[195]

As articulated in the introduction of a 1973 translation of Dumézil's work, C. Scott Littleton summarizes the three Dumézilian functions in the following way:

> As presently formulated, the salient features of this model can be summarized as follows: The common Indo-European ideology, derived ultimately from one characteristic of the Proto-Indo-European community, was composed of three fundamental principles: (1) maintenance of cosmic and juridical order, (2) the exercise of physical prowess, and (3) the promotion of physical well-being. Each of these principles forms the basis for what Dumézil terms a fonction, or "function": that is, a complex whole that includes both the ideological principle itself and its numerous manifestations in the several ancient Indo-European social and supernatural systems. The first function was thus expressed in the presence of distinct priest classes (e.g., the Indic Brahmans), which inevitably stood at the apex of their respective social systems and which were collectively represented, in the Durkheimian sense, by a pair of sovereign gods, such as Mitra and Varuna in Vedic India, Jupiter and Dius Fidius at Rome, and Odin and Týr in ancient Scandinavia. Moreover, there was a clear division of labor between these two co-sovereigns: one, let us call him the "Varuna figure," had charge of cosmic matters, the other, who may be termed the "Mitra figure," was principally concerned with the maintenance of proper juridical relationships among men. Together they stood at the apex of the supernatural system, just as the priests were at the top of the social hierarchy.[196]

Littleton continues focusing on the second function, providing that through a comparative mythological approach:

> The second function was reflected in the presence of a warrior-class, such as the Indic Kşatriyas, whose basic role was to exercise force in defense of the society (or to further its imperialistic ambitions), as well as in the collective representations of this class, such great Vedic warrior divinity Indra, the Roman god Mars, and the Norse war god Thor. The third function was reflected by the society, the herders and cultivators upon whom the priests triors depended for their sustenance (e.g., the Indic Vaiśyas); the principle was collectively represented by yet another stratum of divinities. In the majority of cases the principal occupants of this third divine stratum were conceived as a pair of closely related kins-men, the most usual relationship being that of a set of twins? (e.g., the Greek Dioscuri, the Vedic Aśvins).[197]

Littleton's analysis that only focuses on Indo-European society should not limit our analysis. As indicated earlier, there has been scholarship in applying Dumézilian trifunctionalism to Pre-Columbian Yucatán Mayan societies—a society with no recognizably common roots with Indo-European culture and society given the divide of the Americas and no connection between Asia and the Americas.[198] Likewise, taking a universalist approach is in line with Claude Lévi-Strauss's anthropological analysis and to Mayan society.[199] In such a manner, it seems feasible to at least compare Freud's theories with Dumézil's theories. Given that there exists scholarship applying Dumézil's trifunctionalist theories more universally, such analysis does not amount to using numerology, where all theories with three parts relate. Rather, such analysis consists of taking like ideas and comparing them.

Analogously, the super-ego could be seen as the Dumézilian first function. Like the ego that provides a type of morality, the priestly function can be seen as the purveyor of morality in the community and operated as the most educated class.[200] Furthermore, this class worked with the written word more than any other class.[201]

For the second function, the ego seems most closely associated with the conception of the warlike and military function. The super-ego often is based on forces and morality that help sustain an individual. Much like warlike and military functions focus on winning military engagements, the super-ego operates in a similar manner to sustain the individual.

For the third function, the id appears to be the most consistent force in providing for fertility. In the Freudian conception of the soul, the id relates to

Table 7.2 The Freudian Tripartite Psyche as a Reflection of Dumézil's Trifunctional Hypothesis

	First	Second	Third
	Priestly—Sovereign Function	Warlike—Military Function	Productivity—Fertility Function
Freudian Psychoanalytic Tripartite *Psyche*	Super-ego	Ego	Id

the more emotional and erotically chaotic parts of the psyche.[202] Likewise, these erotic feelings most closely resemble the production and agrarian society. Such a comparison does not perfectly fit with the Freudian and Dumézilian theories. However, by process of elimination and by process of the most comparability in the ideas, the cohesion of the third function and the notion of the Freudian id most closely resembles each other. The relationship between the Freudian tripartite psyche and Dumézil's trifunctional hypothesis is summarized in Table 7.2.

Plato's Soul as an Example of Dumézil's Trifunctional Hypothesis

In parallel to Dumézilian thought, the Platonic soul (ψυχή) consists of three parts: the λογιστικόν (logical), the θυμοειδές (thumotic/spirit), and the ἐπιθυμητικόν (appetitive/erotic). Each part represents an integral part of how societies function anthropologically. But a balance between the parts is necessary for justice to exist.

Specifically, in relation to the military function, the logos (λογιστικόν)[203] in the Platonic sense represents the part of the soul that loves knowledge and the search for knowledge.[204] It emphasizes the moral calculation of consequences, as opposed to "blind passion."[205] This idea can be compared to the section in the Platonic dialogue *Phaedrus* where "Socrates compares the soul to a charioteer who controls two horses—one white and docile, the other black and intemperate. These three figures echo the division of the soul into reason, emotion, and appetite in Book IV of the Republic."[206] The charioteer is logos, keeping control of the two horses.

Compared to the Platonic paradigm, the productivity or fertility function is eros. Eros, in the Platonic sense, represents what Socrates says is "that with which it loves, hungers, thirsts, and feels the flutter and titillation of other desires, the irrational and appetitive—companion of various repletions [*sic*] and pleasures."[207] This, too, seems akin to Freud's conception of the id. Thus, it gives further credence to the theory that the Platonic conception of the soul and Freud's structure of the psyche run in tandem with Dumézil's anthropological analysis of Indo-European society. This author has written previously about the parallel nature of the Platonic system of the soul in relation to the US Constitution.[208]

In the Platonic conception of the soul, the Dumézilian priestly function compares most closely with thumos, which represents the "spirit" unifying with the logos but resisting the erotic part of the soul.[209] This spirit has been described in a:

> [D]istinctively Platonic sense of θυμός as the power of noble wrath, which, unless perverted by a bad education, is naturally the ally of the reason, though as mere angry passion it might seem to belong to the irrational part of the soul, and so, as Glaucon suggests, be akin to appetite, with which it is associated in the mortal soul of the *Timaeus* 69 D. In Laws 731 BC Plato tells us again that the soul cannot combat injustice without the capacity for righteous indignation. The Stoics affected to deprecate anger always, and the difference remained a theme of controversy between them and the Platonists. *Cf.* Schmidt, Ethik der Griechen, ii. pp. 321 ff., Seneca, De ira, i. 9, and passim. Moralists are still divided on the point. *Cf.* Bagehot, Lord Brougham: "Another faculty of Brougham … is the faculty of easy anger. The supine placidity of civilization is not favorable to animosity [Bacon's word for θυμός]." Leslie Stephen, Science of Ethics, pp. 60 ff. and p. 62, seems to contradict Plato: "The supposed conflict between reason and passion is, as I hold, meaningless if it is taken to imply that the reason is a faculty separate from the emotions," etc. But this is only his metaphysics. On the practical ethical issue he is with Plato.[210]

Again, Freud's conception of the super-ego is something that is passed down from a person's parents. Thus, it represents a societal force brought down to an individual level into the psyche, similar to that of the Dumézilian priestly function representing and passing down the morals of society. Often these morals passed by the priestly function are those that are most materialistically relevant and practically valuable for society to support the effective and efficient functioning of society. Table 7.3 summarizes below.

A Summary and Examples to Support Dumézil's Trifunctionalist Hypothesis

So far, this section of the chapter explored Dumézil's trifunctionalist hypothesis. This section provides the evidence that Dumézil wrote and found

Table 7.3 Plato's Tripartite Soul as an Expression of Dumézil's Trifunctional Hypothesis

	First	**Second**	**Third**
	Priestly—Sovereign Function	Warlike—Military Function	Productivity—Fertility Function
Plato's Conception of the Soul in *The Republic* & *Phaedrus*	Thumos	Ego	Eros

Table 7.4 Comparative Summary of Dumézil's Trifunctional Hypothesis and Parallel Theories

	First	**Second**	**Third**
	Priestly—Sovereign Function	Warlike—Military Function	Productivity—Fertility Function
Vedic India	Mitra, Varuna	Indra & Vāyu	The two Ashvins
Mahābārata	Yudhishthira	Arjuna & Bhima	Nakula & Sahadeva
Norse Mythology	Odin & Týr	Thor	Freyr, Freyja, Njord, & the gods Vanes
Roman Mythology—focusing on the Archaic Triad	Jupiter	Mars	Quirinus
Estates of the *Ancien Régime*	First Estate (clergy)	Second Estate (nobility)	Third Estate (commoners)
Ancient Rome	Flamen	Roman citizens	Roman residents
Theories in addition to Dumézil's theories			
Freudian Psychoanalytic Tripartite *Psyche*	Super-ego	Ego	Id
Plato's Conception of the Soul in *The Republic* and *Phaedrus*	Thumos	Ego	Eros

for the trifunctionalist hypothesis. Dumézil's evidence included his analysis of mythology from various Indo-European sources.[211] The author added two other tripartite theories, namely those of Plato's soul and Freud's psychoanalytic theories. Both Freud's and Plato's theories mirror each other.

Table 7.4 represents the theories outlined so far in the chapter as they parallel each other.

Comparing the Structure of the Federal Government to the Dumézilian Trifunctionalist Conception of Indo-European Society

The Judiciary as the Dumézilian First Function

The judiciary[212] in this chapter's paradigm represents the Dumézilian first function. As Chief Justice Marshall stated in *Marbury v. Madison*:

> [T]he particular phraseology of the constitution of the United States confirms and strengthens the principle, supposed to be essential to all written constitutions, that a law repugnant to the constitution is void; and that courts, as well as other departments, are bound by that instrument.[213]

The judicial function is outlined in Article III of the US Constitution. Article III provides that "[t]he judicial Power of the United States, shall be vested in one supreme Court, and in such inferior Courts as the Congress may from time to time ordain and establish."[214] Article III judges—as intended by the Framers of the Constitution—were not and are not politicians seeking re-election. But rather, judges are aloof from the political system, seeking to interpret, apply, and provide rationality for the law. Such a description of modern judges appears similar to the description of the flamen priestly class in Ancient Rome. Moreover, like the flamen chiefly dealing with written words and the word as manifested in religion, so, too, does the judiciary function. This logical analysis—which can be informed with the other elements of the soul—is the guiding principle of the judiciary. The judiciary represents the first function.

Cases and Examples Showing Why the Judiciary Represents the Dumézilian First Function

Dumézil represents the first function as that which interprets what is needed to maintain the consistency of the society. Likewise, Chief Justice Marshall said, "it is emphatically the province and duty of the judicial department to say what the law is."[215] The Supreme Court uses judicial review and interprets the Constitution and legislatively passed statutes to keep them in check, much like the analogy of the rider being the ego in Plato's *Phaedrus*.

When constituent parts of the first function become imbalanced, then unjust results arise, such as *Plessy v. Ferguson*.[216] However, imbalance and stepping out of a role in the separate powers may lead to more just and fair results, such as *Brown v. Board of Education*.[217]

In *Plessy v. Ferguson*,[218] the Supreme Court stepped out of its judicial authority and took on a legislative function, but with an unjust result. The Court declared that a "State, shall provide equal but separate accommodations" for members of different races.[219]

In *Brown v. Board of Education*,[220] the Supreme Court stepped out of its judicial authority and took on a legislative function—in other words, the Supreme Court legislated from the bench—but with a just result. In *Brown v. Board of Education*, the Court noted that "[t]he doctrine of 'separate but equal' did not make its appearance in this Court until 1896 in the case of *Plessy v. Ferguson* ... involving not education but transportation,"[221] showing that the Court in *Plessy* stepped out of its mode of *stare decisis* and made law based on no previous law.

More recently, in *Obergefell v. Hodges*,[222] the Supreme Court took on a legislative role in deciding the case, as Professor Kenji Yoshino writes:

> While Obergefell's most immediate effect was to legalize same-sex marriage across the land, its long-term impact could extend far beyond this context. To see this point, consider how much more narrowly the opinion could have been written. It could have invoked the equal protection and due process guarantees without specifying a formal level of review, and then observed that none of the state justifications survived even a deferential form of scrutiny. The Court had adopted this strategy in prior gay rights cases.[223]

Professor Laurence Tribe supports this position by stating:

> Professor Kenji Yoshino's splendid Comment makes clear just how misguided these glib detractions are, and eloquently elaborates the important doctrinal work done by Justice Kennedy's decision, which represents the culmination of a decades-long project that has revolutionized the Court's fundamental rights jurisprudence. As Yoshino demonstrates, *Obergefell* has definitively replaced *Washington v. Glucksberg*'s wooden three-prong test focused on tradition, specificity, and negativity with the more holistic inquiry of Justice Harlan's justly famous 1961 dissent in *Poe v. Ullman*, a mode of inquiry that was embodied in key opinions from the mid-1960s to the early 1970s.[224]

Over time, society may come to a consensus on whether the Court decided any case correctly or incorrectly, but such cases currently serve as an example of a Court decision stepping out of the bounds of the role of the judiciary and acting in a legislative capacity with an unclear or clear result of justice.

Although ideally the Court would follow the first function, the catch is that the members of the Court are not purely guided by the first function. In the Freudian conception, the idea of a three-part psyche may be intended to understand the basic functions of an aspect of government, each member has an entire psyche governing their mind. This leads to more nuanced decisions, not only in the judiciary but in all three branches of the government.

Justice from the judiciary comes in various forms. In this instance, the Dumézilian first function likely guides to just results by keeping emotional aspects in check. Here, the judiciary is represented through the Dumézilian second function, functioning as a repressive force to keep emotions in check.

The Executive as the Dumézilian Second Function

In this chapter, the executive[225] represents the Dumézilian second function. Analogous to the ego in the Freudian structure that represents a societal force that represses the desires of the id, but through mediation of the super-ego. Likewise, the Dumézilian second function operates to stabilize and provide a force that governs society. In the same way, the executive branch of government provides a way to stabilize society and support sovereignty. In this manner, the president is a type of Dumézilian first function, where the president supports the notions of sovereignty in the country.

As such, the function of the executive indicates that one will likely turn to politics while in the tension of the Dumézilian first function, the judiciary, and the second function. In this sense, the most widely known politician nationwide is usually the president.[226] In Freudian terms, the ego is a force that mediates between the two opposing elements of the id and the super-ego. As such, the ego is more akin to the President, rather than a member of the judiciary, who, in all likelihood, is in search of honors and recognition, much like other politicians. Such recognition of a politician's psyche is not necessarily a negative characteristic for the executive. If the executive of the country did not seek honor or maintain some haughtiness, other politicians and world leaders would take advantage. As president, one must be a decisive president, not merely following the dictates of another Dumézilian function but operating as that of the Dumézilian second function. Yet, each function operates within the context of the other Dumézilian functions.

Cases and Examples Showing Why the Executive Represents the Dumézilian Second Function

Here, the Dumézilian second function manifests itself where a part of the executive branch of government, such as the EPA, would interpret a statute from the legislature and implement it. This occurs through the rules laid out by the Supreme Court and the judiciary, as seen in the *Chevron* case.

Frequently, the president issues executive orders.[227] Conversely, Courts of Appeals frequently declare the executive orders unconstitutional. Regardless of whether the executive orders are eventually upheld as constitutional, they represent the executive branch acting within the justification that executive orders are in line with societal values as solutions to various problems. In this sense, executive orders act as a Dumézilian second function, giving legitimacy to an action. If the orders are upheld as constitutional, then the judiciary or the legislature will deem them to have been the most effective approach at the time to avoid a greater disaster later. If the orders are not upheld to be constitutional, then the judiciary or the legislature will have deemed them not the most effective approach at the time.

Because the executive, and the legislature, in certain contexts, are charged with carrying out the daily activities of the nation, international relations, between spirited leaders who repress the immediate instincts of pleasure, are of paramount importance. This spirited leadership is represented by the Dumézilian third function. Thus, the leadership and executive actions may or may not be based on the Dumézilian first or third function, but through the regulating force of the Dumézilian second function, which this chapter argues fits into the paradigm of the executive branch of government in the US Constitution.

The Legislature as the Dumézilian Third Function

In this chapter, the legislature[228] represents the third function. The Dumézilian third function represents the part of society most closely associated with productivity and agricultural production. In theory, Congress acts according to the will of the people and is the closest interaction most of the population can have with the three main branches of government—arguably other than through taxation that the legislature has and the authority to collect taxes in the executive branch. Thus, many proposals in Congress can represent more emotional responses to issues. Some proposals are passed, and some of those passed proposals are thwarted by the other branches of government.

One of the most difficult things to discern is the legislative intent of a Congressional act. Much like the Dumézilian third function, an act of Congress can exhibit contradictory aims at the same time.

Table 7.5 Mapping the US Federal Government onto Dumézil's Trifunctional Hypothesis

Category	US Branch of Government	Dumézilian Trifunctionalist Category
Functionality Division	Judiciary	First Function—Priestly—Sovereignty
	Executive	Second Function—Warrior—Military
	Legislative	Third Function—Farmers/Commoners/Tradesmen—Productivity

Summary of the Parallel Comparison of the Dumézilian Three Functions

Table 7.5 summarizes the comparison of the Dumézilian functions as compared to the three parts of the US federal government.

Conclusion

This chapter interprets the problems and eventual purpose of the US government, while simultaneously explaining its continued existence, by analyzing its three-part structure as outlined in the Constitution. Through the lens of the Dumézilian structural paradigm of anthropological prehistoric Proto-Indo-European society, this chapter subsequently interprets all three parts of the government: the judiciary being the sovereignty, the executive being the military, and the legislative being the productivity. The major premise of the chapter is Dumézil's tripartite structure of society. The minor premise of the chapter is the three-part structure of the US government. The syllogism is the analysis in the chapter that attempts to show how each part of the Dumézilian anthropological model represents itself in the three branches of the federal government: the judiciary as the first function, the executive as the second function, and the legislative as the third function.

Overall, this Dumézilian anthropological analysis of the Constitution's structure and function could add to the dialogue of Constitutional analysis. There are arguments for living constitution, purposivism in constitutional interpretation, and political process theory, but there also seems to be a basis for a Dumézilian interpretation of the Constitution. In line with balanced societal notions of the polity and a balanced government, each part of government would not reach into another's duties in line with the outline of Federalist No. 47.[229]

Returning to the parallel analogy of Freudian psychoanalysis, there could be parallels in thought that inform each theory respectively. As Freud outlined his theory, each person has the three parts of the psyche. Although an individual may act in one part of the federal government, each person has all three parts of the Freudian structure operating within their psyche. Thus, it is to be expected that different parts of the psyche would manifest in a different part of the federal government from various individuals.

Regardless of the correct formulation of the Dumézilian paradigm, there is an archetype of government that seems suited for long-term existence. Plato touched upon this archetype, and perhaps Freud illuminated it in the individual sense through his theory of psychoanalysis.[230] From a Freudian perspective, it is fair to say that the best government, at least in part, represents the individual or the psyche of the individual. Likewise, it seems fair to say that a firm structure of society or government in Dumézilian terms appears to function in accord with a Jungian archetype of government, based on the studies of one of Freud's students, Carl Jung. The topic of a Jungian archetype or other archetypal type of government would fall into the scope of a different chapter and further research.

Notes

1 Charles Lincoln, *A Structural Etiology of the US Constitution*, 43 Notre Dame J. Legis. 122 (2016).

2 For example, in correspondence with Jaan Puhvel about his book *Epilecta Indoeuropea*, Puhvel wrote that the notion of a trifunctionalist Constitution "has some passing interest as a potential relic of engrained formulaic structure coinciding with inherent triplicity." Email from Jaan Puhvel, Professor of Classics, UCLA, to author (January 9, 2023, 04:11:22 CST) (on file with author).

3 C. Scott Littleton, *The New Comparative Mythology: An Anthropological Assessment of the Theories of Georges Dumézil* (University of California Press ed., 1973).

4 Claude Calame, *Myth and History in Ancient Greece: The Symbolic Creation of a Colony* (Princeton University Press, trans., Daniel W. Berman, 2003).

5 Lincoln, *supra* note 1, at 122.

6 In the author's view, the equally valid, yet mutually exclusive, interpretations make the Constitution a great text in the spirit of the Great Books series of Mortimer J.

Adler and Robert M. Hutchins, *Great Books of the Western World* (Robert Maynard Hutchins et al. eds., Chicago: Encyclopaedia Britannica, Inc., 1952).

7 *See generally* Charles Lincoln, *A Brief Historical Sketch of an Anthropological Analysis of the Development of International and Comparative Law*, 19 FLA. COASTAL L. REV. 221, 225 (2019) (approaching legal analysis through anthropological principles); Charles Edward Andrew Lincoln IV, *A Literary Lens into Constitutional Interpretation and a Possible Synthesis of Natural and Positive Law: The Silmarillion*, 41 MITCHELL HAMLINE L.J. PUB. POL'Y & PRAC. 101, 103–6 (2020) (analyzing the law through the lens of literary traditions).

8 *See generally* cicero, *De Republica* (James E.G. Zetzel ed., Cambridge University Press, 1995) (c. 54 B.C.).

9 Plato, *Timaeus and Critias 18–19* (Oxford University Press, Inc. ed., Robin Waterfield trans. 2008) (c. 360 B.C.).

10 For questions dealing with the notion of whether the demiurge (Ancient Greek: δημιουργός (*dēmiourgós*) to be interpreted as the handicraftsman creator of the universe) made the universe in order or in chaos, see *id.* at 16–18.

11 *Id.*

12 Ludwig Wittgenstein, in full Ludwig Josef Johann Wittgenstein (born April 26, 1889, Vienna, Austria-Hungary [now in Austria]—died April 29, 1951, Cambridge, Cambridgeshire, England):

> Wittgenstein is an Austrian-born British philosopher, regarded by many as the greatest philosopher of the twentieth century. Wittgenstein's two major works, *Logisch-philosophische Abhandlung* (1921; *Tractatus Logico-Philosophicus*, 1922) and *Philosophische Untersuchungen* (published posthumously in 1953; Philosophical Investigations), have inspired a vast secondary literature and have done much to shape subsequent developments in philosophy, especially within the analytic tradition. His charismatic personality has, in addition, exerted a powerful fascination upon artists, playwrights, poets, novelists, musicians, and even filmmakers, so that his fame has spread far beyond the confines of academic life.

Ray Monk, *Ludwig Wittgenstein*, Britannica, https://www.britannica.com/biography/Ludwig-Wittgenstein (October 20, 2023).

13 Alexander Miller & Olivia Sultanescu, *Rule-Following and Intentionality*, STAN. ENCYCLOPEDIA OF PHIL. (April 12, 2022), https://plato.stanford.edu/entries/rule-following/.

14 David Foster Wallace, *Tense Present: Democracy, English, and the Wars over Usage*, HARPER'S MAG. 47 (April 2001), https://harpers.org/wp-content/uploads/HarpersMagazine-2001-04-0070913.pdf. David Foster Wallace wrote:

> The point here is that the idea of a Private Language, like Private Colors and most of the other solipsistic conceits with which this particular reviewer has various times been afflicted, is both deluded and demonstrably false.

In the case of Private Language, the delusion is usually based on the belief that a word such as pain has the meaning it does because it is somehow "connected" to a feeling in my knee. But as Mr. L. Wittgenstein's *Philosophical Investigations* proved in the 1950s, words actually have the meanings they do because of certain rules and verification tests that are imposed on us from outside our own subjectivities, viz., by the community in which we have to get along and communicate with other people. Wittgenstein's argument, which is admittedly very complex and gnomic and opaque, basically centers on the fact that a word like pain means what it does for me because of the way the community I'm part of tacitly agreed to use pain.

Id.

15 Ludwig Wittgenstein, *Philosophical Investigations* 81 (G.E.M. Anscombe trans., 2nd ed. 1953). This raises the question whether randomness really exists or if everything follows a set rule? See, e.g., Ahilan T. Arulanantham, *Breaking the Rules?: Wittgenstein and Legal Realism*, 107 YALE L.J. 1853, 1869–71 (1998); Dennis Patterson, *Wittgenstein and Constitutional Theory*, 72 TEX. L. REV. 1837, 1851 (1994); Scott Hershovitz, *Wittgenstein on Rules: The Phantom Menace*, 22 OXFORD J. LEG. STUD. 619, 639–40 (2002).

16 Wittgenstein, *supra* note 15.

17 Such an example can be seen in literature:

Borges's *The Library of Babel* implicitly undercuts all the written structures—religion, science, art—through which human beings strive to impose order on an unruly world. It consists of a fantastic monologue in which a Librarian, who lives in a Library which is also the universe, tries unsuccessfully to describe the chaotic infinity (or near infinity) that surrounds him. According to the Librarian, the Library may or may not be endless; but it is certainly meaningless, being made up of numberless books in a Babel of tongues. Because it contains all the possible combinations of letters in all languages, many of the books contain only an intelligible word or two, or are only partially true copies of books contained in their proper form elsewhere in the Library. The Librarians spend their time, among other ways, searching for the true catalogue that would bring order and meaning to their incomprehensible collection.

Susan Mann, *The Universe and the Library: A Critique of James Boyd White as Writer and Reader*, 41 STAN. L. REV. 959, 965 (1989).

18 *See* 12 *Great Books of the Western World* (H. A. J. Munro trans., Robert Maynard Hutchins ed. 1952); *see also* Marion Hilligan et al., *Symposium Issue: World Views Collide: A Dialogue on State-Authored Embryonic Stem-Cell Research, Human Enhancements, Physician-Assisted Suicide and the Value of Life: Superhuman-Biotechnology's Emerging Impact on the Law*, 24 T.M. COOLEY L. REV. 1, 31 (2007). Here, the authors directly contrast the Platonic theory of the order of the universe:

The contrary materialist view characterizes archetypes as speculative constructs. Aristotle and Plato had their ancient Greek materialist counterparts in Epicurus, Democritus, and Lucretius, who in his *On the Nature of the Universe* wrote that all things began from "the purposeless congregation and coalescence of atoms." There are uniform and entirely natural causes in a closed system, not ordered or otherwise affected by the presence of a higher mind capable of recognizing and ordering information. Thus, Epicurus could hold that morality was merely a sensual matter of seeking pleasure and avoiding pain, not a sensitivity issue to any particular purpose or design. Aristotle's teleological universe was rejected for an atomistic universe without purpose or form in which biological forms and the ordered universe in which they exist were not the fixed product of information, intelligence, or design but of random accretion. Nobel Prize–winning biologist George Wald, physicist Freeman Dyson, and astronomer George Greenstein explain the improbability of the universe's remarkable order by suggesting either that the universe did not exist until humans observed it and (in Wald's words) that "[t]he universe wants to be known."

Id.

19 Such as the interlocutor suggests, nature represented itself in Athens. Plato, *supra* note 9, at 96; *see also* Robert Birmingham, *Proving Miracles and the First Amendment*, 5 Geo. Mason L. Rev. 45, 60 n.78 (1996). This work suggests that there is an order to the world's structure:

About fifty years ago, a physicist called Paul Dirac asked himself why the number ten to the fortieth power keeps occurring. The square of this number, ten to the eightieth power, is the mass of the visible universe, measured in terms of the mass of the proton. The number itself, ten to the fortieth, is the present age of the universe, expressed in units of time it takes light to travel across a proton. And, get this, the constant that measures the strength of gravity in terms of the electrical force between two protons is ten to the fortieth times weaker! Also, ten to the fortieth to the one-fourth, or ten to the tenth, just about equals the number of stars in a galaxy, the number of galaxies in the universe, and the inverse of the weak fine structure constant!

Id.

20 Claude Lévi-Strauss (born November 28, 1908, Brussels, Belgium—died October 30, 2009, Paris, France):

[Lévi-Strauss] is a French social anthropologist and leading exponent of structuralism, a name applied to the analysis of cultural systems (e.g., kinship and mythical systems) in terms of the structural relations among their elements. Structuralism has influenced not only social science but also the study of philosophy, comparative religion, literature, and film. *Claude Lévi-Strauss*, Britannica, https://www.britannica.com/biography/Claude-Levi-Strauss (October 26, 2023).

21 To illustrate the nature of structuralist theory, this discussion will concentrate on the work of Claude Lévi-Strauss:

Lévi-Strauss has made the search for the fundamental properties of human thought the focus of his work. His basic objective is uncovering the universal, basic structure of human thought, which is deep below the surface but is manfested [*sic*] in myth, language, cooking, table manners, and the general structures of social life. This basic structure, which is termed "deep structure," will identify cross-cultural similarities.

Donald H. J. Hermann, *Phenomenology, Structuralism, Hermeneutics, and Legal Study: Applications of Contemporary Continental Thought to Legal Phenomena*, 36 U. MIA. L. REV. 379, 390–1 (1982).

22 Gary Gutting, *Michel Foucault*, STAN. ENCYCLOPEDIA OF PHIL. (August 5, 2022), https://plato.stanford.edu/archives/fall2022/entries/foucault/.

23 Michel Foucault's compelling and poetic methodological manifesto describes the nature of "critique" and, thereby, the proper role of the critic. For Foucault, "critique" was more than a means to an end; criticism was itself an act of resistance and refusal. Toward this end, Foucault sought to decouple criticism from positive programs for social and political change. Criticism is, according to this view, a negative operation—"essays in refusal"—resisting and rejecting "what is" without regard for "what needs to be done." For this reason, Foucault's views have occasionally been labeled "rejectionist." Such "rejectionist" claims, in turn, exemplify the most feared aspects of a new challenge to traditional legal thought: postmodernism. Derek P. Jinks, *Essays in Refusal: Pre-Theoretical Commitments in Postmodern Anthropology and Critical Race Theory*, 107 YALE L.J. 499, 499–500 (1997); *see also* Tom Frost, *Agamben's Sovereign Legalization of Foucault*, 30 OXFORD J. LEGAL STUD. 545, 545–77 (2010) (discussing Foucault's ideas on law and sovereignty).

24 "Marvin Harris (born August 18, 1927, New York, New York, US—died October 25, 2001, Gainesville, Florida) is an American anthropological historian and theoretician known for his work on cultural materialism. His fieldwork in the Islas ('Islands') de la Bahía and other regions of Brazil and in Mozambique focused on the concept of culture." *Marvin Harris*, Britannica, https://www.britannica.com/biography/Marvin-Harris (October 21, 2023).

25 John W. Ragsdale, Jr., *The Rise and Fall of the Chacoan State*, 64 UMKC L. REV. 485, 528 (1996) ("The reciprocity concept justifies the assumption that one who gives will receive in return, though there are no hard promises as to timing, quality, or quantity."); *see also* Bronislaw Malinowski, Argonauts of the Western Pacific 178–81 (Project Gutenberg ed. 2017) (discussing gift-giving cultures).

26 According to Dumézil, the division of society—government—into three parts was inherent in all Indo-European societies. The trifunctional pattern (and implicit

political separation of powers) is manifest among the Hindus in the original Castes: Brahmana (teachers, priests, keepers of the law), Ksatriya (Warrior Kings), and Vaisya (Farmers, Producers, Merchants and Doctors). For classic development of this so-called tripartite hypothesis concerning the division of social roles in Proto-Indo-European societies, see Georges Dumézil, *Mitra-Varuna: An Essay on Two Indo-European Representations of Sovereignty* 14 (Derek Coltman trans., 2nd ed. 1988).

27 Plato, *Phaedo*, MIT: Internet Classics Archive, http://classics.mit.edu/Plato/phaedo.html (last visited December 29, 2023).

28 Charles E. Lincoln, Ethnicity and Social Organization at Chichen Itza, Yucatan, Mexico (May 1990) (Ph.D. dissertation, Harvard University) (on file with the University Microfilms International).

29 *Id.*

30 Homer, The *Iliad of Homer* 710–14 (Project Gutenberg ed. 2006).

[T]he well known Judgment of Paris, which Homer apparently knew. Although it is not directly recounted in the Iliad, there is a clear reference to it in Book 14, where Hera's displeasure with the other gods (i.e., gods who were urging Achilles to treat Hector's corpse with respect) was attributed to the Judgment of Paris: "because of the delusion of Paris / who insulted the goddesses when they came to him in his courtyard / and favoured her who supplied the lust that led to disaster." The myth of the Judgment of Paris began when Peleus and Thetis did not invite Eris, the goddess of discord, to their wedding. Eris, feeling snubbed, concocted one of literary history's most evil schemes. She procured a golden apple and inscribed it "For the fairest." She then crashed the wedding feast and tossed the apple onto the table. Three goddesses, Hera, Athena, and Aphrodite, each argued that it should be hers. They asked Zeus to decide. He refused because he feared his wife's anger in the event that he did not choose her. He passed the buck and suggested that the Trojan prince Paris, the son of Priam, act as arbiter.

See Russ VerSteeg, *A Contract Analysis of the Trojan War*, 40 ARIZ. L. REV. 173, 192 (1998).

31 Charles Lincoln, *The Dialectical Path of Law* 33 (2021).

32 Baron De Montesquieu, *The Spirit of the Laws* 152 (Thomas Nugent trans. 1949).

33 Lincoln, *supra* note 1, at 126.

34 *Id.*

35 Akiba J. Covitz, *The Soul of the Polity: Beginnings of American Constitutional Thought* (1999) (Ph.D. dissertation, University of Pennsylvania).

36 *Id.* at 155.

37 Lincoln, *supra* note 1, at 123.

38 Covitz, *supra* note 92, at xxii, xxiii.

39 *Id.* at 37–9.

40 *Id.* at iv.

41 *Id.*

42 *See* Calame, *supra* note 4, at 116–18.

43 Phillip E. Hammond, *Constitutional Faith, Legitimating Myth, Civil Religion*, 14 L. & Soc. Inquiry 377, 382 (1989) (reviewing Sanford Levinson, Constitutional Faith (1988)).

44 *See also* Donald Kagan, *New History of the Peloponnesian War* (Cornell University Press, 2013).

45 Covitz, *supra* note 92, at iv, 80–1.

46 *Id.* at 81.

47 *See id.* at 81–2, 159.

48 *Id.* at 82.

49 *Id.*

50 In the majority opinion, Chief Justice Kelly stated:

Stare decisis is short for *stare decisis et non quieta movere*, which means "stand by the thing decided and do not disturb the calm." *Stare decisis* attempts to balance two competing considerations: the need of the community for stability in legal rules and decisions, and the need of courts to correct past errors. This doctrine has been part of the American legal landscape since the country's formation.

Petersen v. Magna Corp., 484 Mich. 300, 314 (2009). The court further noted "[t]he doctrine can be traced back to medieval England." *Id.* at 314 n.34 (citing Thomas Healy, *Stare Decisis as a Constitutional Requirement*, 104 w. Va. L. Rev. 43, 56–62 (2001)).

The article itself notes that very few cases were recorded during the Anglo-Saxon period. However, there were many records of Anglo-Saxon and Norman history. See, e.g., *Anglo-Saxon Chronicle (version D)*, *in* 2 English Historical Documents 103–215 (David C. Douglas & G.W. Greenway eds., S.I. Tucker trans., Routledge 2nd ed. 1981) (1079). There are even artistic representations, such as the Bayeux Tapestry. See, e.g., *The Bayeux Tapestry*, *in* 2 English Historical Documents 247, 247–301 (David C. Douglas & G.W. Greenway eds., Routledge 2nd ed. 1981).

But earlier Roman law was itself a compilation of cases in digests, which Roman lawyers would reference. *See* Shael Herman, *Legacy and Legend: The Continuity of Roman and English Regulation of the Jews*, 66 Tul. L. Rev. 1781, 1797 (1992). Even as early as the first century B.C. "Cicero praised his friend, the jurist Servius Sulpicius Rufus for using dialectic and treating law as [a science]," indicating that—much like the modern method of using case law—Romans treated like cases alike. James Gordley, *The Method of Roman Jurists*, 87 Tul. L. Rev. 933, 947 n.73 (2013); *see generally* Peter Stein, Regulae Iuris: From Juristic Rules to Legal Maxims (1966).

By 1256, Henry de Bracton wrote of the importance of using past precedent he experienced to decide current cases before him, "if any new and unusual matters arise, which have not before been seen in the realm, if like matters arise let them be decided by like since the decision is a good one for proceeding a similibus ad similia." Healy, *supra*, at 56–7.

51 Henry Paul Monaghan, *Stare Decisis and Constitutional Adjudication*, 88 Colum. L. Rev. 723, 749–52 (1988).

52 United States v. Osborne (*In re* Osborne), 76 F.3d 306, 309 (9th Cir. 1996). Moreover, the Court unpacked the etymology of *stare decisis*, writing:

Consider the word "*decisis*." The word means, literally and legally, the decision. Nor is the doctrine *stare dictis*; it is not "to stand by or keep to what was said." Nor is the doctrine *stare rationibus decidendi*—"to keep to the *rationes decidendi* of past cases." Rather, under the doctrine of *stare decisis*, a case is important only for what it decides—for the "what," not for the "why," and not for the "how." Insofar as precedent is concerned, *stare decisis* is important only for the decision, for the detailed legal consequence following a detailed set of facts.

Id.

53 Payne v. Tennessee, 501 US 808, 827 (1991).

54 *Id.*

55 *Id.* at 827–8.

56 *Id.* at 828.

57 Johnson v. United States, 576 US 591, 605 (2015).

58 Nick Rennison, Freud and Psychoanalysis 38–9 (2001).

59 Thomas C. Grey, *Holmes and Legal Pragmatism*, 41 Stan. L. Rev. 787, 861 (1989).

60 Oliver Wendell Holmes, Jr., The Common Law 1 (Mark DeWolfe Howe ed., Harvard University Press 1963) (1881).

61 *Compare id.* (stating that "[t]he life of the law has not been logic: it has been experience"), *with* Andrew P. Morriss, *Codification and the Right Answers*, 74 Chi.-Kent L. Rev. 355, 385 & n.161 (1999) (describing the purely scientifically logical methods proposed by Langdell).

Many legal scholars:

[H]ave long viewed Christopher Columbus Langdell, the Dean of Harvard Law School from 1870 to 1895, as the prototypical American jurist of the late nineteenth century. He portrayed the common law as a conceptually ordered scientific system in which rigorous logical reasoning trumped concerns about the just resolution of particular cases. In Langdell's Orthodoxy, probably the most influential modern article on Langdell, Thomas Grey dubbed this system of legal thought "classical orthodoxy." Others have labeled it "mechanical jurisprudence," "classical legal thought," "liberal legal science," or "Langdellian formalism." Whatever term they have preferred, scholars have long agreed that Gilded Age legal thinkers viewed the common law as a rigidly logical, amoral system.

Lewis A. Grossman, *Langdell Upside-Down: James Coolidge Carter and the Anticlassical Jurisprudence of Anticodification*, 19 Yale J.L. & Humans. 149, 150 (2007).

62 Oliver W. Holmes, Jr., *Book Notices*, 14 AM. L. REV. 233, 234 (1880). Holmes continued a sentence later:

> The form of continuity has been kept up by reasonings [*sic*] purporting to reduce every thing [*sic*] to a logical sequence; but that form is nothing but the evening dress which the newcomer puts on to make itself presentable according to conventional requirements. The important phenomenon is the man underneath it, not the coat; the justice and reasonableness of a decision, not its consistency with previously held views. … As a branch of anthropology, law is an object of science; the theory of legislation is a scientific study; but the effort to reduce the concrete details of an existing system to the merely logical consequences of simple postulates is always in danger of becoming unscientific, and of leading to a misapprehension of the nature of the problem and the data.

Id.

63 Roscoe Pound, *Mechanical Jurisprudence*, 8 COLUM. L. REV. 605, 606 (1908).

64 Oliver W. Holmes, Jr., *Privilege, Malice, and Intent*, 8 HARV. L. REV. 1, 7 (1894).

65 *Id.* at 7.

66 Youngstown Sheet & Tube Co. v. Sawyer, 343 US 579 (1952).

67 *Id.*

68 *Id.* at 584.

69 *Id.* at 585.

70 *Id.* at 587.

71 *Id.*

72 *Id.* at 588.

73 *Id.*

74 *Id.* at 589.

75 *Id.* at 646–7.

76 *Id.* at 629.

77 *Branches of Government*, U.S. House of Rep., https://www.house.gov/the-house-explained/branches-of-government (last visited December 29, 2023).

78 Chevron, USA, Inc. v. Nat'l Res. Def. Council, Inc., 467 US 837, 844 (1984).

79 *Id.* at 839–40 (citation omitted).

80 *Id.* at 840.

81 *See id.*

82 *Id.*

83 *Id.* at 842.

84 *Id.* at 842–3.

85 *Id.* at 843.

86 *Id.*

87 Thomas W. Merrill, *Judicial Deference to Executive Precedent*, 101 YALE L.J. 969, 969 (1992).

88 *Id.* at 969–70.

89 *Prohibition Is Ratified by the States*, History (November 24, 2009), https://www.history.com/this-day-in-history/prohibition-ratified.

90 *21st Amendment Is Ratified; Prohibition Ends*, History, https://www.history.com/this-day-in-history/prohibition-ends (December 4, 2020).

91 *Id.*

92 *Id.*

93 *See* Abbe R. Gluck, *Imperfect Statutes, Imperfect Courts: Understanding Congress's Plan in the Era of Unorthodox Lawmaking*, 129 Harv. L. Rev. 62, 63 (2015).

94 *See* Cristina Marcos & Sarah Ferris, *House Votes to Repeal ObamaCare*, The Hill (February 3, 2015, 5:07 AM), https://thehill.com/policy/healthcare/231638-house-votes-to-repeal-obamacare/.

95 *See* Gluck, *supra* note 150.

96 Pamela S. Karlan, *The Supreme Court 2011 Term: Foreword: Democracy and Disdain*, 126 Harv. L. Rev. 1, 5 (2012).

97 See generally Carlos E. Gonzalez, *Reinterpreting Statutory Interpretation*, 74 n.c. l. Rev. 585, 590 (1996); see also Abbe R. Gluck, *The States as Laboratories of Statutory Interpretation: Methodological Consensus and the New Modified Textualism*, 119 Yale L.J. 1750, 1753 (2010).

98 Gluck, *supra* note 154, at 1754–5.

99 Brian G. Slocum, *Overlooked Temporal Issues in Statutory Interpretation*, 81 Temp. L. Rev. 635, 637–9 (2008) (illustrating how usage of different types of statutory analysis in courts can be problematic because the same method does not work in every court).

100 Glen Staszewski, *The Dumbing Down of Statutory Interpretation*, 95 B.U. L. Rev. 209, 214–15 (2015) (arguing against a uniform system of statutory interpretation).

101 Professor Gluck expands on the terms methodological and formalistic:

> By "formalistic," I mean clearly defined, ex ante interpretive rules arranged to be applied in a consistent order. But the characteristics of the particular rules chosen (for instance, whether and when legislative history may be consulted) need not themselves be rigid. *Cf.* Cass R. Sunstein, *Must Formalism Be Defended Empirically?*, 66 u. Chi. L. Rev. 636, 638 (1999) ("Formalist strategies … entail three commitments: to promoting compliance with all applicable legal formalities (whether or not they make sense in the individual case), to ensuring rule-bound law … and to constraining the discretion of judges.").

Gluck, *supra* note 154, at 1754 n.8.

102 *See generally* Sydney Foster, *Should Courts Give Stare Decisis Effect to Statutory Interpretation Methodology?*, 96 geo. l.j. 1863, 1910 (2008).

103 *See* Saul Levmore, *Parliamentary Law, Majority Decisionmaking, and the Voting Paradox*, 75 Va. L. Rev. 971, 978, 982 (1989) (citing Henry M. Robert III et al., Robert's Rules of Order Newly Revised (11th ed. 2011)).

104 Thomas Jefferson, Manual of Parliamentary Practice (1801) reprinted in John V. Sullivan, Constitution, Jefferson's Manual, and the Rules of the House of Representatives, H.R. Doc. No. 111-57, at 127–330 (2011).

105 Daniel Dubuisson, *Twentieth Century Mythologies: Dumézil, Lévi-Strauss, Eliade* 9 (Routledge, trans., Martha Cunningham, 2nd ed., 2014) (1993).

106 *Id.*

107 *Id.*

108 *See id.*

109 *See id.*

110 *Id.*

111 *Id.*

112 *See id.*

113 *Id.* at 12.

114 LITTLETON, *supra* note 3, at 4–5.

115 *See* Georges Dumézil, *The Destiny of the Warrior,* at x–xi (Alf Hiltebeitel trans., University Chicago Press, 1970) (1969).

116 *Id.* at 3.

117 *Id.*

118 *Id.*

119 Alf Hiltebeitel, *The Ritual of Battle: Krishna in the Mahābhārata* 27, 30 (1976).

120 Dumézil, *supra* note 172, at 4; Littleton, *supra* note 3, at 4, 8.

121 Dumézil, *supra* note 172, at 4.

122 Littleton, *supra* note 3, at 4, 8.

123 *Id.* Regarding the connection of the priestly function and contracts in a legal sense:

> A brief synopsis of Bergaigne and, in particular, Dumézil's thesis may be necessary before proceeding to re-establish the otherwise missing component of *Ṛta*. The Gods in themselves represent distinct functions. Mitra, the more peaceful and peaceable of the two, performs the formal, juridical, and priestly function of sovereignty. His concerns are with harmonious relationships and therefore with contract.

Piyel Haldar, *Sovereignty and Divinity in the Vedic Tradition: Mitra-Varuna, Prajā-Pati and RTA*, 115 *Divus Thomas* 382, 389 (2012).

124 Littleton, *supra* note 3, at 18; *see also* Anders Hultgård, The End of the World in Scandinavian Mythology: A Comparative Perspective on Ragnarök 14 (2022) ("In the Mahābhārata, this is a fairly short period of time. … The good times that follow during the reign of Yudhishthira correspond to the renewal of the world in the Scandinavian myth.").

125 Littleton, *supra* note 3, at 12.

126 Dumézil, *supra* note 172, at 6.

127 Wouter W. Belier, *Decayed Gods: Origin and Development of Georges Dumézil's "Idéologie Tripartie"* 173–5 (1991).

128 Littleton, *supra* note 3, at 124. Here in Dumézil's thought "they are connected with what Georges Dumézil has called the … warrior[] function are Bhīma and Arjuna, sons of Vāyu and Indra." Hiltebeitel, *supra* note 176, at 27.

129 Littleton, *supra* note 3, at 12, 76; Jens Peter Schjødt, Óðinn, Þórr and Freyr: Functions and Relations, in News from Other Worlds: Studies in Nordic Folklore Mythology and Culture 64, 67, 78 (Merril Kaplan & Timothy R. Tangherlini eds., 2012) (regarding the Norse pantheon from an anthropological perspective "of three gods in such wise that the mightiest of them, Thor, … three functions of Dumézil, it is just that there are two gods … success in war, including strategic skills and warlike ecstasy.").

130 Littleton, *supra* note 3, at 68–70 (describing Dumézil's approach of the Capitoline or archaic triad, consisting of Jupiter, Mars, and Quirinus as operating in the warlike function); 6 Structuralism in Myth: Lévi-Strauss, Barthes, Dumézil, and Propp 53, 65, 80 (Robert A. Segal, ed. 1996) (interpreting the Roman pantheon as "Mars, and Quirinus, and this triad [*dieser Dreiverein*] of gods … is also very old, older than Rome, and the functional pair rex … gods, but aligned with the circumstance, which is warlike.").

131 Dumézil, *supra* note 172, at 6.

132 Georges Dumézil, *Gods of the Ancient Northmen* 16 (Einar Haugen ed. & trans., University California Press 1973) (1959).

133 Zdenko Zlatar, *Approaches to the Ur-Mahabharata*, 15 Sydney Stud. in Soc'y & Culture 243, 252–3 (1997) ("Dumézil showed that the group of five heroes of *The Mahabharata*, the Pandava brothers, 'were duplications as to their characters, their actions, and their relationships (beginning with the very order of their birth) of the hierarchised group constituted in the earliest Vedic mythology by the gods of the three functions: the just king Yudhisthira is modelled on Mitra (simply rejuvenated as Dharma), the two kinds of warrior, Bhima and Arjuna, on Vāyu and Indra, and the two twins Nakula and Sahadeva on the Nasatya twins')."

134 "The fertility aspect which Heimdallr shares with Freyja is also appropriate here." Britt-Mari Näsström, Freyja—a Goddess with Many Names, in *The Concept of the Goddess* 82–91 (Routledge 2002).

135 Carl Lindahl, *Book Review: Gods of the Ancient Northmen by Georges Dumézil and Einar Haugen*, 93 J. of Am. Folklore 224, 224–5 (1980) ("When this schema is applied to Norse mythology, Dumézil identifies … Frey and Njord as the paired fertility deities of land and sea"). Vanes is translated to "Vanir" in English, and refers to the god Freyja. *See generally* Dieux Ases et Dieux Vanes: "délimite les positions respectives des grands dieux Odhmrc, Thôrr, Freyr dans la mythologie

Scandinave et se complète par l'étude du mythe de Kvasir." Georges Dumézil, Les Dieux Des Germains: Essai Sur La Formation de La Religion Scandinave (1959).

136 Dumézil, *supra* note 189, at xii.

137 Douglas J. Stewart, *"Mythomorphism" in Greco-Roman Historiography: The Case of the Royal "Gamos,"* 22 Bucknell Rev. 186, 186 (1976).

138 Arnaldo Momigliano, *Georges Dumézil and the Trifunctional Approach to Roman Civilization*, 23 Hist. & Theory 312, 316–17 (1984); *see generally* Belier, *supra* note 184; Littleton, *supra* note 3.

139 See generally Momigliano, *supra* note 195, at 316–17.

140 Donald Kagan, *The Human Sources of History: A Review of the Classical Foundations of Modern Historiography (Sather Classical Lectures) by Arnaldo Momigliano*, New Criterion, https://newcriterion.com/issues/1992/3/the-human-sources-of-history (last visited December 29, 2023).

141 *See generally* Momigliano, *supra* note 195, at 322–4.

142 *See* J. Gonda, *Dumézil's Tripartite Ideology: Some Critical Observations*, 34 J. of Asian Stud. 139, 148 (1974). Dumézil identifies "the Latin flamen 'priest [as part] of a special deity, member of a group of fifteen priests.'"

143 *See* Momigliano, *supra* note 195, at 315–16, 320.

144 Charles Goldberg, *Priests and Politicians: Rex Sacrorum and Flamen Dialis in the Middle Republic*, 69 Phx. 334, 334 (2015).

145 See Greg Woolf, *Religion and Power: Divine Kinship in the Ancient World and Beyond* 238, 241–2 (Nicole Brisch ed. 2008).

146 *Id.* at 238, 242.

147 *See* Momigliano, *supra* note 195, at 316, 325–6.

148 *Id.* at 324–5.

149 *Id.* at 325.

150 *Id.* at 324–5.

151 *See* Jane F. Gardner, Being a Roman Citizen 1 (2010); Seth Kendall, *The Struggle for Roman Citizenship: Roman, Allies, and the Wars* 91–77 BCE 30 (2013).

152 *See generally* Andrew Wallace-Hadrill, *Civilis Princeps: Between Citizen and King*, 72 J. of Roman Stud. 32 (1982). "Since Caracalla's edict of AD 212 virtually all the subjects of the empire had possessed the Roman citizenship." War and Society in the Roman World 7 (John Rich & Graham Shipley eds., 1993).

153 Bruce Bartlett, *How Excessive Government Killed Ancient Rome*, 14 Cato J. 287, 290 (1994).

154 *See* Gardner, *supra* note 208, at 3.

155 *Id.*

156 *See* Momigliano, *supra* note 195, at 326–7.

157 *Id.*

158 Bartlett, *supra* note 210, at 290.

159 *See id.*

160 Arnaldo Momigliano, *An Interim Report on the Origins of Rome*, 53 J. Roman Stud. 95, 133 (1963). Again, this chapter does not take a position on whether Dumézilian theory is correct.

161 *Id.* at 133–4.

162 *Cf.* Bruce Lincoln, Theorizing Myth: Narrative, Ideology, and Scholarship 123–4 (1999). Here, Professor Bruce Lincoln, Caroline E. Haskell Distinguished Service Professor Emeritus of the History of Religions in the Divinity School; also in the Center for Middle Eastern Studies and Committee on Medieval Studies; Associate Faculty in the Departments of Anthropology and Classics of the University of Chicago, wrote:

> Dumézil's [scholarship] won him virtually universal admiration. [He was a] scholar of extraordinary abilities and erudition. … Among his other gifts, he was master of countless languages: virtually all the Indo-European family, including some of its more obscure members (Armenian, Ossetic), as well as most of the Caucasian languages, one of which (Oubykh) he saved from extinction, and a few outliers like Quechua, which he seems to have acquired simply for fun. His oeuvre spanned six decades and includes more than fifty books, all of which are marked by extraordinary lucidity, ingenuity, rigor, and intelligence. His accomplishments have won wide acclaim among philologians, historians of religions, and anthropologists.

Id.

163 Dumézil argues that the Estates General of 1789 led to the end of the tripartite system. Sverre Bagge, *Old Norse Theories of Society from Rígspula to Konungs Skuggsiá*, Univ. of Bergen Open Rsrch. Archive 7 (2000), https://bora.uib.no/bora-xmlui/bitstream/handle/1956/674/Old%20Norse%20Theories%20of%20Society.pdf.

164 Andrea Bierstein, *Millennium Approaches: The Future of the Voting Rights Act After Shaw, De Grandy, and Holder*, 46 Hastings L.J. 1457, 1472 n.51 (1995) ("The Estates General in France, too, consisted of representatives of the three estates recognized in society, the clergy, the nobility, and the common people.").

165 *See id.*

166 *See id.*

167 *See id.*

168 *See* Joseph A. Dane, *The Three Estates and Other Mediaeval Trinities*, 3 Florilegium 283, 284 (1981).

169 Dumézil expressly wrote, "[L]e schéma tripartite est mort en Occident avec les États généraux de 1789, quand la noblesse et le clergé ont baissé le pavillon devant le tiers

état. On a enfin répondu à la question: qu'est-ce que le tiers état? Eh bien, c'était la ruine du système trifonctionnel." Georges Dumézil, *Le Parcours Initiatique d'un "Parasite" des Sciences Humaines, in* Passion du Passé 54, 56–7 (1987).

170 Thomas Piketty (born May 7, 1971, Clichy, France):

[Piketty] is a French economist who was best known for Le Capital au XXIe siècle (Capital in the Twenty-first Century (2013)). Piketty was born to militant Trotskyite parents and was later politically affiliated with the French Socialist Party. After he took the baccalaur … at examination, he spent two years preparing for the École Normale Supérieure (ENS) entrance examination. From the ENS he received (1990) an M.Sc. degree in mathematics. In 1993, he was awarded a Ph.D. in economics from the École des Hautes Études en Sciences Sociales (EHESS) and the London School of Economics European doctoral program for a dissertation on the theory of the redistribution of wealth. After Piketty taught (1993–5) at the Massachusetts Institute of Technology, he returned to France as a research fellow (1995–2000) at the Centre National de la Recherche Scientifique. He became professor of economics at the EHESS (2000) and also at the Paris School of Economics (2007), of which he was the founding director. He was the author of numerous other books and articles and, in collaboration with French American economist Emmanuel Saez, British economist Anthony B. Atkinson, and Facundo Alvaredo of Argentina, was a compiler of the World Top Incomes Database.

Martin L. White, *Thomas Piketty*, Britannica, https://www.britannica.com/biography/Thomas-Piketty (November 13, 2023).

171 Thomas Piketty, *Capital and Ideology 478* (Harvard University Press, trans., Arthur Goldhammer, 2020).

172 *Id.*

173 Idrees Kahloon, *Thomas Piketty Goes Global*, New Yorker (March 2, 2020), https://www.newyorker.com/magazine/2020/03/09/thomas-piketty-goes-global.

174 Piketty, *supra* note 228, at 478 n.92 (citing Didier Eribon, Faut-il Brüler Dumézil? 185–206 (Flammarion 1992)).

175 Kahloon, *supra* note 230.

176 *Id.*

177 Sigmund Freud (born May 6, 1856, Freiberg, Moravia, Austrian Empire [now Příbor, Czech Republic]—died September 23, 1939, London, England):

[Freud] is an Austrian neurologist and the founder of psychoanalysis. Freud may justly be called the most influential intellectual legislator of his age. His creation of psychoanalysis was at once a theory of the human psyche, a therapy for the relief of its ills, and an optic for the interpretation of culture and society. Despite repeated criticisms, attempted refutations, and qualifications of Freud's work, its spell remained powerful well after his death and in fields far removed from psychology as it is narrowly defined. If, as the American sociologist Philip

Rieff once contended, "psychological man" replaced such earlier notions as political, religious, or economic man as the twentieth century's dominant self-image, it is in no small measure due to the power of Freud's vision and the seeming inexhaustibility of the intellectual legacy he left behind.

Martin Evan Jay, *Sigmund Freud*, Britannica, https://www.britannica.com/biography/Sigmund-Freud (November 9, 2023).

178 Winfried Brugger, *Dignity, Rights, and Legal Philosophy Within the Anthropological Cross of Decision-Making*, 9 Germ. L.J. 1243, 1246 (2008).

179 *Id.* at 1246–7.

180 Freud wrote that "the ego is that part of the id which has been modified by the direct influence of the external world. … The ego represents what may be called reason and common sense, in contrast to the id, which contains the passions." Sigmund Freud, *The Ego and the Id* 25 (James Strachey ed. 1923). It is like a tug of war, with the difference that in the tug of war, the teams fight against one another in equality, while the ego is against the much stronger "id." *Id.*

181 Sigmund Freud, *New Introductory Lectures on Psychoanalysis*. 4669 (1933).

182 *Id.* at 4682.

183 *Id.* at 4676.

184 *superego*, Britannica, https://www.britannica.com/science/superego (October 10, 2023).

[The] super-ego, in the psychoanalytic theory of Sigmund Freud, the latest developing of three agencies (with the id and ego) of the human personality. The super-ego is the ethical component of the personality and provides the moral standards by which the ego operates. The super-ego's criticisms, prohibitions, and inhibitions form a person's conscience, and its positive aspirations and ideals represent one's idealized self-image, or "ego ideal."

Id.

185 *Id*, Britannica, https://www.britannica.com/science/id-psychology (August 18, 2023).

Id, in Freudian psychoanalytic theory, [is] one of the three agencies of the human personality, along with the ego and super-ego. The oldest of these psychic realms in development, the id contains the psychic content related to the primitive instincts of the body, notably sex and aggression, as well as all psychic material that is inherited and present at birth. The id (Latin for "it") is oblivious of the external world and unaware of the passage of time. Devoid of organization, knowing neither logic nor reason, it has the ability to harbor acutely conflicting or mutually contradictory impulses side by side. It functions entirely according to the pleasure-pain principle, its impulses either seeking immediate fulfillment or settling for a compromise fulfillment. The id supplies the energy for the development and continued functioning of conscious mental life, though the working processes of the id itself are completely unconscious in the adult (less unconscious in the child). In waking life it belies its content in slips of the tongue, wit, art, and other at least partly nonrational modes of expression. The primary methods for unmasking its content, according to Freud, are the analysis of dreams and free association.

Id.

186 The Pervert's Guide to Cinema (Amoeba Film et al. 2009).

187 *Id.*

188 *Id.*

189 *Id.*

190 *Id.*

191 *Id.*

192 *Id.*

193 *Id.*

194 *Id.*

195 C. Scott Littleton & Udo Strutynski, *Introduction* to Georges Dumézil, *Gods of the Ancient Northmen, at xviii* (Einar Haugen ed. & trans., University of California Press, 1973) (1959).

196 *Id.* at xi.

197 *Id.* at xi–xii.

198 *See* Lincoln, *supra* note 31; see also Charles E. Lincoln, The Chronology of Chichen Itza: A Review of the Literature 141–56 (Jeremy A. Sabloff & E. Wyllys Andrews V eds., 1986) [hereinafter The Chronology of Chichen Itza].

199 *See* Lincoln, *supra* note 31; The Chronology of Chichen Itza, *supra* note 255; *but cf.* Elena K. Lincoln, Yucatec Maya Marriage and Political Alliances (2000) (Ph.D. dissertation, University of California, Los Angeles).

200 Littleton & Strutynski, *supra* note 252, at ix, xi.

201 *See* C. Scott Littleton, *The Comparative Indo-European Mythology of Georges Dumézil*, 1 J. of Folklore Inst. 147, 148–51 (1964).

202 Elizabeth Lunbeck et al., *Sigmund Freud's The Ego and the Id*, JSTOR Daily (September 21, 2019), https://daily.jstor.org/virtual-roundtable-on-the-ego-and-the-id/.

203 Etymologically speaking, The Liddell & Scott's *A Greek-English Lexicon* defines the word as, "λογιστικός from λογιστής 1 I. skilled or practised in calculating, Xen., Plat.:—ἡ λογιστική (sc. τέχνη), arithmetic, Plat. II. endued with reason, rational, Arist.:—τὸ λ. the reasoning faculty, Plat. 2.using one's reason, reasonable, Xen." Henry George Liddell & Robert Scott, *An Intermediate Greek-English Lexicon* (1889), http://www.perseus.tufts.edu/hopper/text?doc=Perseus%3Atext%3A1999.04.0058%3Aentry%3Dlogistiko%2Fs.

204 *See* Plato, Republic bk. IV, at 435e (Paul Shorey trans., Harvard. University Press 1969) (c. 375 B.C.), https://www.perseus.tufts.edu/hopper/text?doc=Perseus%3Atext%3A1999.01.0168%3Abook%3D4%3Asection%3D435e.

205 This can be compared to "*Crito* 46 B (one of the passages which the Christian apologists used to prove that Socrates knew the λόγος), *Theaetetus* 186 C ἀναλογίσματα πρός τε οὐσίαν καὶ ὠφέλειαν, and *Laws* 644 D. Aristotle *Eth.* 1139 a 12 somewhat differently." *Id.* at 439d & n.8, http://www.perseus.tufts.edu/hopper/text?doc=Perseus%3Atext%3A1999.01.0168%3Abook%3D4%3Apage%3D439.

206 Kenji Yoshino, *The City and the Poet*, 114 YALE L.J. 1835, 1856 (2005).

207 Plato, *supra* note 261, at 439d.

208 *See generally* Lincoln, *supra* note 1; Lincoln, *supra* note 31; see, e.g., Robert C. Bordone et al., *The Negotiation Within: The Impact of Internal Conflict over Identity and Role on Across-the-Table Negotiations*, 2014 J. OF DISP. RESOL. 175, 180 (2014).

209 *See* Plato, *supra* note 261, at 439e.

210 *Id.* at 439e n.11.

211 Georges Dumézil, *The Destiny of a King, 10–15* (University Chicago Press, trans., Alf Hiltebeitel, 1973) (1971).

212 US Const. art. III, § 1.

213 5 US (1 Cranch) 137, 180 (1803).

214 US Const. art. III, § 1.

215 *Marbury*, 5 US at 177; *accord* United States v. Nixon, 418 US 683, 703 (1974).

216 163 US 537 (1896).

217 347 US 483 (1954).

218 163 US 537.

219 *Id.* at 540 (internal quotation marks omitted).

220 347 US 483.

221 *Id.* at 490–1.

222 576 US 644 (2015).

223 Kenji Yoshino, *A New Birth of Freedom?: Obergefell v. Hodges*, 129 HARV. L. REV. 147, 147 (2015). Illustrating the differences of originalist and evolutionary document theories of interpreting the Constitution, Andrew W. Schwartz writes, discussing the *Obergerfell* case:

The majority and dissenting opinions in *Obergefell v. Hodges*, the Supreme Court's recent decision finding that same-sex marriage is a constitutional right, offer a lucid comparison of originalism with evolutionary document theories of interpretation. The majority point out that the institution of marriage "has evolved over time." *Obergefell v. Hodges*, No. 14–556, slip op. at 6 (US, June 26, 2015). Finding that the right to marry the person of one's choice, regardless of their gender, was compelled by the due process clause of the Fourteenth Amendment, the majority described its task as interpreting a constitutional provision that sets forth broad principles rather than specific requirements. History and tradition guide and discipline this inquiry but do not set its outer boundaries. That method respects our history and learns from it without allowing the past alone to rule the present. The nature of injustice is that we may not always see it in our own times. The generations that wrote and ratified the Bill of Rights and the Fourteenth Amendment did not presume to know the extent of freedom in all of its dimensions, and so they entrusted to future generations a charter protecting the right of all person to enjoy liberty as we learn its meaning. When new insight reveals discord between the Constitution's central protections and a received legal stricture, a claim to liberty must be addressed. *Id.* at 10–11 (citations omitted). In sharp contrast, Chief Justice Roberts and Associate Justice Alito, in their dissenting opinions, refused to recognize contemporary views of marriage, asserting that the notion of marriage as solely between a man and a woman is "deeply rooted in this Nation's history and tradition." *Id.* at 14 (Roberts, C.J., dissenting); *id.* at 2 (Alito, J., dissenting) (quoting Washington v. Glucksberg, 521 US 701, 720–1 (1997)). Justice Scalia, in a separate dissent, relied on the public understanding of the meaning of marriage at the time the due process clause was ratified in 1868, which, he argued, universally confined marriage to a man and a woman. *Id.* at 4 (Scalia, J., dissenting).

Andrew W. Schwartz, *No Competing Theory of Constitutional Interpretation Justifies Regulatory Takings Ideology*, 34 STAN. ENV'T L.J. 247, 259 n.43 (2015).

224 Laurence H. Tribe, *Equal Dignity: Speaking Its Name*, 129 HARV. L. REV. F. 16, 16 (2015).

225 The Executive Branch's source of power is derived from the Article II of the US Constitution. *See* US Const. art. II, § 1, cl. 1.

226 Medical exams in the United States consider the idea of who the president is so ubiquitous that it is used as a basis for establishing whether one has cognitive function orienting them to the present day. In other words, asking who the Senator or Representative from one's state is would likely not be as universally helpful as asking who the President. *See* Jeff Hersh, *What Questions Are Asked on a Mental Status Exam?*, Taunton Daily Gazette (October 30, 2023, 6:21 PM), https://www.tauntongazette.com/story/lifestyle/health-fitness/2020/07/23/whats-up-doc-what-questions-are-asked-on-mental-status-exam/114523550/. Such an inquiry in itself is fairly philosophical as an assumption—the zeitgeist of the country is known and that is a test of basic consciousness as seen through the president of the United States.

227 *The Executive Branch*, White House, https://www.whitehouse.gov/about-the-white-house/our-government/the-executive-branch/ (last visited December 29, 2023); *see Executive Orders (Beginning with J.Q. Adams)*, AM. PRESIDENCY PROJECT, https://www.presidency.ucsb.edu/documents/presidential-documents-archive-guidebook/executive-orders-beginning-with-jq-adams (last visited December 29, 2023).

228 The power of the Legislative Branch generally emanates from Article I of the US Constitution. *See* US Const. art. 1.

229 The Federalist No. 47, at 303 (James Madison).

230 *Lincoln*, *supra* note 31, at viii.

Conclusion

Overall, this book on the trifunctionalism of law strove to show how social thought can help explain the US Constitution. But the book also attempted to show how the structure of the US Constitution could help interpret social thought. In short, it shows how both social thought and the US Constitution are a two-way street providing information to each other; both provide reciprocal information and means of interpretation of the other.

Likewise, this book employed various means to interpret the Constitution. The means were poetical through Homer, philosophical through Plato, political through the *Federalist Papers* and Montesquieu, psychological through Freud, and anthropological through Dumézil. As such, the book presents its thought in the following way. These modes of interpretation and their corresponding thinkers are summarized in Table 8.1.

These means are all forms of social thought. These means of interpretation and the thinkers are not the only sources for each means. Indeed, Akiba Covitz's thought represents the background of much of the origin of this book. But also, structuralists such as Claude Lévi-Strauss also influenced the writing and thinking behind this book in the context of anthropological thought. Moreover, this book presented a Straussian theme interwoven throughout. The Straussian

Table 8.1 Modes of Interpretation and Corresponding Thinkers in the Analysis of the US Constitution

Interpretation Means	Thinker
Poetic	Homer
Philosophical	Plato
Political	Montesquieu and *The Federalist Papers*
Psychological	Freud
Anthropological	Dumézil

idea of esoteric thought existing within writings that cannot be openly expressed finds potential validity in the writings of the early James Madison during the Constitutional debates of 1788. In other words, arguably, James Madison—and even Alexander Hamilton—wished to give more power to the central federal government than they suggested in their writings. Giving much more power to the federal government than Madison, Hamilton, and Jay admit is the esoteric meaning of *The Federalist Papers*.

The result of such "esoteric" thought became exoteric thought in the Nullification Crisis of 1832 and 1833 under President Andrew Jackson's administration, with the conclusion that federal law invalidated state law. Furthermore, Abraham Lincoln settled such questions in the Civil War. Thus, the primary document to be interpreted is the US Constitution of 1787 with all its relevant amendments. That text is the basis of the United States.

Given that the Constitution is the primary text of US government and all US law, it is therefore incumbent on those concerned with the United States to use all means of analysis to interpret the Constitution. This book represents an attempt to interpret the text through social thought.

Epilogue

Social thought influences political thought. Law influences social norms, and culture influences law. But are there static aspects of culture and human society that don't change? From a textual perspective, one of the forms of law that hardly changes in the United States is the text of the Constitution. But theoretically, the Constitution is subject to constant change through Article V of the Constitution, allowing for Amendments—whether those are actualized or not. Likewise, all the relevant case law, common law, executive orders, regulations, and administrative state decisions all affect the periphery that the Constitution affects.

This book focused on interpreting the Constitution, but can the peripheries be analyzed through the lens of trifunctionalism? One could show how the legislative function represents one of the trifunctional approaches. But could each actor or person in the legislative function represent all three branches? Or could one actor—or the main actor—in the executive role have all three functions represented in oneself? The answer is likely, yes. This raises a deeper question outside the immediate scope of this book: What are the implications of such functions for the structure and future of the American Republic?

Whether the constitutional function of a political actor whose powers are outlined in the US Constitution is analyzed through Plato, Freud, Dumézil, Polybius, the writings of the Framers of the 1789 US Constitution, or Montesquieu does make a difference. But as shown, they all have a similarity as exhibited through the US Constitution.

So, then the question for future research is what are the implications—if any—if every person—in a governmental or power role—has all three functions outlined in this book operating within them at different times. Such a moment of the legal and political actor realizing itself as itself through self-realization would be difficult to empirically test. That is to say, it would be difficult to test how often political actors realize they are a political actor in a role outlined by a complex history. It is even harder to observe when their decisions are influenced by the vast anthropological and social traditions that inform the laws they are bound to follow or enforce.

If the Constitution reflects a mythopoetic archetype, and each actor potentially embodies all three functions—priest, warrior, and legislator—then how might our Republic evolve when its leaders recognize this within themselves?

Perhaps the best answer for now comes from William Shakespeare's play *As You Like It*, in a speech by the character Jacques:

All the world's a stage,
And all the men and women merely players;
They have their exits and their entrances;
And one man in his time plays many parts,
His acts being seven ages. At first the infant,
Mewling and puking in the nurse's arms;
And then the whining school-boy, with his satchel
And shining morning face, creeping like snail
Unwillingly to school. And then the lover,
Sighing like furnace, with a woeful ballad
Made to his mistress' eyebrow. Then a soldier,
Full of strange oaths, and bearded like the pard,
Jealous in honour, sudden and quick in quarrel,
Seeking the bubble reputation
Even in the cannon's mouth. And then the justice,
In fair round belly with good capon lin'd,
With eyes severe and beard of formal cut,
Full of wise saws and modern instances;
And so he plays his part. The sixth age shifts
Into the lean and slipper'd pantaloon,
With spectacles on nose and pouch on side;
His youthful hose, well sav'd, a world too wide
For his shrunk shank; and his big manly voice,
Turning again toward childish treble, pipes
And whistles in his sound. Last scene of all,
That ends this strange eventful history,
Is second childishness and mere oblivion;
Sans teeth, sans eyes, sans taste, sans everything.

Future Research

This book follows from my previous book, *The Dialectical Path of Law* (2021). The ideas explored in that book focus on the contours of the philosophy of Hegelian dialectics and law. This current book focused on theories of trifunctionalism and the law originating with Plato's Republic. A future book and avenue of researchers interested in the topic would focus on the triads of Hegelianism and trifunctionalism through the viewpoint of Hegel's theory of sublation.

Possible ideas for future research could build off the ideas of esotericism (not to be confused with esoteric mysticism) from Leo Strauss's writings. Such future research could focus on the esoteric ideas in *The Federalist Papers*, common law, case law in the United States, the US Constitution, legislative history, regulations and regulatory history, rules for legal procedure, and, of course, the vast corpus of tax law.

Such research into Straussian ideas of esotericism in law could extend to Europe and international law as well. New insights on international treaties, especially tax treaties and the Vienna Convention on the Law of Treaties (1969), could engender a whole new study of law.

Moreover, in line with Straussian thinking, notions of Athens and Jerusalem could use new and refreshed eyes in analyzing these subject areas of law.

Aside from Straussian studies, poetry, philosophy, political science, government, psychologic, and anthropology could come together for future research on law. If such ideas could come together in a unified field with empirical data, then there could be a revolution in law. New think tanks and institutes could focus on the combination of these ideas this book has attempted to break ground examining.

For example, based on the Freudian chapter, there perhaps exist parallels between the Freudian conception of the psyche and Plato's conception of the soul. Indeed, the id does not precisely correlate to eros. The id from a Freudian perspective is the reservoir of all emotions. In Plato's conception, eros is more the erotic portion of the soul. Moreover, thumos does not precisely correlate either. Plato conceived thumos as anger and spiritedness seeking honor. In this sense, the Freudian id would encompass both the Platonic conception of thumos and eros.

Nevertheless, Freud likely explored in a different way through his psychoanalytic theory at the individual level through Plato's paradigm of a long-lasting government archetype. Freud's paradigm seems suitable as a heuristic regardless of the "correct" Freudian application to the three-part structure of the US government as outlined in the US Constitution.[1] From a Freudian perspective, is it fair to say that the best government, at least in part, represents the individual or the psyche of the individual? Likewise, it seems fair to say that an anthropological archetype of government could exist based on the psychology of humans. The topic of such a connection of the psychological archetype of government would fall into the scope of a different article and further research. Arguably, such a government based on an archetype could correlate to Jungian—after the psychoanalytic theories of Carl Jung that represent the earliest and compelling counter arguments to Freud—notions of individual archetypes. But instead, such research could seek to find a "Jungian archetypal" form of government.

Note

1 Charles Lincoln, *The Dialectical Path of Law*, viii (2021).

Bibliography

Books and Articles Consulted

Abbott, Edwin A. *Flatland: A Romance of Many Dimensions*. New York: Harper & Row, 1963.

Adler, Mortimer J. *The Syntopicon: "The Great Ideas,"* Vol. 1, Angel to Love. Chicago, IL: Encyclopaedia Britannica, 1971.

Adler, Mortimer J., ed. *The Syntopicon: An Index to the Great Ideas. Vol. 2, Man to World, of The Great Books of the Western World*. Chicago, IL: Encyclopaedia Britannica, 1952.

Alighieri, Dante. *Inferno*. Translated by Dorothy L. Sayers. New York: Modern Library, 1949.

Alighieri, Dante. *Paradiso*. Translated by Dorothy L. Sayers. New York: Modern Library, 1962.

Alighieri, Dante. *Purgatorio*. Translated by Dorothy L. Sayers. New York: Modern Library, 1961.

Aristotle. *De Anima* 412a1–413a10. Edited by W. D. Ross. 1956.

Aristotle. *Ethica Nicomachea* 1105b20–28.

Aristotle. *Metaphysics*. Translated by Joe Sachs. 2nd ed. Newburyport, MA: Focus Philosophical Library, 2002.

Aristotle. *Nicomachean Ethics*, in *Aristotle: Nicomachean Ethics*. Translated by H. Rackham, 1139a12. Loeb Classical Library 73. Cambridge, MA: Harvard University Press, 1926.

Aristotle. *Nicomachean Ethics*. Translated by Joe Sachs. Newburyport, MA: Focus Philosophical Library, 2002.

Aristotle. *On the Soul and On Memory and Recollection*. Translated by Joe Sachs. Newburyport, MA: Focus Philosophical Library, 2001.

Aristotle. *Poetics*. Translated by Joe Sachs. Newburyport, MA: Focus Philosophical Library, 2006.

Aristotle. *Politics*. Translated by Carnes Lord. Revised ed. Chicago, IL: University of Chicago Press, 2013.

Arulanantham, Ahilan T. "Breaking the Rules?: Wittgenstein and Legal Realism." *Yale Law Journal* 107 (1998): 1853–71.

Aurelius, Marcus. *Meditations*. Translated by Gregory Hays. Foreword by Ryan Holiday. New York: Modern Library, 2003.

Austin, John. *The Province of Jurisprudence Determined* (1832), reprinted in *The Province of Jurisprudence Determined and The Uses of the Study of Jurisprudence*, 132. New York: Noonday Press, 1954.

Barber, James David. *The Presidential Character: Predicting Performance in the White House*. New York: Routledge, 2017.

Baudrillard, Jean. "The Precession of the Simulacra." in *Simulacra and Simulation*, Translated by Sheila Faria Glaser, 1–42. Ann Arbor: University of Michigan Press, 1997.

Bederman, David J. "The Classical Constitution: Roman Republican Origins of the Habeas Suspension Clause." *Southern California Interdisciplinary Law Journal* 17 (2008): 405–30.

Belier, Wouter W. *Decayed Gods: Origin and Development of Georges Dumézil's "Idéologie Tripartite."* Leiden: E. J. Brill, 1991.

Benedict, Ruth. *The Chrysanthemum and the Sword*. Boston, MA: Mariner Books, 2006.

Bergman, Matthew P. "Montesquieu's Theory of Government and the Framing of the American Constitution." *Pepperdine Law Review* 18 (1991): 1–70.

Birmingham, Robert. "Proving Miracles and the First Amendment." *George Mason Law Review* 5 (1996): 45–60.

Bix, Brian. *Jurisprudence: Theory and Context*. 8th ed. London: Sweet & Maxwell, 2019.

Bloom, Harold. *A Map of Misreading*. New York: Oxford University Press, 1975.

Bloom, Harold. *Possessed by Memory: The Inward Light of Criticism*. New York: Alfred A. Knopf, 2019.

Bloom, Harold. *The Anxiety of Influence: A Theory of Poetry*. New York: Oxford University Press, 1973.

Bloom, Harold. *The Western Canon: The Books and School of the Ages*. Cambridge, MA: Houghton Mifflin Harcourt, 2014.

Bok, Hilary. "Baron de Montesquieu, Charles-Louis de Secondat." *The Stanford Encyclopedia of Philosophy*, Edited by Edward Zalta. Winter 2018 edition. https://plato.stanford.edu/entries/montesquieu/.

Bordone, Robert C., Cara J. Grand, and Roscoe M. Pound. "The Negotiation Within: The Impact of Internal Conflict over Identity and Role on Across-the-Table Negotiations." *Journal of Dispute Resolution* 2014 (2014): 175–80.

Borges, Jorge Luis. *Labyrinths: Selected Stories and Other Writings*. Edited by Donald A. Yates and James E. Irby. New York: New Directions, 1964.

Borges, Jorge Luis. "The Library of Babel." in *Labyrinths: Selected Stories and Other Writings*, Edited by Donald A. Yates and James E. Irby, 51–8. New York: New Directions, 1964.

Bowen, Margaret R. and Cynthia J. Bowling. "Executive Orders and Administrative Control." *Public Administration Review* 68 (2008): S20–S28.

Bracton, Henry de. *De Legibus et Consuetudinibus Angliae*. c. 1256.

Bronislaw Malinowski. *Argonauts of the Western Pacific*. London: Routledge, 1922.

Brutus. Essay I, in *The Essential Anti-Federalist*. Edited by W. B. Allen and Gordon Lloyd, 2nd ed. Indianapolis: Liberty Fund, 2002.

Bubuison, Daniel. *Twentieth Century Mythologies: Dumézil, Lévi-Strauss, Eliade*. Translated by Martha Cunningham. New York: Routledge, 2014.

Calame, Claude. *Myth and History in Ancient Greece: The Symbolic Creation of a Colony*. Translated by Daniel W. Berman. Princeton, NJ: Princeton University Press, 2003.

Cass, Ronald A. "Delegation Reconsidered: A Delegation Doctrine for the Modern Administrative State." *Harvard Journal of Law & Public Policy* 40 (2017): 147–96.

Caudill, David S. "Freud and Critical Legal Studies: Contours of a Radical Socio-Legal Psychoanalysis." *Indiana Law Journal* 66 (1991): 651–59.

Chaucer, Geoffrey. *The Canterbury Tales*. Barnes & Noble Classics. Introduction by Robert W. Hanning. Translated by Peter Tuttle. New York: Barnes & Noble Books, 2007.

Chemerinsky, Erwin. "Rethinking State Action." *Northwestern University Law Review* 80 (1985): 503–35.

Cicero, Marcus Tullius. *De Legibus*. Translated by Clinton Walker Keyes. Cambridge, MA: Loeb Classical Library, 1928.

Cornell, Saul. "The People's Constitution vs. the Lawyer's Constitution: Popular Constitutionalism and the Original Debate over Originalism." *Yale Journal of Law & Humanities* 23 (2011): 295–343.

Covitz, Akiba J. *The Soul of the Polity: Beginnings of American Constitutional Thought*. PhD diss., University of Pennsylvania, 1999.

D'Amato, Anthony, ed. *Analytic Jurisprudence Anthology*. Durham, NC: Carolina Academic Press, 2001.

Dane, Joseph A. "The Three Estates and Other Medieval Trinities." *Florilegium* 3 (1981): 283–95.

Dane, Perry. "Jurisdictionality, Time, and the Legal Imagination." *Hofstra Law Review* 23 (1994): 1–106.

De Sutter, Laurent. "Legal Shandeism: The Law in Laurence Sterne's *Tristram Shandy*." *Law & Literature* 23 (2011): 224–33.

Driesen, David M. "President Trump's Executive Orders and the Rule of Law." *UMKC Law Review* 87 (2018): 489–520.

Dubuisson, Daniel. *Twentieth Century Mythologies: Dumézil, Lévi-Strauss, Eliade*. Translated by Martha Cunningham. New York: Routledge, 2014.

Dumézil, Georges. *The Destiny of a King*. Translated by Alf Hiltebeitel. Chicago, IL: University of Chicago Press, 1973.

Dunn, Sarah. "How John Adams Established the Peaceful Transfer of Power." *History.com*, January 14, 2021. https://www.history.com/news/peaceful-transfer-power-adams-jefferson.

Durkheim, Émile. *The Elementary Forms of Religious Life*. New York: The Free Press, 1995.

Dyson, Freeman. *Disturbing the Universe*. Oxford: Oxford University Press, 1979.

Elhauge, Einer. *Statutory Default Rules: How to Interpret Unclear Legislation*. Cambridge, MA: Harvard University Press, 2008.

Eliot, Thomas Stearns. *The Waste Land: Authoritative Text, Contexts, Criticism*. Edited by Michael North. Norton Critical Editions. New York: W. W. Norton, 2006.

Euclid. *The Thirteen Books of Euclid's Elements*. Edited by Dana Densmore. Translated by T. L. Heath. Santa Fe, NM: Green Lion Press, 2002.

Federalist Papers. Nos. 4, 6, 10, 34, 38, 41, 47, 63, 70, 75. New York: Signet Classics, 2003.

Federalist Papers. *The Federalist: A Commentary on the Constitution of the United States*. By Alexander Hamilton, John Jay, and James Madison. Edited by Clinton Rossiter. New York: Signet Classics, 2003.

Fiennes, Sophie, dir. *The Pervert's Guide to Cinema*. Amoeba Film, 2009. Film.

Fisher, Bruce D. "The Ethical Consumer: A Rejecter of Positive Law Arbitrage." *Seton Hall Law Review* 25 (1994): 230–45.

Fisher, Louis. "The Korean War: On What Legal Basis Did Truman Act?" *American Journal of International Law* 89, 1 (1995): 21–39.

Ford, Matt. "The Fifth Circuit Court of Appeals Rules Against Obama's Executive Actions on Immigration." *The Atlantic*, November 10, 2015. Accessed May 19, 2021. https://www.theatlantic.com/politics/archive/2015/11/fifth-circuit-obama-immigration/415077/.

Foster, Sydney. "Should Courts Give Stare Decisis Effect to Statutory Interpretation Methodology?" *Georgetown Law Journal* 96 (2008): 1863–910.

Foucault, Michel. "Essays in Refusal." *Yale Law Journal* 107 (1997): 499–500.

Founders Online, National Archives. Additional Memorandums on Ancient and Modern Confederacies, [ante 30 November 1787]. https://founders.archives.gov/documents/Madison/01-10-02-0183.

Founders Online, National Archives. Notes on Ancient and Modern Confederacies, [April–June 1786]. https://founders.archives.gov/documents/Madison/01-09-02-0001.

Freud, Sigmund. *The Ego and the Id (1923). In The Standard Edition of the Complete Psychological Works of Sigmund Freud*, Vol. 19. Edited and Translated by James Strachey. London: Hogarth Press, 1961.

Freud, Sigmund. *The Interpretation of Dreams*. Translated by James Strachey. New York: Avon, 1965.

Frosio, Giancarlo F. "Rediscovering Cumulative Creativity from the Oral Formulaic Tradition to Digital Remix: Can I Get a Witness?" *Journal of Marshall Review of Intellectual Property Law* 13 (2014): 341–56.

Frost, Tom. "Agamben's Sovereign Legalization of Foucault." *Oxford Journal of Legal Studies* 30, 3 (2010): 545–77.

Gangi, William. "A Scholar's Journey on the Dark Side." *Chapman Law Review* 11 (2007): 1–15.

González, Carlos E. "Reinterpreting Statutory Interpretation." *North Carolina Law Review* 74 (1996): 585–621.

Gordley, James. "The Method of Roman Jurists." *Tulane Law Review* 87 (2013): 933–64.
Grand, Cara J. "Zivotofsky v. Kerry: Of Passports, Politics, and Foreign Policy Powers." *Duke Journal of Constitutional Law & Public Policy* 10 (2014): 39–58.
Gray, Thomas C. "Holmes and Legal Pragmatism." *Stanford Law Review* 41 (1989): 787–887.
Grossman, Lewis A. "Langdell Upside-Down: James Coolidge Carter and the Anticlassical Jurisprudence of Anticodification." *Yale Journal of Law & the Humanities* 19 (2007): 149–82.
Harris, Marvin. *The Rise of Anthropological Theory*. New York: Columbia University Press, 1968.
Healy, Thomas. "Stare Decisis as a Constitutional Requirement." *West Virginia Law Review* 104 (2001): 43–62.
Hegel, Georg Wilhelm Friedrich. *Phenomenology of Spirit*. Translated by A. V. Miller. Oxford: Oxford University Press, 1977.
Hegel, Georg Wilhelm Friedrich. *The Philosophy of History*. Translated by J. Sibree. Barnes & Noble Library of Essential Reading. New York: Union Square, 2009.
Herman, Arthur. *The Cave and the Light: Plato Versus Aristotle, and the Struggle for the Soul of Western Civilization*. New York: Random House, 2013.
Hermann, Donald H. J. "Phenomenology, Structuralism, Hermeneutics, and Legal Study: Applications of Contemporary Continental Thought to Legal Phenomena." *University of Miami Law Review* 36 (1982): 379–412.
Herodotus. *The Landmark Herodotus: The Histories*. Edited by Robert B. Strassler. Introduction by Rosalind Thomas. Translated by Andrea L. Purvis. New York: Anchor Books, 2009.
Hersh, Jeff. "What Questions Are Asked on a Mental Status Exam?" *Taunton Daily Gazette*, October 30, 2023. https://www.tauntongazette.com/story/lifestyle/health-fitness/2020/07/23/whats-up-doc-what-questions-are-asked-on-mental-status-exam/114523550/.
Hershovitz, Scott. "Wittgenstein on Rules: The Phantom Menace." *Oxford Journal of Legal Studies* 22 (2002): 619–40.
Hesiod. *Theogony*. Translated by Dorothea Wender. London: Penguin Classics, 1973.
Hilligan, Marion, Nelson P. Miller, Don Petersen, and Chris Hastings. "World Views Collide: A Dialogue on Superhuman-Biotechnology's Emerging Impact on the Law." *T. M. Cooley Law Review* 24 (2007): 1–26.
Holmes, Oliver Wendell Jr. "Privilege, Malice, and Intent." *Harvard Law Review* 8 (1894): 1–29.
Holmes, Oliver Wendell Jr. *The Common Law*. Edited by Mark DeWolfe Howe. Cambridge, MA: Harvard University Press, 1963.
Homer. *Homeric Hymns*. Translated by Jules Cashford. London: Penguin Books, 2003.
Homer. *The Iliad*. Translated by Richmond Lattimore. Chicago, IL: University of Chicago Press, 1976.

Homer. *The Iliad*. Translated by Samuel Butler. Project Gutenberg, 2006. https://www.gutenberg.org/ebooks/6130.

Homer. *The Odyssey*. Translated by Robert Fitzgerald. New York: Farrar, Straus and Giroux, 1998.

Horton, Sir Arthur, Translated. *Theophrastus: Enquiry into Plants and Minor Works on Odours and Weather Signs*. London: William Heinemann, 1916.

Hunt, Albert R. "Republican Haste Warps Tax Bills." *Bloomberg View*, November 29, 2017.

Hutchins, Robert Maynard. *The Great Conversation: The Substance of a Liberal Education*. Chicago, IL: Encyclopædia Britannica, 1952; repr. 1955.

Jay, Martin Evan. "Sigmund Freud." *Encyclopaedia Britannica*. Last modified November 9, 2023. https://www.britannica.com/biography/Sigmund-Freud.

Jefferson, Thomas. *A Manual of Parliamentary Practice*. Washington, DC: Government Printing Office, 1801.

Jinks, Derek P. "Essays in Refusal: Pre-Theoretical Commitments in Postmodern Anthropology and Critical Race Theory." *Yale Law Journal* 107 (1997): 499–559.

Johnson, Calvin H. *Righteous Anger at the Wicked States: The Meaning of the Founders' Constitution*. New York: Oxford University Press, 2005.

Johnson, George. *A Fire in the Mind: Science, Faith, and the Search for Order*. New York: Random House, 1996.

Judiciary Act of 1789, ch. 20, § 13, 1 Stat. 73 (1789).

Judiciary Act of 1801, ch. 4, 2 Stat. 89 (1801).

Kahloon, Idrees. "Thomas Piketty Goes Global." *The New Yorker*, March 2, 2020. https://www.newyorker.com/magazine/2020/03/09/thomas-piketty-goes-global.

Kar, Robin Bradley. "Western Legal Prehistory: Reconstructing the Hidden Origins of Western Law and Civilization." *University of Illinois Law Review* 2012 (2012): 1499–530.

Karlan, Pamela S. "Foreword: Democracy and Disdain, The Supreme Court 2011 Term." *Harvard Law Review* 126 (2012): 1–45.

Katyal, Neal Kumar. "Internal Separation of Powers: Checking Today's Most Dangerous Branch from Within." *Yale Law Journal* 115 (2005): 2314–45.

Kearley, Timothy G. "From Rome to the Restatement: S.P. Scott, Fred Blume, Clyde Pharr, and Roman Law in Early Twentieth-Century America." *Law Library Journal* 108 (2016): 55–82.

Klein, Kenneth S. "Weighing Democracy and Judicial Legitimacy in Judicial Selection." *Texas Review of Law & Politics* 23 (2018): 269–84.

Lacan, Jacques. "Some Reflections on the Ego." *International Journal of Psycho-Analysis* 34 (1953): 11–19.

Lacan, Jacques. *The Ego in Freud's Theory and in the Technique of Psychoanalysis, 1954–1955*. New York: W. W. Norton, 1991.

Lawson, Gary. "The Rise and Rise of the Administrative State." *Harvard Law Review* 107, 6 (1994): 1231–54.

Levmore, Saul. "Parliamentary Law, Majority Decisionmaking, and the Voting Paradox." *Virginia Law Review* 75 (1989): 971–1044.

Liddell, Henry George and Robert Scott. *An Intermediate Greek-English Lexicon.* Oxford: Clarendon Press, 1889.

Liddell, Henry George and Robert Scott. *An Intermediate Greek-English Lexicon.* Oxford: Clarendon Press, 1889. (Entries for λογιστικός, ἐπιθυμητικός, θυμοειδής, ψυχή accessed online May 19, 2021.)

Lincoln, Charles E. *Ethnicity and Social Organization at Chichen Itza, Yucatan, Mexico.* PhD diss., Harvard University, 1990.

Lincoln, Charles Edward Andrew IV. "A Literary Lens into Constitutional Interpretation: The Silmarillion." *Mitchell Hamline Law Journal of Public Policy & Practice* 41 (2020): 101–28.

Lincoln, Charles Edward Andrew IV. "A Structural Etiology of the U.S. Constitution." *Journal of Legislation* 43 (2016): 122.

Lincoln, Charles Edward Andrew IV. *The Dialectical Path of Law.* Notre Dame, IN: University of Notre Dame Press, 2021.

Lincoln, Elena K. *Yucatec Maya Marriage and Political Alliances.* PhD diss., University of California, Los Angeles, 2000).

Littleton, C. Scott. "The Comparative Indo-European Mythology of Georges Dumézil." *Journal of the Folklore Institute* 1, 2 (1964): 147–51.

Littleton, C. Scott and Udo Strutynski. Introduction to *Gods of the Ancient Northmen.* Edited by Einar Haugen. Berkeley: University of California Press, 1973.

Locke, John. *The Second Treatise of Government.* In Great Books of the Western World, Vol. 35, Edited by Robert Maynard Hutchins. Chicago, IL: Encyclopaedia Britannica, 1952.

Lucian. *Dialogues of the Gods.* Translated by A. M. Harmon. Loeb Classical Library. Cambridge, MA: Harvard University Press, 1915.

Lucretius. *On the Nature of Things.* Translated by H. A. J. Munro. In Great Books of the Western World, Vol. 12, Edited by Robert Maynard Hutchins. Chicago, IL: Encyclopaedia Britannica, 1952.

Lunbeck, Elizabeth, Amber Jamilla Musser, and Todd McGowan. "Sigmund Freud's *The Ego and the Id.*" *JSTOR Daily*, September 21, 2019. https://daily.jstor.org/virtual-roundtable-on-the-ego-and-the-id/.

Lyons, Edward C. "Reason's Freedom and the Dialectic of Ordered Liberty." *Cleveland State Law Review* 55 (2007): 157–210.

Madison, James. "For the National Gazette." *National Gazette*, February 18, 1792. https://founders.archives.gov/documents/Madison/01-14-02-0203.

Madison, James. *Notes of Debates in the Federal Convention of 1787.* Athens: Ohio University Press, 2022.

Madison, James. *Notes on Ancient and Modern Confederacies*, [April–June?] 1786, Founders Online, National Archives. https://founders.archives.gov/documents/Madison/01-09-02-0001.

Malinowski, Bronislaw. *Argonauts of the Western Pacific*. London: Routledge, 1922. Reprint, 1961.

Manning, John F. "Separation of Powers as Ordinary Interpretation." *Harvard Law Review* 124 (1939, 2004 (2010)).

Marcos, Cristina and Sarah Ferris. "House Votes to Repeal ObamaCare." *The Hill*, February 3, 2015. https://thehill.com/policy/healthcare/231638-house-votes-to-repeal-obamacare.

Meacham, Jon. *American Lion: Andrew Jackson in the White House*. New York: Random House, 2008.

Melville, Herman. *Moby-Dick; or, The Whale*. Chapter 135. Great Books of the Western World, Vol. 48. Chicago, IL: Encyclopaedia Britannica, 1952.

Mendelson, Wallace. "The Judiciary Act of 1789: The Formal Origin of Federal Judicial Review." *Judicature* 76 (1992): 133–42.

Merrill, Thomas W. "Judicial Deference to Executive Precedent." *Yale Law Journal* 101 (1992): 969–1015.

Meyer, Linda. "'Nothing We Say Matters': Teague and New Rules." *University of Chicago Law Review* 61, 2 (1994): 423–92.

Milton, John. *Paradise Lost*. Edited by Gordon Teskey. Norton Critical Edition. New York: W. W. Norton, 2005.

Moe, Terry M. and William G. Howell. "Unilateral Action and Presidential Power: A Theory." *Presidential Studies Quarterly* 29, 4 (1999): 850–73.

Mollin, Alfred. *An Introduction to Ancient Greek*. 3rd ed. Lanham, MD: University Press of America, 1997.

Momigliano, Arnaldo. "Georges Dumézil and the Trifunctional Approach to Roman Civilization." *History and Theory* 23 (1984): 312–32.

Monaghan, Henry Paul. "Stare Decisis and Constitutional Adjudication." *Columbia Law Review* 88 (1988): 723–52.

Montesquieu. *The Spirit of the Laws*. In Great Books of the Western World, Vol. 38, Edited by Robert Maynard Hutchins. Translated by Thomas Nugent. Chicago, IL: Encyclopaedia Britannica, 1952.

Morriss, Andrew P. "Codification and the Right Answers." *Chicago-Kent Law Review* 74 (1999): 355–402.

Natelson, Robert G. "A Republic, Not a Democracy? Initiative, Referendum, and the Constitution's Guarantee Clause." *Texas Law Review* 80 (2002): 807–39.

National Archives. "Executive Orders Disposition Tables." August 15, 2016. https://www.archives.gov/federal-register/executive-orders.

Nektarios, Peter Yioutsos. "Order in Ancient Greek Dance Rituals: The Dance of Pan and the Nymphs." *Dramaturgias* 5 (2017): 211–34.

Nietzsche, Friedrich. *On the Genealogy of Morals and Ecce Homo*. Translated by Walter Kaufmann and R. J. Hollingdale. Edited with commentary by Walter Kaufmann. New York: Vintage Books, 1967.

Nussbaum, Martha C. *Commentary on Aristotle, De Motu Animalium*. Chicago, IL: University of Chicago Press, 1978.

Ovid. *Heroides*. Translated by Harold Isbell. London: Penguin Classics, 1990.

Oxford English Dictionary, 2nd ed. 1989.

Patterson, Dennis. "Wittgenstein and Constitutional Theory." *Texas Law Review* 72 (1994): 1837–51.

Pausanias. *Description of Greece*. Translated by W. H. S. Jones and H. A. Ormerod. Loeb Classical Library. Cambridge, MA: Harvard University Press, 1918.

Perseus Digital Library. "Greek Word Study Tool." Accessed October 14, 2023. http://www.perseus.tufts.edu/hopper/morph

Piketty, Thomas. *Capital and Ideology*, 478 n.92, citing Didier Eribon, *Faut-il brûler Dumézil?* Paris: Flammarion, 1992, 185–206.

Piketty, Thomas. *Capital and Ideology*. Translated by Arthur Goldhammer. Cambridge, MA: Harvard University Press, 2020.

Plato. *Crito*, in *Plato: Euthyphro. Apology. Crito. Phaedo. Phaedrus*. Translated by Harold North Fowler, 46b. Loeb Classical Library 36. Cambridge, MA: Harvard University Press, 1904.

Plato. *Gorgias*. Translated by James H. Nichols Jr. Agora Editions. Ithaca, NY: Cornell University Press, 1998.

Plato. *Laws*, in *Plato: Laws, Volume I*. Translated by R. G. Bury, 644d. Loeb Classical Library 187. Cambridge, MA: Harvard University Press, 1926.

Plato. *Meno*. Translated by George Anastaplo and Laurence Berns. Newburyport, MA: Focus Philosophical Library, 1998.

Plato. *Parmenides*. Translated by Albert Keith Whitaker. Newburyport, MA: Focus Philosophical Library, 1996.

Plato. *Phaedrus*. Translated by Christopher J. Rowe. 1986, 248d–e.

Plato. *Phaedrus* 248d–e. Translated by Christopher J. Rowe. 1986.

Plato. *Republic*. Translated by Paul Shorey. Cambridge, MA: Harvard University Press, 1969. https://www.perseus.tufts.edu/hopper/text?doc=Perseus:text:1999.01.0168:book=4:section=435e.

Plato. *Sophist: The Professor of Wisdom*. Translated by Eva Brann. Newburyport, MA: Focus Philosophical Library, 1996.

Plato. *Theaetetus*, in *Plato: Theaetetus. Sophist*. Translated by Harold North Fowler, 186c. Loeb Classical Library 123. Cambridge, MA: Harvard University Press, 1921.

Plato. *Theaetetus*. Translated by Joe Sachs. Newburyport, MA: Focus Philosophical Library, 2004.

Plato. *Timaeus*. Translated by Peter Kalkavage. New York: Focus Philosophical Library, 2001.

Plato. *Timaeus*. Translated by Robin Waterfield. Oxford: Oxford University Press, 2008.

Polybius. *The Histories of Polybius*. Translated by Evelyn S. Shuckburgh. Bloomington: Indiana University Press, 1962.

Popper, Karl. *The Logic of Scientific Discovery*. London: Routledge, 2002.

Pound, Roscoe. "Mechanical Jurisprudence." *Columbia Law Review* 8 (1908): 605–46.

Poundone, Abbe R. "Imperfect Statutes, Imperfect Courts: Understanding Congress's Plan in the Era of Unorthodox Lawmaking." *Harvard Law Review* 129 (2015): 62–96.

Pradeau, Jean-François. *Plato and the City*. Exeter: University of Exeter Press, 2002.

Prakash, Saikrishna and Steven D. Smith. "How to Remove a Federal Judge." *Yale Law Journal* 116 (2006): 72–137.

Pseudo-Apollodorus. *Bibliotheca*, E.3.2. Translated by Sir James George Frazer. London: William Heinemann, 1921.

Ragsdale Jr., John W. "The Rise and Fall of the Chacoan State." *UMKC Law Review* 64 (1995): 485–538.

Rakove, Jack N. *Original Meanings: Politics and Ideas in the Making of the Constitution*. New York: Alfred A. Knopf, 1996.

Reid, Charles J. "America's First Great Constitutional Controversy: Alexander Hamilton's Bank of the United States." *University of Saint Thomas Law Journal* 14 (2018): 105–30.

Republic, Plato. *The Republic of Plato*. Edited by and Translated by Allan Bloom. 2nd ed. New York: Basic Books, 1991.

Ricks, Thomas E. *First Principles: What America's Founders Learned from the Greeks and Romans and How That Shaped Our Country*. Oxford: Oxford University Press, 2020.

Robert, Henry M., *Robert's Rules of Order Newly Revised*. 12th ed. Cambridge, MA: Da Capo Press, 2020.

Schwartz, Andrew W. "No Competing Theory of Constitutional Interpretation Justifies Regulatory Takings Ideology." *Stanford Environmental Law Journal* 34 (2015): 247, 259 n.43.

Schweller, Randall L. *Maxwell's Demon and the Golden Apple: Global Discord in the New Millennium*. Baltimore, MD: Johns Hopkins University Press, 2014.

Scuillo, Nick J. "Žižek/Questions/Failing." *Willamette Law Review* 47 (2011): 287–325.

Shakespeare, William. "Antony and Cleopatra." In *The Oxford Shakespeare: The Complete Works*, 2nd ed., Edited by John Jowett, William Montgomery, Gary Taylor, and Stanley Wells, 1021–60. Oxford: Oxford University Press, 2005.

Shakespeare, William. *As You Like It*.

Shakespeare, William. *Coriolanus*. In *The Oxford Shakespeare: The Complete Works*, 2nd ed., Edited by John Jowett, William Montgomery, Gary Taylor, and Stanley Wells, 1301–44. Oxford: Oxford University Press, 2005.

Shakespeare, William. *Julius Caesar*. In *The Oxford Shakespeare: The Complete Works*, 2nd ed., Edited by John Jowett, William Montgomery, Gary Taylor, and Stanley Wells, 957–86. Oxford: Oxford University Press, 2005.

Shakespeare, William. *Romeo and Juliet*. Act 2, Scene 2, lines 133–6.
Shear, Michael D. "Obama to Appeal Immigration Ruling to Supreme Court." *New York Times*, November 10, 2015. Accessed May 19, 2021. https://www.nytimes.com/2015/11/11/us/politics/supreme-court-immigration-obama.html.
Shuckburgh, Evelyn S., Translated. *The Histories of Polybius*. London: Macmillan, 1962.
Slocum, Brian G. "Overlooked Temporal Issues in Statutory Interpretation." *Temple Law Review* 81 (2008): 635–54.
Smith, Adam. *An Inquiry into the Nature and Causes of the Wealth of Nations*. Edited by Edwin Cannan. Chicago, IL: University of Chicago Press 1976 (1776).
Smith, Adam. *The Theory of Moral Sentiments*. London: A. Millar, 1759.
Sommer, Carol A., Panagiotis Markopoulos, and Shana L. Goggins. "Mentoring Master's Level Students: Drawing upon the Wisdom of Athena as Mentor in Homer's *Odyssey*." *Journal of Poetry Therapy* 26, 1 (2013): 1–12.
Staszewski, Glen. "The Dumbing Down of Statutory Interpretation." *Boston University Law Review* 95 (2015): 209–40.
Stein, Peter. *Regulae Iuris: From Juristic Rules to Legal Maxims*. Oxford: Oxford University Press, 1966.
Stolberg, Sheryl Gay and Robert Pear. "Obama Signs Health Care Overhaul into Law." *New York Times*, March 23, 2010. Accessed May 19, 2021. https://www.nytimes.com/2010/03/24/health/policy/24health.html.
Strachey, James, ed. and Translated. *The Standard Edition of the Complete Works of Sigmund Freud*. Vol. 2: *New Introductory Lectures on Psycho-Analysis*. London: Hogarth Press, 1966.
Strassler, Robert B., ed. *The Landmark Thucydides: A Comprehensive Guide to the Peloponnesian War*. Translated by Richard Crawley; revised and annotated by Robert B. Strassler et al. New York: Free Press, 1996.
Strauss, Leo. *Persecution and the Art of Writing*. Chicago, IL: University of Chicago Press, 1952.
Strauss, Leo. *The City and Man*. Chicago, IL: University of Chicago Press, 1964.
Sunstein, Cass R. "Must Formalism Be Defended Empirically?" *University of Chicago Law Review* 66 (1999): 636–51.
The Editors of Encyclopaedia Britannica. "superego." Encyclopedia Britannica, June 7, 2025. https://www.britannica.com/science/superego.
The Patient Protection and Affordable Care Act, Pub. L. No. 111–48, 124 Stat. 119 (2010).
Tribe, Laurence H. "Equal Dignity: Speaking Its Name." *Harvard Law Review Forum* 129 (2015): 16.
U.S. *Constitution of the United States*. 1787.
U.S. *Declaration of Independence*. 1776.
U.S. House of Representatives. "Branches of Government." https://www.house.gov/the-house-explained/branches-of-government.
United States Constitution. Article I.

United States Constitution. Article II, Section 1, Clause 1.

United States Constitution. Article III, Section 1.

VerSteeg, Mila. "Unpopular Constitutionalism." *Indiana Law Journal* 89, 3 (2014): 1133–77.

VerSteeg, Russ. "A Contract Analysis of the Trojan War." *Arizona Law Review* 40 (1998): 173–200.

Wald, George. "Life and Mind in the Universe." *International Journal of Quantum Chemistry* 2, S1 (1968): 5–16.

Walsh, James J. *Education of the Founding Fathers of the Republic: Scholasticism in the Colonial Colleges*. New York: Fordham University Press, 1970.

Weber, Max. *The Protestant Ethic and the Spirit of Capitalism*. Translated by Talcott Parsons. New York: Charles Scribner's Sons, 1958.

White, Martin L. "Thomas Piketty." *Britannica*. Last modified November 13, 2023. https://www.britannica.com/biography/Thomas-Piketty.

White House. "Executive Orders (Beginning with J.Q. Adams)." *American Presidency Project*. Accessed December 29, 2023. https://www.presidency.ucsb.edu/documents/presidential-documents-archive-guidebook/executive-orders-beginning-with-jq-adams.

White House. "The Executive Branch." Accessed December 29, 2023. https://www.whitehouse.gov/about-the-white-house/our-government/the-executive-branch/.

Wittgenstein, Ludwig. *Philosophical Investigations*. 2nd ed. Translated by G. E. M. Anscombe. Oxford: Blackwell, 1953.

Wittgenstein, Ludwig. *Tractatus Logico-Philosophicus*. Translated by C. K. Ogden. London: Routledge & Kegan Paul, 1922.

Wittgenstein, Ludwig. *Tractatus Logico-Philosophicus*. Translated by David F. Pears and Brian F. McGuinness. London: Routledge, 1961.

Wuttke, Alexander. "The Pleasure Principle: Why (Some) People Develop a Taste for Politics: Evidence from a Preregistered Experiment." *Politics and the Life Sciences* 40, 1 (2021): 19–39.

Yoshino, Kenji. "A New Birth of Freedom?: *Obergefell v. Hodges*." *Harvard Law Review* 129 (2015): 147.

Yoshino, Kenji. "The City and the Poet." *Yale Law Journal* 114 (2005): 1835–65.

Žižek, Slavoj. *Less Than Nothing: Hegel and the Shadow of Dialectical Materialism*. London: Verso, 2012.

Žižek, Slavoj. "Revenge of Global Finance." *In These Times*, May 21, 2005. Accessed June 11, 2025. https://www.lacan.com/zizekfinance.htm.

Žižek, Slavoj. *The Sublime Object of Ideology*. London: Verso Books, 1989.

Žižek, Slavoj. *Welcome to the Desert of the Real*. 2nd ed. London: Verso, 2002.

Periodicals Consulted

Columbia Law Review
Harper's Magazine
Harvard Journal of Law & Public Policy
Harvard Law Review
Η Καθημερινή (Kathimerini)
Le Monde
National Geographic
Smithsonian Magazine
Stanford Law Review
The Atlantic
The Economist
The Guardian
The New York Review of Books
The New York Times
The New Yorker
The Wall Street Journal
The Washington Post
University of Chicago Law Review
University of Pennsylvania Law Review
Yale Law Journal

Table of Cases

Vanhorne v. Dorrance, 2 U.S. (2 Dall.) 304 (1795).
Marbury v. Madison, 5 U.S. (1 Cranch) 137 (1803).
Eakin v. Raub, 12 Serg. & Rawle 330 (Pa. 1825).
Plessy v. Ferguson, 163 U.S. 537 (1896).
Youngstown Sheet & Tube Co. v. Sawyer, 343 U.S. 579 (1952).
Brown v. Board of Education, 347 U.S. 483 (1954).
United States v. Nixon, 418 U.S. 683 (1974).
Chevron U.S.A. Inc. v. NRDC Inc., 467 U.S. 837 (1984).
Payne v. Tennessee, 501 U.S. 808 (1991).
In re Osborne, 76 F.3d 306 (9th Cir. 1996).
Petersen v. Magna Corp., 773 N.W.2d 564 (Mich. 2009).
Johnson v. United States, 576 U.S. 591 (2015).
Obergefell v. Hodges, 576 U.S. 644 (2015).

Index

Page numbers followed by n denote endnotes.

About the Author

Charles Lincoln is a lawyer. The author of *The Dialectical Path of Law*, he lives in Austin, Texas. He is currently a PhD student at the University of Groningen (abbreviated as UG in English; in Dutch: *Rijksuniversiteit Groningen*, abbreviated as RUG in Dutch) in the Netherlands. Previously he received his LLM in Tax Law (*Magister Legum ad Vectigalia Pertinentium*) at Boston University in May 2018. Prior to that, he received his Advanced LLM (*Magister Legum*) in International Tax Law from the University of Amsterdam abbreviated in English and Dutch as UvA (Dutch: Universiteit van Amsterdam). Before embarking to study in the Netherlands, he received his JD from Texas A&M University School of Law in May 2016. He received his bachelor's degree from Harvard University with a concentration in Government in May 2013. Finally, he finished high school at Harmony Science Academy in Austin in May of 2010, the same school he went to from sixth grade starting in 2003 through twelfth grade.

www.ingramcontent.com/pod-product-compliance
Ingram Content Group UK Ltd.
Pitfield, Milton Keynes, MK11 3LW, UK
UKHW021906150926
475560UK00003B/206

9 781666 957761